Celebrity

To Emmeline with all my love

Celebrity

Capitalism and the Making of Fame

Milly Williamson

polity

The right of Milly Williamson to be identified as Author of this Work has been asserted in accordance with the UK Copyright, Designs and Patents Act 1988.

First published in 2016 by Polity Press

Polity Press
65 Bridge Street
Cambridge CB2 1UR, UK

Polity Press
350 Main Street
Malden, MA 02148, USA

ISBN-13: 978-0-7456-4104-1
ISBN-13: 978-0-7456-4105-8(pb)

A catalogue record for this book is available from the British Library.

Library of Congress Cataloging-in-Publication Data

Names: Williamson, Milly, author.
Title: Celebrity : capitalism and the making of fame / Milly Williamson.
Description: Malden, MA : Polity, 2016. | Includes bibliographical references and index.
Identifiers: LCCN 2016017839 (print) | LCCN 2016041834 (ebook) | ISBN 9780745641041 (hardback) | ISBN 0745641040 (hardcover) | ISBN 9780745641058 (paperback) | ISBN 0745641059 (paperback) | ISBN 9781509511426 (mobi) | ISBN 9781509511433 (epub)
Subjects: LCSH: Celebrities. | Mass media. | Performing art. | Fame--Social aspects. | BISAC: SOCIAL SCIENCE / Media Studies.
Classification: LCC HM621 .W535 2016 (print) | LCC HM621 (ebook) | DDC 305.5/2--dc23
LC record available at https://lccn.loc.gov/2016017839

Typeset in 10.5 on 12 pt Sabon by Toppan Best-set Premedia Limited
Printed and bound in Great Britain by CPI Group (UK) Ltd, Croydon

The publisher has used its best endeavours to ensure that the URLs for external websites referred to in this book are correct and active at the time of going to press. However, the publisher has no responsibility for the websites and can make no guarantee that a site will remain live or that the content is or will remain appropriate.

Every effort has been made to trace all copyright holders, but if any have been inadvertently overlooked the publisher will be pleased to include any necessary credits in any subsequent reprint or edition.

For further information on Polity, visit our website: politybooks.com

Contents

Acknowledgements

I am lucky enough to have excellent friends in academia, whose emotional and intellectual support is unfailing. I would like to thank them for their friendship and much laughter – and for reading draft chapters of this book, which has, without question, been improved as a result. I would particularly like to thank Natalie Fenton, Des Freedman and Gholam Khiabany. Natalie spent long hours discussing the ideas in this book on our travels to and from swimming pools, rivers and ponds, helping me to clarify my ideas and sharpen my arguments. She also made invaluable comments and suggestions on two chapters and pointed me in the direction of important ideas and further work which were essential to the latter half of the book. Des, with characteristic insight, explained to me what my book was about, which was handy. He also provided invaluable feedback on chapters, pointed me in the direction of new evidence and, with well aimed questions, got me to look at things in a new way. Gholam has, with great generosity, read every draft chapter of this book (some more than once). He has provided me with endless encouragement, critical commentary, and new ideas. He has been a great resource for Marxist thought and has helped me to clarify my ideas through our many conversations.

I would also like to thank Jo Littler who kindly read two chapters of this book and for making wonderful suggestions and much needed encouraging noises as the work on this book was coming to a close. Thank you also to Mila Steele for reading the opening chapter of the book and for her excellent suggestions. Thank you to Geoff King for reading and commenting on the second chapter, and for good advice.

Thank you to Sheela Banerjee for our many conversations and laughs in the British Library while we were both working on our respective projects. I also want to thank Chris Williamson who read the whole manuscript, which must be beyond the call of duty for a sibling – thanks for being a great brother.

I would very much like to thank all of my colleagues and friends in Film and Television Studies at Brunel University whose understanding of the mad realities of our world, including as they appear in the Higher Education system, make day-to-day working life in neoliberal times possible. A special thanks to those colleagues whose humour and tendency to gently take the mickey out of me, manage also to make it fun – Mike Wayne, Leon Hunt, Sean Holmes, Caroline Ruddell, Piotr Cieplak and Craig Haslop. Without the supportive environment created by all of my Film and TV colleagues, research, thinking and writing would be impossible.

Brunel University provided me with a sabbatical which enabled me to complete the manuscript for this book, for which I am grateful. A special thanks and love to my parents, Nancy and Joe.

1

What is Celebrity?
The Changing Character of Fame

Introduction

Every epoch has its own form of fame, and celebrity is a form of fame commensurate with capitalist society, both economically and culturally. The rise of celebrity corresponds to the enormous social changes wrought by the emergence of capitalism: the rise of bourgeois modernity, the commercialization of culture, the development of technology and the processes of industrialization, the growth of democracy and its curtailment. In particular, celebrity is seen to be intimately bound up with the development and extension of the mass media.

But fame has been a feature of society throughout the history of civilization. Different periods of history in different parts of the globe possess ways of being well known and publicly renowned, which are shaped by the structure of public life as it is created by the particular social, political and economic conditions that prevail. Fame is not an unchanging human condition, attached inevitably to 'Great Men' and the occasional 'Great Woman'. Instead, fame is part of the historical process, and as such it helps to illuminate the balance of power in any society between different social forces and values. Perceptions of fame and its social meanings change in times of social transformation often highlighting the transition between epochs.

Famous figures from history can tell us a great deal about their period, the values of their society, the shape of power and challenges to it. Leo Braudy's (1986) epic history of fame charts the key changes in the ideas and practices of fame since ancient times. According to Braudy, we find in Alexander the Great the origins of fame, for he was the first person in Western history to have the urge to be seen as unique and to be universally known (although perhaps not the first person, for 900 years prior to the life of Alexander, the Egyptian Pharaoh Ramses II immortalized himself in his lifetime as the greatest pharaoh of all time). Braudy argues that Alexander presented himself as the direct descendent of the Homeric Gods – his grandiose persona corresponding with his status. His career became a guide for future generations of conquerors, and even centuries later Roman emperors emulated Alexander in their quest for absolute power, while the Roman aristocracy considered Rome to be superior by divine providence. In this atmosphere, every 'true' Roman strove to make himself worthy of his place in the Roman order, producing what Braudy terms 'the Roman urge to fame' (1986: 49).

The ostentatious and god-like fame inspired by Alexander remained the model for renown in the West for many centuries until it was challenged by the Roman emperor Augustus. Augustus did not emulate the heroes of the past, but instead developed a new form of fame which stressed civic duty and loyalty to Rome as the basis for public prominence. In this context Augustus presents himself as an imperial symbol, his importance tied to the destiny of Rome and its empire rather than to the gods. This marks one of the earliest shifts in the meanings of fame – from god-heroes to imperial-heroes, from grandiose display to an emphasis on civic duty.

Zygmunt Bauman (2005) also identifies the broad shifts in the changing patterns of fame but offers an alternative historical analysis. While for Braudy transformations in fame are related to social values, for Bauman, fame is also connected to *social function* and reveals the human condition in any period. Bauman contrasts the prominence of the 'martyr' figure in early Christian societies with the fame of the emerging 'hero' figure of early modern societies in the throes of nation-building. While the death of the martyr suited a world predicated on the self as a sacrifice to God and the salvation of the immortal soul, the death of the hero is a sacrifice, not to the immortality of the soul, 'but the immortality of the nation' (2005: 44). For Bauman, like others (Anderson, 2006; Calhoun, 2007), the nation must be understood as an 'imagined' community, the consolidation of which needed patriotic heroes prepared to die to ensure its success. Echoing but updating the Augustan link between public prominence and service to the state, the promotion of the early modern hero figure served the interest of nation states wanting to become stable and 'solid' at a time when the success of nation-building was not a foregone conclusion. The patriotism and the possibility of the death of the warrior-hero figure enacted and legitimatized these aims (Bauman 2005: 43). This period required patriotic heroes.

But for Bauman, if the hero embodied the needs of fame for a 'solid' modernity, then celebrity is the figure *par excellence* of what he terms 'liquid modernity'. He characterizes our era as one in which community is not only 'imagined', as in the society of the 'solid' modern era, 'but also *imaginary*, apparition-like; and above all loosely knit, frail, volatile, and recognized as ephemeral' (Bauman 2005: 50). All is unstable in this characterization of the present, including, according to Bauman, the sovereignty of the nation state itself, which is no longer seen to entirely control culture and the economy and thus no longer commands the commitment of patriotic heroes. Bauman suggests that celebrities are symptoms of a new set of conditions; 'celebrities are so comfortably at home in the liquid modern setting' because they are 'as episodic as life itself', as are the 'imaginary communities' that wrap around 'eminently restless celebrities who hardly ever outstay their public welcome [and] call for no commitment; still less for a lasting, let alone "permanent" commitment' (2005: 50). For Bauman, then, celebrity comes to be an emblem of contemporary ephemera and is an expression of profound social changes.

Bauman's account perhaps overemphasizes the reduction of the role of the nation state in contemporary capitalism as a political, economic and particularly military entity, but also as a force for identification. But this is part of his diagnosis of the present as one in which huge changes to the human condition have occurred in the shift away from the 'solid' modern and towards the 'liquid' modern era. However, once must consider whether Bauman's insight about the ongoing 'cavalcade of celebrities, each one leaping out of nowhere only to sink shortly into oblivion' (2005: 51) is a symptom of a shift to a new epoch, or, as this book argues, a continuing and intensifying product of capitalist modernity. We must ask what the function of ephemeral celebrity is. Is it a symptom of a total cultural transformation, or an ongoing product of commercialized culture which extends back to the late eighteenth century? This book argues the latter; that it is a form of fame that emerges with the transition to capitalism and which first becomes a *system* in the commercial Georgian theatre in the latter half of the 1700s as a result of the growth of commercialism at the time.

Celebrity and the Cultural Decline Narrative

However, Bauman is not alone in his characterization of the present as a decisive break from the past, one that privileges the momentary and favours appearances over content. Nor is he alone in suggesting that the celebrity is a symbol of the prevailing zeitgeist. A number of commentators have suggested that contemporary celebrity is a symptom or a symbol of these cultural transformations and indeed represents cultural decline (Boorstin 1961; Debord 1984 [1967]; Gitlin 2002; Lowenthal 1961; Schickel 1985; Walker 1970). Perhaps the most frequently quoted is Daniel Boorstin who bemoans the decline of greatness that once purportedly characterized fame. For Boorstin, the 'man of truly heroic stature' (1961: 62), who scorned publicity, has been replaced by the image-obsessed publicity seeker. Boorstin argues that the graphic revolution in the nineteenth and into the twentieth century led to an increased valuation of style over substance. According to Boorstin, the widespread dissemination of the image through photography, film and television has meant that the circulation of the image has superseded the circulation of ideas, so that the media now rely on pseudo-events – events staged in order to be reported upon in the media – often before they occur. For Boorstin, celebrities are human 'pseudo-events' because, unlike heroes of the past who performed great deeds in the real world, celebrities since the early twentieth century are entirely constructed for media consumption. Boorstin claims that in the past the famous were known for their great achievements while today's celebrities are simply 'well known for their well-knownness' (1961: 58). They are no longer great, he claims, but mediocre mirrors of ourselves.

Boorstin has been identified, rightly in my view, as a conservative cultural elitist and a pessimist by more than one critic for harking back to an age that never was (Evans and Hesmondhalgh 2005; Ponce de Leon 2002). However, while there is a great deal of validity to this criticism, Boorstin's concept of the pseudo-event does point to an important dimension in the structure of information circulation which often relies on planned press conferences and prearranged events rather than spontaneous happenings. Nonetheless, it is important to recognize that concerns about 'cultural decline' are not new, but instead have a long history in modernity's language of critique, setting the 'serious' against the 'frivolous' at a time when both were emerging as important elements in an emerging contradictory structure of feeling that characterized a period in great turmoil. Celebrity has from its inception produced both sides of the coin, fame as achievement (serious) and fame as personality (frivolous). And, this duality still persists today.

For even as early as the sixteenth century, as a harbinger of debates to come, the Renaissance philosopher Michel de Montaigne expressed deep concerns about the dangers of the 'mediocre' in art and culture. In his work *Essais* (2015 [1580]), de Montaigne values the ability of both folk culture and high art to alleviate inner pain through diversion, but he considered the 'in-betweeners' (by which he probably meant various forms of theatrical performance) to be dangerous because of their perceived mediocrity. Interestingly, Montaigne was criticized at the time of publication for the endless digressions in his essays and for insisting on making himself their central subject matter (Sichel 1911). A century later, Montaigne's successor, Blaise Pascal advances the critique of mediocrity by suggesting that *diversion* itself is dangerous. In *Pensées*, Pascal (1983 [1670]) criticizes the entertainment afforded by the new forms of art of his day because he considers them to be a diversion from inner contemplation and elevated pursuits. Pascal considered the theatre to be the most dangerous diversion of all, because he thought it could deceive man into believing he has all of the noble qualities he sees portrayed on the stage. As we shall see below, the theatre is one of the earliest arenas for modern fame so perhaps it is not coincidental that early concerns about diversion and identification should originate there. Leo Lowenthal (1961) argues that Pascal's critique of entertainment, 'prefigures one of the most important themes in modern discussions on popular culture: the view that it is a threat to morality, contemplation, and an integrated personality, and that it results in a surrender to the mere instrumentalities at the expense of the pursuit of higher goals' (1961: 17). Hence the discourse on 'cultural decline', the concerns about the disintegration of the 'solid' for the 'fragmented', and the 'serious' for the 'frivolous', the 'great' for the 'mediocre', are themselves part of the transition to modernity rather than a new language with which to describe its perceived decline. Celebrity does not point to social transformation that has moved beyond capitalism into liquid or postmodernity; instead, celebrity is the condition of fame that emerges with the development of capitalist modernity, including its complex structure of feeling, and its consolidation with the rise of the mass media and the industrialization of the fields of art and culture.

However, this is not to suggest that because celebrity has a history as long as capitalism that we ought not to offer critiques of its meanings and functions. Instead, this book offers a critical view of celebrity as a significant factor in the industrialization of culture and the commercial character of media. It is also worth noting that there are critiques from the left which share some of the concerns set out above. The Marxist cultural critic, Guy Debord, writing just a few years after Boorstin in France, also suggested that authentic social life has been replaced by representation. In his book *The Society of the Spectacle* (1967), Debord outlines 221 theses on contemporary culture in which capitalism, or more specifically, the consumer capitalism inaugurated in the twentieth century, has colonized social life beyond the arena of production and has expanded into leisure time and all areas of civil society. For Debord, this is because we now live in a society which is dominated by consumption and by the image – the society of the spectacle. Consumer capitalism presents a spectacle of the good life that depends on the separation of the individual from the collective, and rests upon the alienation of work. Because the individual is divorced from the collective, s/he is reduced to consuming corporate ideas and images. Writing about Debord, Richard L. Kaplan puts it thus:

> In these media-packaged and corporate-supplied depictions of the good life, all the social attributes actually denied to the general populace – independent power, freedom, social connection and meaningful social action – are repackaged as 'consumer choice', or as features of the lives of celebrities in Hollywood and Washington, DC suitable for vicarious consumption. (Kaplan 2012: 461)

Debord was one of a number of critics who theorized late modernity or 'postmodernity' as characterized by the dominance of simulation on social life, the descent of the population into passive consumption of the spectacle, and the subsequent destruction of the cultural fabric of society, or the 'real' (Baudrillard 1983; Jameson 1991; Ritzer 2007). Figures like Debord provide a much needed critique of our increasingly corporate-dominated, commodity-saturated and mass-mediated world, particularly now, when many celebrate the consumer power of audiences and users of new technology, embrace relativism, and rewrite the language of consumerism in the rhetoric of rebellion, while media capital consolidates its dominance even further. There are valuable insights in these works that are worth revisiting. Still, there are a number of issues too. For example, Debord privileges the power of media over and above all other powers, including the nation state, its institutions of coercion, such as the prison system and the military, supranational organizations such as the World Bank, the European Bank and the International Monetary Fund, or other sectors of corporate capitalism, including powerful sectors such as pharmaceuticals and the arms industries. This is a problematic formulation which overemphasizes the power of the media and the dominance of spectacle. Also, the collapse of the banking system in 2008, and the wars in Iraq, Syria and Afghanistan are horrifying reminders that there is life (and death and destruction) outside of the image. While the spectacle and the image are highly significant social forces, they are not the only ones.

Celebrity and Commodity Fetishism

The Frankfurt School also provided an important critique of modern media culture which sought to explain the role of culture in the maintenance of the existing order, which they argued was characterized by a lack of freedom. Two of the most prominent members of the Frankfurt School were Theodor Adorno and Max Horkheimer, whose critique of the culture industry is well known. For Adorno and Horkheimer, the industrialization of culture and the emergence of the cultural industry (from which celebrity grows) is not a break with modern capitalist society, but a continuation and intensification of its logic. In *The Dialectic of Enlightenment* (1973 [1944]), Adorno and Horkheimer argue that capitalism is not on a linear march towards greater freedom, as its apologists often claim, but is moving towards greater domination and the integration of every aspect of life into capitalist rationalism. The cultural industry plays a key role in domination because it has expanded into the last arena of freedom – culture itself. The culture industry now organizes 'free' time and has integrated it into the logic of capital, that is, production for exchange (rather than need) and standardization (rather than genuine individuality). In the process, the culture industry silences the reflective and critical essence of art and replaces it with an homogenized mass culture which is only an 'escape from the mechanized work process...to recruit strength in order to be able to cope with it again' (Adorno and Horkheimer 1973 [1944]: 135).

For Adorno and Horkheimer, culture has lost its critical capacity because 'it had become commodified, a thing to be bought and sold' (Hesmondhalgh 2007: 15). They argue, from a Marxist perspective, that culture under the system of capitalist commodity production is characterized by production for exchange rather than for use. This has resulted in a universalizing of things that should be particular. By treating everything as a commodity, the intrinsic values of things are displaced onto a universal exchange value (Adorno 1973, 2008). Adorno and Horkheimer argued that the products emanating from the culture industry are subject to this logic and so produce an illusory universalism or unity which not only promotes the dominant ideology, but also represses the idea that there is any alternative to the status quo, to the logic of capital, or to unfreedom.

Adorno reiterates this view in his essay 'Culture industry reconsidered' (1991 [1963]): 'The cultural commodities of the industry are governed...by the principle of their realization as value, and not by their own specific content and harmonious formation. The entire practice of the culture industry transfers the profit motive naked onto cultural forms' (p. 86). For Adorno, the star system is central to the fusing of the economic to the ideological. He argues that:

> Each product affects an individual air; individuality itself serves to reinforce ideology, in so far as the illusion is conjured up that the completely reified and mediated is a sanctuary from immediacy and life. Now, as ever, the culture industry exists in the 'service' of third persons, maintaining its affinity to the declining circulation process of capital, to the commerce from which it came into being. Its ideology above all makes use of the star system, borrowed from individualistic art and its commercial exploitation. The more dehumanized its methods of operation and content, the more diligently and successfully the culture industry propagates supposedly great personalities and operates with heart throbs. (1991 [1963]: 87)

Adorno and Horkheimer have been heavily criticized by academics (see During 2007) who refute the view of the pervasive manipulation of the culture industry. Such critics wanted to re-examine popular culture for moments of opposition to domination, often locating subversion and transgression in the practices of audiences. We shall see how some of the inheritors of such a perspective discuss celebrity news in chapter 4. However, Adorno and Horkheimer's analysis of commodity fetishism in the cultural industries points to the key organizing principle of culture in modern capitalist society – that is, that the production of culture is primarily a pursuit of profit. But this does not mean it is a straightforward business, for we have seen above some of the complexities and specificities of celebrity image-making. Also, cultural industries sociologists, such as Bernard Miège (1989), criticized the Frankfurt School for collapsing together what are quite different industries which produce different types of products (for a film is different from a newspaper) and also for refusing to see the innovative possibilities in new technology, although Miège conceded that industrialization did lead to greater commodification (1989: 11). But Adorno points out that he is suggesting that the term industry not be taken too literally, 'It is industrial more in a sociological sense, in the incorporation of industrial forms of organization even when nothing is manufactured – as in the rationalization of office work – rather than in the sense of anything really and actually produced by technological rationality' (1991 [1963]: 87).

Murdock and Golding also offer an important critique of the Frankfurt School. While they agree that Horkheimer and Adorno's critique is an indispensable starting point for any Marxist analysis of the production of culture under capitalism, they suggest that it is not sufficient simply to assert that the capitalist base of the culture industry necessarily results in the production of cultural forms which are consonant with the dominant ideology. It is also necessary to demonstrate how this process of reproduction actually works by showing in detail how economic relations structure both the overall strategies of the cultural entrepreneurs and the concrete activities of the people who actually make the products the 'culture industry' sells. (Murdock and Golding 1977: 18–19)

One of the central tasks of this book is to examine the business decisions made in particular cultural industries at specific times which resulted either in the increase of celebrity-based content, or the heightened prominence of celebrity in promotional strategies. This book examines why these decisions made sense in context and asks what the consequences were.

For me, though, the main problem with Adorno and Horkheimer's account of the cultural industries is not their identification of the dominance of commodity fetishism, which seems fairly indisputable; instead, it is the evacuation of the notion of contradiction central to Marx's writings, including his writing on the character of the commodity. The perception of the populace as passive, atomized and sutured into consumer capitalism, due to alienation and separation from the collective, only presents one side (although an important one) of the relations of production under capitalism which are at their heart, contradictory.

For Marx, capitalism is essentially contradictory, not because of contradictory ideas, as the philosopher Hegel had previously argued, but due to its contradictory material reality. For instance, those forces which atomize and alienate workers (in particular the division of labour and the processes of exploitation) are the same forces that bring workers together in collective labour, the springboard for collective working-class organization, solidarity and the extension of rights. In the pursuit of profit, capitalists must try to keep wages low to keep profits high, while workers must organize to defend wages in order to live. Capital cannot progress without labour and labour cannot eat unless it is employed by capital, and yet their interests are opposites. Thus, a central material contradiction in the relations of production can never be fully resolved through the operations of cultural or ideological domination – oppositional material interests confront one another.

There is also a contradiction in the character of the commodity (that which is the product of the worker's labour), which Adorno and Horkheimer's analysis omits and which pertains to the question of the function of celebrity. In capitalism, products are commodities because they are produced for exchange (profit) rather than use. For Marx, as for Adorno and Horkheimer, there is a generalized or standard value to a commodity, despite its specificity, which is its exchange value, that is, how much it can be sold for and still make a profit once all of the costs of production have been accounted for. For Adorno and Horkheimer, use value and exchange value are unified, and it is this which leads to standardization – products seem to offer uniqueness when all they really offer is the same standardized product whose basic value is its selling power. But for Marx the commodity form is more contradictory in itself, and this contradiction resides in the opposition between use value and exchange value. In *A Contribution to the Critique of Political Economy* (2014 [1859]), Marx argued that the use value of a commodity appears to be independent of its exchange value. Its use value seems to be based on its ability to satisfy a need and therefore is understood in qualitative terms. That is, the quality of the commodity seems to have an independent existence. However, use values can only be realized in the process of exchange, i.e. in the process of being sold. In the process of being sold, the commodity loses its specificity as a use value because the seller and the system of selling are only concerned with its exchange value; that is, its quantitative value – its profitability in relation to other commodities. So far, Marx and the Frankfurt School seem to be in accord. But Marx goes on to point out that on the other hand the product cannot be exchanged at all unless it has a specific use value. Its generalized or standardized value (profit) can only be generalized through exchanging specific use values for money or its equivalent. Use values are not illusions – a car is not a telephone. But under capitalism, their use value is only meaningful once it has entered the market and becomes a generalized exchange value. Both use value and exchange value, which are opposites, can only be realized in the exchange relationship. We have to understand the generalized system of exchange value if we are to have any hope of understanding how capitalism works. Still, use values do not disappear, the specific value of a commodity is part of the selling process. It seems an obvious point that commodities are not all the same, even though at a fundamental level they all are because they only have value if they can be sold. Marx considered that the commodity was based on a 'whole complex of contradictory premises, since the fulfilment of one condition depends directly upon the fulfilment of its opposite' (2014 [1859]: 112). Adorno and Horkheimer treat the specificity or use value of a commodity as a pseudo-reality, an illusion in the face of standardization. But for Marx, while standardization dominates, it is also predicated upon its opposite.

Marx returns to the commodity and its dual existence as something with a specific property (use value) and also something with a general property (exchange value) in the *Grundrisse* (1993 [1858]). Exchange value is the property that all commodities share, despite their specificity, and that specificity can only be realized if a commodity can be exchanged. But specificity also matters, because exchange could not take place without it – there is no point in selling cheese sandwiches to a micro-processing plant – electronic components would be more appropriate. But capital invests in the production of cheese sandwiches not to satisfy a need per se, but to make a profit, and this lack of planning in the economy has had, and continues to have, dire consequences of overproduction and underproduction, including the grotesque reality of starvation when substantial amounts of food is wasted because it is not sold. Here we see the complexity and the instability of the commodity form. For capital, the rationale of production is profit rather than use, but it depends upon sets of (use) values that it is not designed to address as a system – despite claims to the contrary, and so contradiction is internal to the commodity form.

Cultural production is even more complex because the use values of cultural products are more complex, as are the needs they address – the desire for meaning itself. Predicting the kind of cheese that makes for a profitable sandwich is not straightforward, but it is not as complicated as predicting which story, accompanied by which images and/or sounds, will address a set of far more intangible needs. We shall see that one of the functions of celebrity has been to assist in the process of unifying use values and exchange values in the media and cultural industries, but that this is a complex process which can and does go wrong. This is an important point. A major feature of cultural commodities is precisely the unpredictability of demand. Star and celebrity systems are one approach to the reduction of risk and for addressing unpredictability, as we shall see throughout this book. But this is also a complex process because celebrity in itself does not guarantee success – films and television shows can flop spectacularly despite starring popular celebrities.

Thus what specific celebrities and types of celebrity *mean* is not irrelevant in this process, for their specificity has a role to play in the process of exchange. All celebrities have a value in common – to sell products, media and otherwise. But celebrities are not identical; there are typologies of celebrity (Dyer 2004 [1986]; Geraghty 2000; Rojek 2001); their specific types are not an illusion and unlike other commodities, they are far more unpredictable because they are also living breathing humans, with all the complexity of our species.

Contradiction is also realized in the relations of production. Workers lose control over their labour and over the products of their labour (commodities) because they do not have control in the production process. Their labour and the products of their labour belong not to them, but to the capitalist. For this reason, labour itself is a commodity; it is bought from the worker and controlled by capital.

Celebrities are commodities in both senses discussed here. Their labour is commodified; it produces performances which are only realized in the act of exchange and, unless they are producers themselves, they have no control over the final product. But celebrities are commodities in a third sense. As Richard Dyer argues, 'Stars are involved in making themselves into commodities; they are both labour and the thing that labour produces' (2004 [1986]: 5). All labour is commodified, but while most labour produces either things, or knowledge, or cultural works, stars and celebrities produce *themselves* as commodities too. The image they construct and the persona they produce are central to their value as a commodity, that is, as a figure that can help to sell a film, or a perfume, or a television show.

There has been important scholarship on the differences between stars and celebrities, such as the difference between cinematic aura and televisual immediacy (Langer 1981), and on the specific and changing meanings of individual stars and celebrities (including the pioneering work of Dyer 1979, 2004 [1986]). The specific meanings of stars and celebrities are necessarily multifarious and complex. But they also all have something important in common, for all that variation; what they have in common is that 'they are made for profit' (Dyer 2004 [1986]: 5). In Marxist terms, we can say that they have exchange values in common, and despite the huge variety of specific (use) values (what we might call their meanings), those values are realized in the relationship of exchange. In this book, while I acknowledge important difference in the meanings of stars and celebrities, I am also concerned with the *function* of stars and celebrities and thus what they have in common – their role in the exchange process in media and cultural industries. Sometimes in this book I use the terms stars and celebrities interchangeably, particularly when I am discussing the scholarship on stardom, not because I want to suggest that stars and celebrities have identical meanings, but because the focus of this book is the role that modern fame has played in the development of the media and cultural industries and the reasons that these industries made use of modern fame (called both celebrity and stardom) at particular historical moments in that development. I am focusing therefore on what is shared in common, the function of celebrity in the system of profit. However, also important is the way that this function is realized in very different cultural industries and in specific sets of circumstances, which this book seeks to investigate. This necessarily means examining the specific economic conditions in which it made sense for businesses to develop their celebrity systems and grow celebrity-based output and also necessarily to examine the specific and differing social meanings of celebrity that are tied to these contexts.

In general, celebrities are a central part of the way that media commodities are sold. But as Dyer argues, the image-making system is complex, different agencies inflect images differently, as do different media organizations. A studio may want a polished image of a celebrity to circulate while a tabloid newspaper will invest significant resources into capturing 'unkempt' images of celebrity (Holmes 2005). Even the image of a single star or celebrity is complex, as Dyer reminds us, 'not only do different elements predominate in different star images, but they do so at different periods in the star's career. Star images have histories, and histories that outlive their own lifetime' (Dyer 2004 [1986]: 3). And so too do celebrities; Jade Goody is a prime example of this. Goody became famous during her appearance on the UK version of *Big Brother* in 2002. Goody's early image was as a figure of derision to poke fun at, and she provided many column inches with her lack of education. This image changed in 2007 when she was accused of racially abusing Indian actor Shilpa Shetty when they both appeared on the UK *Celebrity Big Brother*. Her image changed again when she became terminally ill with cervical cancer and died in 2009, and her final depiction was as a dignified mother battling cancer. What Goody shares with the stars that Dyer analysed 30 years ago in *Heavenly Bodies*, is not the historical specificities of image content and how they speak to and of their moment, but her image as a selling point for media. Indeed, that is what unified her own chequered career, and even after her death *Sky Living* profited from these changing images by broadcasting five tribute shows about her life between 2009 and 2012.

Goody's specificity, however, is also tied to the rise of 'ordinary' celebrity, which became an important cultural and economic phenomenon in the 1990s, as we shall see in chapter 5. We shall examine why this form of celebrity becomes a key factor in the restructuring of the television industry and we will also look at the balance of class forces that are articulated by the spread of this form of fame.

The commodity form and the celebrity commodity are contradictory phenomena; cultural value in capitalism is fundamentally economic, but is also reliant on specific cultural meanings. This form is the consequence of relations of production that arise with capitalist

society. But the transition to capitalist modernity is a much broader
transformation that impacted on the economy, politics, society and
culture. It is therefore important to examine the transition to capitalism, which produced both new relations of production and also new
social relations which enable new ways of being famous, and so we
will now turn to that history.

The Transition to Capitalism and the Origins of Celebrity

By the end of the eighteenth century, the cultural politics of fame had
altered drastically because of the enormous political, economic and
social transformations that mark that period of history. This was a
turbulent time that was beginning to shake the old order to its foundations. It was marked by widespread dissent and rioting across
Europe, and in France it culminated in the storming of the Bastille
on 14 July 1789, which inaugurated the first French Revolution. In
August of that year the French National Assembly declared the abolition of feudalism and decreed the Declaration of the Rights of Man
and the Citizen. This swept aside the power of the feudal monarchy
and the clergy and replaced it with a system reaching for democracy,
equality and freedom. Insurrection has a tendency to spread and the
British establishment were deeply troubled. Indeed, prominent Whigs
feared that the 1791 celebrations of the fall of the Bastille would lead
to 'widespread sedition and disorder' in England (Rogers 1998: 192).
    A number of scholars identify the French Revolution as inaugurat-
ing the social conditions that made modern celebrity possible (Braudy
1986; Inglis 2010; Rojek 2001). In the fixed society of pre-
Revolutionary France, fame was predominantly the property of the
monarchs, lords and ladies of Court society. Fame and social prominence was inherited or, in Chris Rojek's term 'ascribed' (2001: 28).
The revolutionary movement that did away with old forms of power
and prominence, he suggests, also elevated the idea of the 'common
man'. In this age, 'ascribed' fame gives way to 'achieved' celebrity;
that is, fame based on achievement rather than bloodline. For Rojek
then, 'celebrity only becomes a phenomenon in the age of the common
man' (2001: 28), so that celebrity is the direct descendent of the
'revolt against tyranny' (2001: 29). This may seem to speak to celebrity as a democratized form of fame as some claim (Ponce de Leon
2002), but the reality is more complex.
    The new social mobility arising from this revolutionary period
gave rise to new ideologies of the self; crucially, alongside the

ideology of the common man grew the ideology of individualism. These new ways of understanding the self began shaping new modes of public prominence that broke with the ideologies of the old order. In addition, the explosion of print culture in the eighteenth century marked the rise of public culture and the widespread dissemination of the image. In this context, European society saw the rise to fame and renown of people from many walks of life, including, significantly, those associated with the incipient mass entertainment industries. Some even suggest that this was the age of the personality as much as it was the age of reason (Luckhurst and Moody 2005). However, this is not to suggest that celebrity is simply a more democratic version of fame as we shall see below.

It is also important to recognize that the revolution sped up political and social tendencies that were already in motion throughout the seventeenth and eighteenth centuries. So while the French Revolution altered politics and society irrevocably, the social movements that culminated in revolution had already began shaping bourgeois notions of public prominence in the late seventeenth and early eighteenth centuries and we can begin to discern competing values for legitimate public renown.

Joseph Addison, for instance, who was famous in the early eighteenth century for his play about classical heroism, *Cato* (2004 [1713]) identifies the existence of two competing forms of fame in an article in the literary journal *The Tatler* (Addison 1987 [1709]). For Addison, fame can be 'that which the Soul really enjoys after this Life, and that imaginary Existence by which Men live in their Fame and Reputation'.[1] We can see in Addison's description two competing forms of fame which have jostled with each other for public attention and legitimacy throughout the modern period (discussed above); the notion of the self-abnegating and hence virtuous hero versus the self-aggrandizing celebrated personality. Addison goes on to describe his dream about joining the ranks of the famous on their path to immortality, who, he notes, are no longer heroic warriors, but artists, writers, explorers and scientists. Addison describes hearing his own name proposed on the roll call of fame and then rejected in favour of the mythical figure of Robin Hood. It is significant that at the beginning of the tumultuous eighteenth century, when Addison expresses concerns about modern fame, it is the figure of Robin Hood who haunts him and overturns his conception of proper renown. The mythical Robin Hood belongs to that category of fame which pits the rebel against the powerful – an icon for the people rather than the elite. So while fame has long been structured by the dualism of 'duty' versus 'display', a third version of fame has also long existed – the figure of the rebel (Hobsbawm 2003 [1969]). In periods of social upheaval and uncertainty, it is always an image of the people that unsettles those of established rank and their spokesmen. Today the British comedian and film and television star Russell Brand might be seen as our Robin Hood figure; he is controversial, anti-establishment and has recently dedicated most of his public image to political activism and questions of redistribution of wealth. And for this dimension of his public persona he is roundly condemned or ridiculed in the media.

Alongside the political revolution was an economic one – the industrial revolution. As the political revolution brought feudalism to an end, the industrial revolution utterly transformed the processes of production and the economy, introducing commodity-based relations of production. It even transformed the landscape as industrial factory production brought large numbers of working people into rapidly growing cities. Britain saw the growth of the immense industrial cities of Birmingham, Sheffield, Leeds, Manchester and Glasgow, while the population of London rose from 900,000 in 1801 to 3,000,000 in 1851 (Booth 1991: 3). These changes altered society irreversibly and the pace and scale of change was startling. A reminder that capitalist modernity has never been 'solid' but subject to constant change, Karl Marx and Frederick Engels wrote:

> Uninterrupted disturbance of all social conditions, everlasting uncertainty and agitation distinguishes the bourgeois epoch from all earlier ones. All fixed, fast-frozen relations, with their train of ancient and venerable prejudices and opinions, are swept away, all new-formed ones become antiquated before they can ossify. All that is solid melts into air. (Marx and Engels 1970 [1848]: 38)

The concerns about 'cultural decline' (discussed above) are rooted in this period of rapid change – a time in which social position is unsettled and there is great uncertainty about rank as new classes come to the fore. Everything was altered in this period, including ways of being publicly renowned and famous. Because of the challenges to aristocratic political and cultural domination, new classes of people attempted to thrust themselves into the public eye and the idea of inherited rank and fame were being questioned as much as the classical idea of fame as bound up with public action, self-abnegation and posthumous reward. This was the period in which the biographer James Boswell and author Laurence Sterne both avidly sought celebrity status.[2] It is also the moment of the rise of the satirist and mimic Samuel Foote, who became famous precisely for satirizing the desire for fame in others. He perfected performances centred on the twin cultural obsessions of the chattering classes of the day, the manipulation of the image to create fame and the destruction of the reputations of public figures (as we shall see in the next chapter).[3]

Foote used mimicry and theatre to satirize the most celebrated characters from the metropolitan world of his day – actors, authors, orators, 'blue-stockings', religious figures, and the occasional aristocrat. In the process of satirizing the desire for fame in others, Foote carefully created his own public image based on mischief and deviance, with more than a hint of danger.[4] Yet Foote's self-invention and theatre of mimicry coincided with a public mood that went beyond the theatre, to permeate all of Georgian culture. The Romantic poets were also subject to rumours and gossip (McDayter 2009; Mole 2009). Indeed, Elizabeth Wilson argues, in her fascinating account of bohemia, that Lord Byron's reputation 'anticipated' twentieth-century forms of 'fame, glamour and notoriety' (2004: 54). Byron seems to exemplify the paradoxes of the period; he was aristocratic, yet an anti-bourgeois rebel; he personified everything the rising bourgeoisie rejected, and 'yet his audiences thrilled to him in his embodiment of artist-as-outlaw' (p. 55). As Leo Braudy argues 'the eighteenth century seemed particularly preoccupied with the question of fame in the modern sense – as a way of defining oneself, making oneself known, beyond the limitations of class and family' (1986: 14). But that preoccupation was infused with an intense uncertainty about the ensuing class mobility and the ability of public figures to create their own fame through manipulation and control of institutions, images and performances. It is also a phenomenon that is deeply paradoxical. Foote also seemed to embody the contradictions and ambivalences of this new approach to the celebrity figure. Foote positioned himself on the fine line between respectability and transgression and at the same time he promoted himself as one who exposed hypocrisy and dissimulations, but 'his self-aggrandising rhetoric conveniently masked a mixture of less glorious motives: money, malice and a desire for power' (Moody 2000: 67).

The Age of the Personality and the Contradictions of Revolution

Although the effects of the political and industrial revolutions of the late eighteenth to mid nineteenth century were permanent, they were also deeply paradoxical, and this leaves a lasting imprint on all of bourgeois culture including the structure of fame. The revolutionary aims of equal rights and citizenship for all were established in theory,

but not fully in practice. Women, for instance, were excluded from
the Third Estate, as were the enslaved populations of the European
empires, including those of post-revolutionary France under the
control of Napoleon. Most poignant of all paradoxes is perhaps when
leader of the Haitian revolution Toussant L'Ouverture led his slave
army into battle against the French in 1791, both armies were singing
the same revolutionary songs of equality and freedom (James 2001
[1938]). As Terry Eagleton points out, 'progress and...deterioration
are closely linked aspects of the same narrative', because 'the conditions which make for emancipation also make for domination' (2004:
179). Eagleton reminds us that in Marxist thinking, dialectical
thought is paramount. He writes,

> [m]odern history has been an enlightened tale of material welfare,
> liberal values, civil rights, democratic politics and social justice, and
> an atrocious nightmare. These two fables are by no means unrelated.
> The condition of the poor is intolerable partly because the resources
> to alleviate it exist in abundance. Starvation is appalling partly because
> it is unnecessary. Social change is necessary because of the lamentable
> state of the planet, but also possible because of material advances.
> (2004: 180)

Chris Rojek observes that the movement to eliminate privilege,
paradoxically and 'unintentionally laid the foundations for the emergence of new forms of distinction' (2001: 29). For Rojek, this is to
do with the bureaucratization of life and the rise of acquisitive society,
'The democratic ideal of being recognized as extraordinary, special
or unique collides with the bureaucratic tendency to standardize and
routinize existence' (2001: 149). But for Wilson and others, it is to
do with the contradictions of the revolutionary moment, particularly
the French revolutions of 1789 and 1848. Certainly, the overthrow
of the old feudal order was contradictory. There were domestic and
foreign assaults on the revolution; Napoleon's rise to power saw the
demise of the Republic, and his reinstatement of the French Empire
(Napoleon gave himself the title of Emperor) saw the degeneration
of the aims of the revolution. His defeat and the restoration of the
Bourbons then ushered in an even more deeply repressive era which
attempted to re-establish the monarchy and turn back the clock,
aided by the foreign intervention of Austria, Russia and Prussia. This
period, poised between revolution and reaction, looking forward and
backward simultaneously, did indeed invent new forms of privilege.
However, despite the setbacks, the trends set in motion by the French
Revolution were irreversible as 1789 was followed by 1848 – and
this includes the paradoxical nature of bourgeois society and culture.

While old forms of inherited power were overturned during the period of revolution, new ones were being created. Mass revolution resulted in constitutional democracies which established the principle of freedom, but not the fact. From the outset, constitutional democracies were shaped by the class interests of an economic elite (Marx and Engels 1970 [1848]).

In addition, the gap between the political revolution and the industrial revolution meant that while equal rights were formally conferred, and the *idea* of equality was widely heralded, there continued to be huge disparities between rich and poor. Thus, while the revolution had been fomented by the common people of Paris and the peasantry of the French countryside, the main beneficiaries of the revolution were the bourgeois class whose wealth and power rose with the growth of industrial society and a centralized nation state that enabled trade and quelled opposition. Engels writes of the 1848 revolutions, 'The people had been victorious, they had won freedoms of a decisively democratic nature, but the immediate ruling power passed not into their hands but into the big bourgeoisie [....] in short the revolution was not complete' (Marx and Engels 1970 [1848]: 64–5). The ideology of equality and freedom was confronted by the reality of a new class heirarchy and associated power. For instance, Marx and Engels argued that the establishment of constitutions, rather than protecting rights and freedoms, became the legal means of curtailing freedom of workers and the poor. Indeed for Marx, 'freedom' becomes class interest disguised as universal value. He writes in *The Eighteenth Brumaire* that the laws of the constitution regulated all liberties granted 'in such a manner that the bourgeoisie in its enjoyment of them finds itself unhindered by the equal rights of other classes' (Marx 2008 [1852]: 159).

It might be said that the industrial revolution merely altered the economic and social forms of inequality – the lord and the peasant tied to his land was replaced by the capitalist and the 'free' worker. The worker might not be tied to the land and was free to join the wave of people engulfing the new industrialized cities, but as Elizabeth Wilson puts it, 'it soon became clear that the new freedom was for some merely the freedom to starve' (2004: 17).

The rise of capitalism saw social mobility on a scale unknown previously, as cities swelled with new populations, but also witnessed the entrenchment of new class power. Modernity meant that individuals from different classes could come to the fore but there were also significant limits to those possibilities and to the social meanings attached to some new forms of prominence as we shall see in the following chapter when we look at the nineteenth-century theatrical star. The political revolution and the creation of an industrial economy revolutionized all belief systems – *all* traditional relationships were disrupted.

Celebrity and the Ideology of Individualism

Certainly, social mobility was an enormously significant aspect of the destruction of feudal social relations and it becomes a central idea in the social meanings of celebrity. The wide scale movement of populations, the shift from fixed and allotted social positions to unfixed and more fluid social positions created both opportunities for new classes of people to gain success while at the same time creating immense uncertainty about social roles in the latter half of the eighteenth century. Alongside the fluidity of social position grew the ideology of individualism, which also becomes central to the values of celebrity. Elizabeth Wilson argues that the dynamic free-for-all that marks modern capitalism generated the belief system of liberal individualism; 'This was a philosophy of personal autonomy, freedom and continual change; freedom of capital; freedom from authority of established religion; freedom from the ties of custom and deference; a demand for the individual democratic rights of every citizen' (2004: 18). Indeed the romantic poets and thinkers such as Jean-Jacques Rousseau were embodiments of the revolutionary side of this new individualism, by living life according to one's passions and advocating this new guide to action.

Fred Inglis reminds us that ideas about the self are as historically constituted as any other phenomenon and they also shifted in the eighteenth century from ones that can be summed up in the difference between Hume's *Dissertation on the Passions* to the redefinition of the self in the Romantic movement. For Hume, morality drives passion towards appropriate and reasonable conduct and there is a strong sense that social man acts in and for the gaze of others. However, by the end of the century this sense of the social self was challenged by the more revolutionary but also more individualized notion of passion emerging out of the Romantic movement. Social man acting in the gaze of others gives way to Romantic man acting 'true to the self'. Morality shifts from the idea of reciprocal moral conduct to centre on the self, the individual, and on spontaneity. Jean-Jacques Rousseau, for instance, scorns Hume's dependence on the gaze of others to advance a philosophy in which being true to one's own feelings is the surest guide to proper conduct. Here action is guided by the individual rather than social obligation.

However, like almost everything else connected to the rise of capitalism, notions of individualism are contradictory. As Wilson notes, while the new industrialists approved of economic individualism (which benefited them so greatly), political and cultural freedom alarmed them and there were repeated attempts to restrict it, including through the development of legal restrictions as Marx demonstrates so forcefully in *The Eighteenth Brumaire* (2008 [1852]). Nonetheless, individualism takes on a force beyond the economic interests of the bourgeoisie and becomes a guide to action, including action in the public sphere.

Individualism and celebrity are inextricably bound together, as many critics have noted. Dyer explains that individualism continues to be a major moving force in our culture. Capitalism 'justifies itself on the basis of freedom (separateness) of anyone to make money, sell their labour how they will, to be able to express opinions and get them heard (regardless of wealth or position)' (2004 [1986]: 10). The narrative of individualism contains a sense of freedom, but also of domination. For, as P.D. Marshall (1997) suggests, celebrity articulates forms of subjectivity that support the value of individuality and the prominence of personality. But for Marshall, this is a means of governing the population and ensuring that compliance to social norms are adhered to. However, Dyer reminds us that while stars and celebrities 'articulate these ideas of personhood, in large measure shoring up the notion of the individual, [they are]...also at times registering doubts and anxieties attendant upon it' (2004 [1986]: 10). The symbolic meanings of celebrity are thus also contradictory integration of opposites.

The Structure of the Book

The symbolic meaning of celebrity is as contradictory as the system from which it emerged. Celebrity speaks both to the arrival of greater freedoms in the modern period, but also demonstrates the limits to those freedoms; it is a sign of the dominance of the commodity form and the idea of culture for profit, and yet it speaks to desires and cultural values outside of the logic of the economic – if it did not, it would have no economic value.

With this in mind, this book has two linked purposes: the first is to ask under what circumstances celebrity grows and spreads, and the second is to examine the role of celebrity in the development of the media industries at key moments and in key sectors. This book argues that the growth of celebrity has occurred primarily for

economic reasons. Celebrity has played a significant role in the fortunes of important media sectors: the press and the news media, the
cinema, the television industry and the internet. Celebrity has become
a key selling mechanism in each of the arenas and this has had an
important impact on the forms and meanings of the products of each
in quite distinct, but connected ways. We will therefore examine
important moments when celebrity becomes central to each of these
industries. In the process of these detailed examinations, the book
challenges three widespread views; that the growth of celebrity is a
product of audience demand, or that it is an inevitable form of public
renown, or that it is necessarily a symbol of the increased democratic
character of public culture.

This book also argues that celebrity burgeons in capitalist society
when particular circumstances collide. These include a general
increase in commercialization, both as an organizing force in cultural
and media industries (and other sectors), and as a set of values that
underpin business decisions. This book therefore begins by examining
the commercial theatre in Britain which produced the first celebrity
or star system (chapter 2). We saw above that there were enormous
social changes that enabled new forms of fame and new types of
famous people, so chapter 2 does not argue that the theatre invented
celebrity, which surely must have multiple points of origin, but instead
that it was the first instance when celebrity becomes a system in the
economics of the cultural form. It is significant that Georgian theatre
is a commercial theatre, for it was subject to commercial pressures
that other European theatres did not face, based as they were on
patronage. Theatrical celebrity emerges as a response to financial
pressures as we shall see. By the mid-Victorian era, after the 1843
Theatre Regulation Act (which consolidated the power of theatrical
management that was allied to speculative commercial capital), the
star system dominated. This was the beginnings of the industrialization of the theatre, witnessed in the rise of theatre ownership and
investment divorced from the production or performance of plays.

Industrialization in the cultural and media sphere is an important
condition in the rise of celebrity systems. We will therefore also
examine the moment of industrialization in both the press and the
cinema, for in both instances the arrival of mass production coincides
with the growth of celebrity as systems of fame become central marketing mechanisms. Chapter 3 begins with an examination of the
growth of the industrialized mass newspaper press which developed
some of the main conventions of celebrity journalism, such as the
celebrity interview, the gossip column, the celebrity human interest
story and the reporting of private scandal. It looks at the economic

conditions that saw this type of journalism replace radical political populist news. This chapter demonstrates that this new type of news was not developed to cater to mass audiences, but in order to cater to advertisers and investors who favoured a suitably consumerist environment for their advertisements and investment and were prepared to pay for it.

The conditions of celebrity growth also include the development of new technology in a context of commercial expansion and/or competition; technology which either transforms existing industries, such as the industrial printing press in the case of the early mass press, or digital technology, again in the case of the press a century later. The arrival of new media technology in an atmosphere of capitalist competition also marks that new media, as we shall see in the case of the cinema in the US, where intense competition led to the kinds of marketing pressure not found in other national cinemas, and which resulted in the entrenchment of the star system in the US, which eventually spread internationally. The commercial climate also marks the introduction of new technology in the case of the internet later in the twentieth century, as chapter 6 examines.

The circumstances in which celebrity grows also include moments of transition in media industries, when uncertainty about profit leads companies to reach for the selling power of celebrity to attract audiences and advertising revenue. Chapter 4 examines the huge increase in celebrity content in the news media at just such a moment in the late 1990s and early 2000s. Celebrity expanded with the arrival of the internet, the growth of news platforms, and increased competition for advertising revenue. Chapter 4 argues that the news media solved the challenges of these circumstances as they migrated online, by increasing celebrity content as 'click bait' to restore profitability to an ailing industry. But it will also ask at what cost to the news as profitable celebrity content pushes out other forms of news such as international news, features sections and investigative journalism.

Celebrity simultaneously expanded due to the radical expansion of commercial television with the introduction of satellite, cable and digital technologies, and with the exponential increase in commercial competition that resulted, as we shall see in chapter 5. The technological developments that restructured the television industries occurred at a time when the ideals of public service broadcasting were under attack, and while those advocating commercial competition as a system for television production were in the ascendant, politically and economically. In this context, which included high levels of competition, new business models were developed which centred on cheap but popular new reality TV formats and the 'ordinary' celebrity which they produced. Ordinary celebrity and interactive television are heralded by some as examples of 'democratainment' (Hartley 2008) and the greater input and power of ordinary people in the media. This chapter will argue that the opposite is true. The rise of ordinary celebrity occurred for economic reasons, which involved a strategy of attacking the conditions of the people who work in the industry, including the ordinary people who perform on the shows. This chapter also examines what 'ordinary celebrity' means in this context to suggest that many of the representations of ordinary people in the media are derisory and injurious, at a time when numbers of working-class people in media professions is in significant decline.

Chapter 6 concludes the book with a discussion of social media and celebrity. This chapter specifically examines social media because we have looked at the development of celebrity in the online news world and the growth of online paparazzi organizations as part of the significant rise in the circulation of images of celebrity online. This chapter instead examines the arrival of social media software as a new space for the celebrification of the self. It examines the contradictory values that structured the development of social media software which has resulted in a simultaneous tendency for software to encourage the celebrification of online participation and the use of new technology for more radical political projects. It argues that many social media platforms embed celebritization in everyday practices online, but suggests that this is not in the character of the technology itself. Rather, it is in the character of the Web 2.0 entrepreneurs who shaped this new media form.

I have chosen to look at these specific moments because they have been central moments in the growth and entrenchment of celebrity. These are moments when new technology, commercialization and uncertainty come together to provide the context in which businesses develop celebrity-oriented strategies of marketing and sales. In the early period of the industrialization of the cultural field, the industries of the mass press and the cinema entrench celebrity as a central economic organizing force – the cinema borrowing much from the earlier theatrical star system. In the late twentieth century, increased commercialization set the scene for the arrival of new technology that could have completely revolutionized media communication to the benefit of humanity, by abolishing information and communication scarcity and by making the means of production accessible to all. But this potential was hampered by the context of its emergence – the dominance of the profit motive as the purpose for cultural production and hence of commodity fetishism – the basic value of cultural production being based in its sellability. It is this same commodity fetishism which produces systems of celebrities in media and cultural industries, shaping and tailoring content around the celebrity commodity.

In providing the necessary detailed examination of these key moments, which I suggest have been central to the expansion of celebrity, this book also has necessary omissions. For instance, it does not examine the rise of public relations in the twentieth century and the place of celebrity in that particular industry. Nor does it examine advertising as an industry, which has certainly both relied upon and expanded the circulation of celebrity images in society (although I do examine the importance of advertising in other media and the role of celebrity in attracting it). The role of celebrity in both of these industries requires book-length studies of their own. This book has also not examined the music industry, another sector where celebrity is a central exchange value but which also produces complex use values as the popularity of pop stars must be one of the most difficult things to predict. Again, this topic is for a longer study in its own right. Nor has this book examined the way the processes of celebritization have impacted on fields outside of media industries, such as political celebrity, sports celebrity, humanitarian celebrity, etc. The celebritization of public culture is an enormous and enormously important topic (for a detailed discussion, see Redmond 2013). However, celebrity is so ubiquitous a phenomenon that to examine each instance would take a dozen book-length studies, which is one of the reasons why the study of celebrity is a growing area of academic concern; its ubiquity and cultural importance cannot be underestimated.

This book provides one of the first book-length studies on the economic character of celebrity. It seeks to examine when, where and why celebrity became a central economic component in the media industries, and to what effect. This book is therefore asking less what celebrity is, and more, what do systems of celebrity do? In the process this book inevitably examines some of the contours of celebrity meanings as they are constituted in each of these industries and in each of these specific moments. Chapter 2 examines the contradictions in fame for female actors in the British theatre; chapter 3 examines how one set of (populist political) values came to be replaced by celebrity and entertainment values in the early mass press and it also looks at the way that cultural and economic meanings were fused in the early cinema star in the US. Chapter 4 examines the extent to which traditional news values are currently being replaced by 'celebrity news' and why. Chapter 5 looks specifically at the category of ordinary celebrity and questions the extent to which this manifestation of fame is an opening up of the public sphere; a democratic inclusion of ordinary people in the media. It argues that much of the meaning of ordinary celebrity vacillates between denigrating those who are seen to lack middle-class values to celebrating those who embrace neoliberal values of the self. Finally, chapter 6 examines the contradictions of constructions of the self in social media; a form which encourages producing an online self that echoes the commodity structure of the celebrity self, but simultaneously provides the means for radical political activism and organization. The book concludes by suggesting that celebrity is without question part of our system of hierarchy and domination; facilitating the economic domination of mainstream media outlets, providing images of the famous (and possibilities for selfhood) that supports consumerism and neoliberalism, or else maligning and excluding those who do not 'fit', and doing so for profit. But domination is seldom absolute, and the contradictions in celebrity culture are a reminder that there continue to be competing ideals and values about what it means to be human.

2

Celebrity and the Theatre: Modernity and Commercial Culture

Introduction

This chapter begins our examination of the growth of celebrity at key moments in the development of commercial culture, to suggest that the theatre in Britain in the late eighteenth century was one of the first of such moments, providing shape and purpose to the promotional role of celebrity for the coming commercial entertainment and media industries. Ways of understanding public figures as celebrities (famous for their private lives as much as their public achievements) begins in the European culture of the late eighteenth century, as modern ways of thinking about the self and about greatness were emerging at this time with the challenges to the existing order. This chapter argues that the processes that accelerate in the nineteenth century with the growth of the mass media are to be found in incipient form with the rise of public culture and that in this context, the British theatre produces the first system of stardom.

In fact, it is widely accepted in studies of the theatre that the eighteenth century is the historical moment when fame takes a recognizably modern form (Luckhurst and Moody 2005). This chapter argues that the British theatre is one of the first examples of the development of a *system* of fame that was used not only to confer prestige but also to promote productions to audiences, and it also argues that it is not an accident that this system emerges in Britain's theatre because of its long commercial history. This chapter suggests that theatrical celebrity was the result of the combined pressures of the commercial organization of the theatre, the development of new technologies and important legislative changes that shifted the balance of power in the theatre towards entrepreneurial capital. In this sense, this examination of the British theatre begins this book's political economy of celebrity, in particular an examination of its promotional and marketing functions in the growth of entertainment and media capital.

However, this chapter also examines some of the contradictions that emerge with this new political economy of fame. With theatrical celebrity we see the spread of fame and social power to new social groups (what some have called the democratization of fame, a formulation that will be interrogated throughout this book) but we also see the simultaneous development of new forms of hierarchy which circumscribe or exclude the possibilities for the public to participate in public life. Theatrical women provide a clear example of this and so the chapter concludes by examining the celebrity status of early female theatrical stars to reveal this dichotomy. It argues that the importance of blurring the public image and the private life of the celebrity and star begins in this period, and that this public/private paradox is revealed to be deeply gendered from its earliest formation. We find the growing power of women in the theatre and also significant limits to their full and equal participation. As Inglis suggests, it is the theatre that gives us the public/private dichotomy, 'where private turns out to be synonymous with sexual' (2010: 41). Women's growing role in the theatre came at a cost as we shall see, because the 'sexual' is a highly gendered field, defining and constraining female actors and managers (Powell 1997).

Celebrity and Restoration Theatre: the Wider Context

Celebrity is a modern form of fame commensurate with capitalist society, both culturally as well as economically, and as we saw in the previous chapter, the rise of celebrity corresponds to the enormous social changes wrought by the emergence of capitalism – the rise of the bourgeoisie, the spread of democracy and its curtailment, the development of technology, the processes of industrialization, urbanization, the rise of consumerism, and the development of new forms of leisure. The role of celebrity in society is related to these wider social transformations, and so the key moments in the political economy of celebrity are part of a set of wider interrelated socio-economic processes that played a part in the development of modern fame. For instance, Fred Inglis reminds us that by the middle of the nineteenth century, the rise of great cities, first London, then Paris, followed by New York, replaced the European monarchy as the centre of western society (2010: 40) and provided the stage for the new forms of leisure in which celebrity comes to be central – London, the theatre, Paris, haute couture, and New York, the industrialized mass press.

Yet, there is little agreement between academic disciplines about the specific historical emergence of modern celebrity. It is a common belief that celebrity is a relatively recent phenomenon, emerging in the late nineteenth or early twentieth century. Traditional film scholars assume that celebrity is an outgrowth of the star system that emerged in relation to the infant film industry and the subsequent development of Hollywood (Gabler 1994; Hampton 1970 [1931]; Morin 1960; Schickel 1985). Although Hollywood has an important place in celebrity and stardom, the phenomenon has, as this chapter demonstrates, a much longer history. For others, the origins of celebrity can be located in the developing journalistic practices of the mass circulation press in the nineteenth century. Scholars such as Ponce de Leon suggest that it was the development of certain reporting conventions that cultivated the treatment of public figures as celebrities and he emphasizes the importance of the news media in creating and sustaining celebrity culture (2002: 5). There is evidence of a long symbiotic relationship between the press, commercial entertainment and celebrity, which extends back before the nineteenth century, and which is a central theme of this book. The broad social changes that enabled the possibility of fame for new classes of people, including theatrical players, also simultaneously contributed to the growth of newspapers and other print culture in the eighteenth century. This led to the rise of public culture and the national and even international dissemination of the public face. However, while the rapidly expanding print culture was crucial for the dissemination of celebrity by building mass audiences, it was in the Georgian theatre that a *system* of stardom first came into being and theatrical players in the eighteenth century reached an extraordinary level of fame.

But theatrical celebrity did not arise spontaneously, nor was it simply a response to audience desires (Staiger 1991). In fact, desires and feelings, as Fred Inglis points out, are as historically constituted as anything else (2010: 19). The desire to be or to see celebrities is connected to the reality of the 'flashy, jumbled world of London' (Inglis 2010: 22) of the late eighteenth century, where old bonds of class, family and duty still existed but were significantly undermined; as Inglis puts it '[a] vehement and counterposed riptide was...beginning to tear across these long undulations of European feeling by the end of the century' (2010: 25). Importantly, the rise of the Romantic movement in arts and politics spoke in the language of revolution, egalitarianism, but also in the growing idiom of a new individualism. The rules of correctness and decorum were being supplanted by spontaneity and iconoclasm, while the notion of duty was confronted with a new guide to action based on 'being true to one's feelings' (Inglis 2010: 25). New social classes arose in this period and also in the theatre, shaping the economic structure of the theatre, its place in society and a new cultural hierarchy, as we shall see below.

The British Theatre and Early Celebrity: the Birth of Modern Fame

First we will turn our attention to the processes by which a system of celebrity came into being in the Georgian theatre. The growth of theatrical celebrity did not arise spontaneously either from the expansion of the range of actors nor from the desires of audiences. Changes in the structure of feelings contributed to a public interest in the previously private realm of the emotions, and a prurient interest in the private lives of actors, female actors in particular, was cultivated in this context through theatre managers, the press and the publication of memoirs, all trying to profit from the rumour mill, as we shall see below. What then, was the cause of this early star system? What were the economic reasons for the development of a system of celebrity stardom in the theatre? A close examination of the rise of the theatrical stardom in Britain does not suggest that it was simply a case of responding to the demands of the public taste for stars. Instead, we find that stardom occurs as a result of important struggles for economic power and control. In fact, in the theatre as in other cultural spheres, it was the commercial status of the theatre, followed by the consolidation of capitalist economic relations and the drive towards industrialization of this subfield of culture, that saw first (1) the rise of its system of stardom, then (2) its firm establishment as part of the system of the production and circulation of plays and, finally, (3) the export of this system to other emerging entertainment industries such as the cinema.

It is common to assume that the coming of the star system in the theatre was a product of the way that audiences responded to prominent actors and clamoured to see them in performances. However, the British theatre had a long tradition of stock companies without a star performer. Stardom was not a characteristic of traditional theatrical culture in Britain, which had been dominated by the stock system until the early eighteenth century. The stock system was a system of fairly stable acting companies who were attached to a theatre and who performed a repertory of a number of plays, rotating them nightly. The lead roles in plays performed by stock companies rotated between a variety of experienced and prominent actors, and despite differences in salaries, actors in a company shared the same conditions of service. Thus in this period theatre goers were drawn to the theatre because of a play or a whole company, rather than an individual performer, and people from all walks of life attended the theatre, including the new working classes and the poor who were able to afford cheap seats in the pit. But the stock system was undermined and eventually replaced by the star system and so, although it is difficult to identify an exact date for the coming of the theatrical star, it is certainly the case that by the 1820s the star system in the theatre was firmly in place and the stock system was in its death throes (Booth 1991; Rowell 1978; Taylor 1989; Wanko 2003).

How did the star system replace the stock system in the British theatre? According to Cheryl Wanko (2003: 217), theatrical celebrity resulted from the increased commercial control of the theatre and the arts, and we shall see below why this is the case. However, unlike other European countries such as France, where, under the *ancien régime*, a system of patronage operated to fund the arts (the traditional clientele for art was the aristocracy and clergy), in England, the theatre had always run along commercial lines – it was not directly subsidized by the aristocracy, privilege was accorded in a different manner. In 1737 the Licensing Act established a form of indirect patronage by giving Royal Patents to two London theatres, Drury Lane and Covent Garden, to perform 'legitimate' plays (by which was meant Shakespeare) and licenses to other theatres under the direction of the Lord Chamberlain's office (Davis 2004: 31). The 1737 Act protected the profits of 'legitimate' theatres by making it illegal for competitors to perform 'serious' spoken plays. The Act also gave the state the power to raid and shut down 'illegitimate' theatres, which it did on a regular basis (Moody 2000).

While the intention of the Act was to secure the profits of the legitimate theatres, it also, as an unintended consequence, conferred enormous prestige on Drury Lane and Covent Garden Theatre Royals in London, giving a great deal of power to their managers and enhancing the reputation of the leading actors (Thomas 1984). Charles Fleetwood (manager of Drury Lane), for instance, poached David Garrick from Goodman's Field theatre in Whitechapel after his successful performance as *Richard III*. Fleetwood then used his patents letter to have his competitors at Goodman's Field theatre closed down in 1742. The actor David Garrick went on to become one of the most influential figures in eighteenth-century theatre and on Fleetwood's retirement, managed Drury Lane for 29 years. Thus figures such as Garrick began to develop individual reputations linked to the legitimate theatre. They also attempted to enhance their own reputations through a refined publicity and they tried to improve the overall reputation of the theatre as an arena of high culture. Inglis argues that not only did Garrick make himself the theatre's 'first celebrity' (2010: 42), he also replaced popular programmes of light opera and song with 'serious' plays: 'Shakespeare was the key and this is the moment – the moment of more or less conscious nation-building...during which Shakespeare was canonized as the greatest *English* writer, and pride of the nations literature' (2010: 42).

Yet, despite the growing prominence of individual actors such as Garrick and his leading lady Peg Woffington, or Sarah Siddons, the stock system continued to persist in the British theatre. What began to undermine the stock system was the advent of single touring stars. Touring becomes an important factor in the rise of the star system at two distinct junctures of the British theatre: the first was when prominent players from the legitimate theatre in London begin to tour the provinces after 1737, and then again in the mid to late nineteenth century when a new breed of actor-manager begins to take an entire show on the road, completely displacing provincial stock companies. In the first period, esteemed actors from Drury Lane and Covent Garden began touring the provincial Theatre Royals during the summer months when Covent Garden and Drury Lane were closed, performing as a temporary attraction in a local stock company (Booth 1991: 16). It was these touring actors from the legitimate London theatre that laid the ground work for the star system, crucially, by undermining the traditional stock company system. Although there was a long tradition of touring among provincial theatres, including circuits of provincial Theatre Royals, these companies had toured as relatively stable troupes and they coexisted with the non-touring stable stock company; it was the independence of the touring 'legitimate' London actors that first destabilized the stock system. Not only did they command much higher salaries than the stock players with whom they performed, they had different conditions of employment. While on tour in the provinces, they were independent, freelance actors who were able to negotiate high fees and sometimes a proportion of the box office receipts. In turn, managers made savings by reducing the salaries of the stock actors. More expensive competent actors were replaced by cheaper but less competent actors. George Rowell claims that the invitation by provincial theatres to London performers was 'ruinous to the pride and standards of the resident company' (1978: 155). Playwright Shirley Brooks bemoans the decline of the acting company and the rise of the single star in a House of Commons Select Committee Report in 1866: plays are now composed of 'one good central figure, while the rest are stocks and puppets...There is no single company now which is wholly composed of good actors'.[1] In a cycle of scarcity of talent that resulted from the undermining of the stock system, managers of provincial theatres became even more dependent on touring stars from the West End as the quality of acting in local stock companies deteriorated. According to Luckhurst and Moody, local theatres thus began to market the coming performances of well-known West End performers in order to try to boost ticket sales (2005: 3) and, in an atmosphere of competition between theatre managers, fees for West End stars rocketed (prefiguring the artificial scarcity of talent found in the cinema and television in the following century, as we will see in chapters 3 and 4).

The stock company did not disappear overnight, however. George Taylor argues that for the first half of the nineteenth century, the stock system and the star system existed simultaneously, but eventually the star actor-manager came to dominate, so that by the mid century the stock system was gone (1989: 22). Booth argues that it was the touring company that finally ended the stock system (1991: 19), while George Rowell (1978) suggests that it was the theatrical 'long run' of a single play which undermined the stock system. In fact, there is evidence to suggest that it was the combined force of each of these elements that led to the demise of the stock system: actor-managers were keen on touring, despite the initial expense, because the rewards could be high, the touring company grew out of the needs of the touring star, and in turn, the expense of the touring company contributed greatly to the development of the long-run play, as will be explained below. Each of these connected elements not only contributed to the demise of the stock system, but as a consequence, rendered the theatre more reliant on the performances of star actors from the legitimate London theatre.

Touring and the Establishment of Theatrical Stardom

The expense of contracting a touring West End player – as we have seen – diminished the quality of player in stock companies as expensive experienced actors were replaced cheaply. This meant that managers of local theatres came to be even more dependent on touring 'star' performers to draw in audiences who would not pay to watch poor acting. Also, as the standard of acting in stock companies continued to deteriorate, with low salaries and fewer roles (which, recall, is a result of the single touring West End actor), a number of touring actors took the decision to enter management themselves and to insist upon touring with their own supporting actors, and this led to the eventual dominance of the actor-manager which in turn further undermined the stock system. Although there had long been individual actor-managers in the British theatre, as a system of theatrical management – that is, a star-led touring theatre – it did not come to dominate until the mid nineteenth century. As we shall see throughout this book, the introduction of new technology is a factor in the growth of stardom and celebrity and this is not necessarily confined to media technology. For example, the star-led touring theatre was helped significantly by the expansion of the railway and other transport systems of the industrial revolution that made travel to and from London much easier, both for touring stars, and also for theatre goers coming into London from the surrounding towns and villages. The railway enabled not just actors, but sets and costumes to be transported more easily. For some actor-managers, touring was necessary for survival. Charles Anderson had bankrupted himself trying to manage Drury Lane in the 1850s, so he used his star prestige and turned to touring which proved to be extremely lucrative (Booth 1991).

The connections between touring and the advent of the 'long run' actually come together in the figure of James R. Anderson, who, at odds with repertory theatre's tradition of regular rotation of plays, played Hamlet for 12 consecutive nights – a long enough run, he judged, to produce original scenery for the play. Original scenery and its transportation costs began to make a significant contribution to the running costs of a troupe. Other star actor-managers of the day, such as Charles Macready, Dion Boucicault and Henry Irving, offset the rising costs of theatrical production in London (due not only to more elaborate sets, but also to more expensive leases on theatres in London), by touring. The quintessential star actor-manager, Henry Irving, who managed the Lyceum from 1877 to 1899, toured the provinces and America extensively (Bingham 1978). According to Booth, his tours 'handsomely subsidised the Lyceum and showed other managers that international touring was desirable and lucrative' (1991: 54). The Lyceum was the first English company to be acclaimed internationally. And touring actor-managers not only destabilized the stock system in Britain, but they also exported the star system to the US, undermining the stock system that had operated there (Bernheim 1932).

Theatrical Reform, Power and Celebrity

Another key aspect of nineteenth-century theatre was the reform of aristocratic power by the Theatre Regulation Act in 1843. This Act shifted the balance of power in the theatre towards actor-managers allied with entrepreneurial and speculative capital, and away from the capital of the traditional landed gentry. It was this shift in power that eventually made possible the industrialization of the theatre. By the turn of the nineteenth century the power of legitimate theatre contended with claims coming from a range of theatre managers; those with a licence but no patent to perform legitimate drama, the managers of well-established minor and provincial theatres who operated on the edge of the law, and the managers of illegitimate and penny theatres which catered for the working class and poor. By the 1830s in Britain, minor houses routinely performed legitimate repertoire no matter how often they were raided. Their share of the market made it profitable and worthwhile to perform Shakespeare without a license.

The 1843 Theatre Regulation Act is heralded by some as spelling an end to protectionism and the introduction of egalitarian theatrical free trade. But the reform really simply put into law what the established minor theatres had been doing for years, ending the protectionism that legitimate theatre owners expected from their allegiance to the aristocracy. However, by this stage, the prestige lent to the legitimate theatres and the actors who performed in them (and who took this prestige with them when they toured local theatres), had already established the importance of star performers in the marketing of plays, and the system of theatrical stardom. Equally significant is the way that the Act also destroyed the theatre of the working class and poor by insisting that for a theatre to be licensed, it had to be a permanent structure and purpose built (Taylor 1989: 17). In the process, and using the language of free trade, the Act suppressed the illegitimate penny theatre that was frequented by the working class and urban poor (these performances often contained radical politics and frequently induced riots which was a major incentive to close these theatres). In fact, the Act gave the Lord Chamberlain's office greater power to censor and veto drama across the nation and this new power was used primarily to censor political material from plays aimed at working-class audiences, purging them of 'rioting-inducing ideas' and, according to some, attempting to indoctrinate the people 'to the tastes and politics of the ruling elite' (Davis 2004: 37). Thus the free market rules that the Act was intended to promote did not increase competition or support the majority theatre – the 'people's theatre'. Instead the Act resulted in the loss of the neighbourhood theatres that catered to the politics and tastes of the working class and poor. Taylor argues that (just like the famous repeal of the Corn Laws in 1845) 'the Theatre Act was passed to benefit the managerial class more than the theatrical "hands" (actors), or even the consumers (the audiences)' (Taylor 1989: 17). By the second half of the nineteenth century, most of London's East End theatres, which had grown up in the 1820s and 1830s, had closed.[2] The only option for working-class audiences was to take up the cheapest seats in the licensed legitimate theatres, to watch 'serious' plays that, as we have seen, were by this stage dominated by the performance of a star actor-manger.

It is important to pause to consider the implications of this history for our understanding of the rise of stardom: the star system in the theatre did not emerge in order to cater to popular taste – in fact the opposite is true. Nor did it emerge simply because the audiences desired to 'see stars' (and Janet Staiger (1991) argues persuasively that this is true of the US theatre too); indeed, it may be suggested that this desire was deliberately manufactured (Davis 2004). The star system in the British theatre is actually consolidated by the very processes that ensured the *decline* of the popular theatre in the nineteenth century. The establishment of stardom and celebrity in the theatre coincides with the demise of popular and radical theatre and the expansion of middle-class commercial theatre. The 1843 Act embedded the existing commercial structure into the British theatre and eventually led to the industrialization of the theatre. It also enshrined in law the middle-class taste culture that was simultaneously being disseminated by the burgeoning press (Rojek 2001: 104). The development of theatrical celebrity is intimately connected to the rise of commercial theatre and the development of theatre as a business. It is the power of the actor-manager which initially fuses celebrity to the economic structures of the theatre.

The Rise of the Actor-Manager, the 'Long Run' and the Industrialization of the Theatre

As we have seen, the power of the theatre manager arose first in the legitimate theatres that were protected by the 1737 Licensing Act which gave them enormous power by protecting their profitability and conferring status. Managers had considerable power not only to decide a theatre's repertory, to hire and fire actors and to allocate roles, but also to promote and legitimate traditional cultural values. In an atmosphere of increased competition and commercialization, the power and status of managers was extended after 1843 to managers from a range of theatres. Rising actors, who wanted more power and control over their careers, took the decision to go into management in order to stand at the apex of the Victorian theatrical hierarchy (Booth 1991: 27).[3] Despite the financial risks (for the manager had to finance his or her theatre entirely out of their own pocket), managers could and did amass fortunes (Booth 1991: 31). But as important was the ambition to enhance one's own status and power. Prominent actor-managers were the 'theatrical equivalent of the rising middle-class' who sought to assert political supremacy (Taylor 1989: 17). According to Taylor, actor-managers such as Charles Macready, Charles Kean and Samuel Phelps thought they had a duty towards the culture of their country (1989: 17). They were self-appointed defenders of the 'best interest of English drama' (Booth 1991: 43). Actor-managers, as we saw above, contributed to the erosion of the stock system by touring with their own supporting cast, and while they benefited from the star system, they also depended on their own star status for the success of their theatre, further embedding the star system into the theatre.

In order to maintain profitability, more and more actor-managers turned not only to touring, but later to producing a single play for a long run. Touring became more expensive as actor-managers travelled with their own supporting cast rather than relying on the lowered standards of local stock companies. So rather than duplicating the rising costs of production, actor-managers began to play their more successful plays on many consecutive nights, instead of rotating a repertory. This became known as the 'long run' and it was practised both in West End theatres and on tour. Many star actor-managers in the mid to late nineteenth century had been trained in repertory theatre and those who were committed to the repertory system saw their fortunes wane. Thus the repertory theatre of actor-manager Samuel Phelps (1804–78) gave way to the long run theatre of actor-managers such as Dion Boucicault, the Bancrofts and Henry Irving. The crucial decades of change were the 1860s and 1870s, which, according to Taylor, transformed the whole structure of the acting profession (1989: 6). In 1860 Dion Boucicault ran a production of *The Colleen Bawn* for 230 consecutive nights at the Adelphi Theatre (Taylor 1989: 8). Boucicault himself claimed that he was creating a 'new order of theatrical affairs' (Taylor 1989: 8). Irving repeated the success of the long run with a production of *Hamlet* which ran for

100 nights at the Lyceum in 1878. The following year he produced his most successful Shakespearian play, *The Merchant of Venice*, which ran for 250 nights (Booth 1991: 54). The long run was a growing trend across the late nineteenth century. In the 1850s, for example, only 13 productions ran for 100 nights or more. By the 1860s, this had risen to 45 productions and by the 1870s to 107 productions (Booth 1991: 13).

The long run was also, of course, facilitated by the rising populations of big cities, by extending the potential audiences for a play that is repeated each night. Paradoxically, the long run also made theatres more dependent on their star performances, as theatres competed with each other for the now predominantly middle-class theatre-going audiences. The long run also reduced the number of possible stars by reducing the changeover time in performed material. So while it was the touring of independent West End actors that initiated the decline in the stock system, and inaugurated the use of star performers to market plays, in the Victorian period, the long run system saw the stock system completely replaced by the star system, with star actor-managers at the top of the theatrical hierarchy.

The British theatre in this period was undergoing industrialization. The long run brought about a separation of theatre ownership from that of play producing for the first time. Theatre ownership became a business in itself, as real estate. For example, the New Theatre Royal in Bristol was opened in 1867 (later renamed The Prince's Theatre) with a resident acting company, but before long, the company was disbanded and the theatre became exclusively a touring house for visiting star actor-managers and their own companies (Rowell 1978: 156). By the 1870s there were chains of large well-equipped provincial theatres without a resident company who catered entirely to housing touring long-run productions from London's West End theatres (Rowell 1978: 84). Thus the theatre went from being a single enterprise to two enterprises, with competition between theatres and between those who produced plays. It also led to financial wrangling between theatre owners and managers of plays. This produced a third enterprise in the form of booking agents who acted as middle men and who profited well from the competition in the theatre world.

In both Britain and the United States, the theatre transformed from a 'stock system' to a 'star system', not, as Janet Staiger rightly argues, because of a demand from the public to 'see stars' (1991: 10), but because of changes in the economic structure of the theatre business and its industrialization. The star actor was a marketing tool initially for the provincial theatres in Britain, whose audiences were predominantly the wealthy and well-to-do. Prior to the 1843 Act, the working class and the poor had mostly frequented a different sort of theatre, a bawdy, irreverent, and often politically charged theatre populated by stock troupe actors. It is only after the 1843 Act that star actors came to dominate the theatre, and they did so as much for economic reasons as for cultural.

Alfred Bernheim (1932) has suggested that the stock system in the US was undermined by the arrival of the British theatrical star system from the 1790s on. Just as in the UK, early theatre in the US was a 'stock system' made up of individual theatre managers who controlled a fairly permanent company of actors who either toured or were attached to a theatre leased by the manager for a season (or occasionally owned outright by him or her). However, by the 1820s the stock system (still at its height) began to be undermined by what Bernheim calls the 'combination system' which was made up of 'temporary producing units, each organized for one play' and unconnected to a specific theatre (1932: 26). These temporary units contained a combination of a star actor and a number of stock players. By the 1820s a large number of British stars visited the US, including Edmund Keane, Charles Matthews, Junius Brutus Booth, William Charles Macready and Charles and Fanny Kemble (who were all actor-managers) (Bernheim 1932: 27). These theatrical stars toured the US for special engagements and demanded independence from the theatre company who toured with them. And just as in the case of the British theatre, these touring stars undermined the existing stock system as resources were redirected from employing experienced stock company actors to paying for expensive (but hopefully lucrative) touring productions from the UK. By the 1860s the stock system had been undermined by the independent star system, giving birth to the combination system (Bernheim 1932: 29) with one star and one or two supporting leads. The dependence on visiting stars tended towards touring with a single play (the long run) which gradually replaced the practice of a theatre company with a repertoire of plays. The star-led touring theatre was also helped by the advances in the systems of transportation in both the US and UK, particularly the development in steam ships which made transatlantic travel much faster and safer. In fact, the shipping lanes between the US and UK were some of the busiest in the world in the latter half of the nineteenth century and the first decades of the twentieth.

Bernheim argues that 'the star becomes a new kind of actor-manager' (1932: 29) who no longer needed any local support. He (although there were exceptions, most of these transatlantic actor-managers were male) had total control over the production and eventually took his own scenery, stage hands and even orchestra with him on tour. And so by the 1870s the stock system had more or less vanished in the US also and had been replaced by the theatrical star system.

According to Bernheim, after the 1870s the 'combination' system was replaced by what he terms the 'syndication' phase of theatre in the US, as in the UK, taking the theatre into the era of big business. In fact, the combination system led to the next phase of economic organization in the theatre because of its emphasis on temporary touring companies. As a result of theatrical companies travelling across the US, networks or circuits of theatres developed across the US in line with the route growth of the railways and those regularly travelled. Increasingly, these theatres were not owned by theatre managers but by businessmen for whom the theatre was a real estate investment. Under the separation of theatre ownership from production, booking touring productions became a business in itself. American entrepreneurial penchant for middle-man profiteering could be found in the role of theatre booking agents. Theatre booking agents took advantage of this separation by supplying contracts between individual theatre circuits and touring theatrical companies. This developed into a centralized system of syndication (which the cinema grafted onto as we shall see in the following chapter). In August 1896, three agencies (Klaw & Erlanger, Hayman & Frohman and Nixon & Zimmerman) formed the Theatrical Syndicate (Staiger 1991: 8), which asserted a monopoly control of theatrical booking by drawing up contracts that demanded that touring productions use its services exclusively. The key feature of syndication was the centralization of both the producing side of the business and of the booking side. So in the decades prior to the monopoly trusts of the early film industry, the theatre was controlled by trust-style booking agents, as businessmen and entrepreneurs attempted to gain financially from the ownership and distribution of cultural forms. In this context, the star performer of the star-led touring play became a significant marketing tool for those whose business it was to book tours and pull in American audiences, who had to be taught, as Staiger (1991) comments, to want to see stars. One of the ways that audiences were encouraged to find stars appealing was through the public/private paradox and in the case of female actors by encouraging a prurient interest in matters sexual. Female actors often had greater wealth and independence than most women outside of the aristocracy, but they were almost entirely defined in sexual terms in order to appeal to male audiences, as we shall see below. Thus the public/private paradox itself is more than partly developed as a marketing ruse, with a significant emphasis on female sexuality. Female audiences were also drawn by displays of sexuality and of love, for as Inglis argues, the space for social action for women was circumscribed and still firmly located in the private sphere. While men of the Romantic movement had the twin impulsive passions of money and love, Romantic woman 'could only be spontaneous in the tiny area of passionate love' (2010: 27), and so even the new feeling structures of the eighteenth century – including the modern sensibility of individuality – contributed to the blurring of the private/public realm through the publicization of passion as the next section demonstrates.

The Fame of Women in the Theatre and the Private/ Public Paradox

Celebrity, even in the early period, is a form of fame obsessed with collapsing the divide between public and private, and with the developments of its consorts, rumour and scandal. Many early theatrical stars were women, who, like other groups in society, found greater freedom as a result of social upheaval. However, gender provides one of the salient examples of the paradoxes of modernity. The changing sexual landscape meant that for the first time women beyond the realms of the aristocracy were thrust into the public eye. But even so, the public definition of femininity was confined to the private realm. This contradiction found expression in the public definition of the actresses of the time which had a luridly sexual side and this points to the deep gender inequalities that also shaped the new era of 'freedom' (Williamson 2014). The greater possibilities opened up to women were severely limited both by the commercial imperatives of the theatre and the press and because of normative values about different social roles for men and women which were becoming entrenched as the social and political power of the bourgeoisie solidified.

Fame for women in the theatre was won at a cost. Actresses' financial independence depended upon acquiescence to public insinuations about their sexuality, and here we see that the theatrical star system and that of celebrity (with its emphasis on the private and personal) combine. We also see the early symbiotic value of celebrity to the theatre and to the burgeoning press. The press mercilessly targeted prominent women and accusations of sexual wrongdoing were regularly voiced. Highly popular was the printing of scandal, the attempted destruction of reputations, and women were a favourite target, particularly where crime and sexuality could be linked (Kinservik 2007). Two crime stories in particular caught the imagination of the British commercial press and its readers in the late eighteenth century: the stories of Caroline Rudd, on trial for forgery, and the Duchess of Kingston, on trial for bigamy (Moody 2000). Both had been indicted for crimes involving accusations of adultery and the use of sexuality to manipulate the opposite sex and both seemed to challenge society's basic assumptions about femininity. Both trials produced a frenzy of interest, for each seemed to undermine the institution of marriage and gave expression to concerns about changing roles of women. These cases also highlight an early example of the symbiotic relationship between the scandal-mongering of the press and the activities in other spheres of culture, including the theatre. For instance, Samuel Foote, a theatre manager operating on the edge of legality himself (who built a reputation on the theatre of mimicry and of sexual scandal-mongering) drew on these two stories in his plays, *The Cozeners* (1774) and *A Trip to Calais* (1775). Foote capitalized on the notoriety of these two women and his theatre of mimicry provides more than one example of sexual scandal-mongering. Foote's plays contributed to the press interest in these cases and contributed, in particular, to the construction of the trial of the Duchess in 1776 as a huge society event; after the play, tickets were being sold to the trial for the enormous sum of 20 guineas. Foote's career was on a knife-edge as a result though, as those intervening on behalf of the Duchess sought to destroy his reputation and business.

Exposing the private lives of notorious women was accompanied by sexually satirizing actresses at a time of growth in the theatre. Even the highly popular actress, Elizabeth Barry, was venomously attacked as 'that mercenary "Prostitute Dame"' (Howe 1992: 27). The treatment of actresses in the newspapers and by satirists echoes the preoccupations about actresses in the theatre of the time, and is both an indication of the greater freedoms for women and the limits to that freedom. Celebrity culture is often lauded as an expression of growing democracy (as we shall see in the coming chapters), as expanded categories of people are able to take to the public stage. This is partly true – even in the late eighteenth century, before the emergence of celebrity – circulated by the mass media, the fame of actresses was part of a process of growing cultural democracy. But this is only one side of the coin, for with fame came the notoriety that accompanied social uncertainty and that notoriety was located in ideas that upheld the subjugated position of women. Also, rather than actresses entering the public domain per se, there was instead a blurring of the public and private realms in the lives of actresses. Until 1660, women were banned from playing in the legitimate theatre. However, by the mid to late eighteenth century, women's indispensability to the commercial theatre was firmly established as actresses, writers and theatrical managers (Nussbaum 2005: 149). Indeed, actresses were earning a living wage and many were the heads of households which certainly upended accepted gender roles. However, this was accompanied by the widespread view that the theatre had a corrupting influence and that women were both responsible for the corrupting influence of the theatre and more susceptible to it. Actresses were considered to be immodest, and 'Society assumed that the woman who displayed herself on the public stage was probably a whore' (Nussbaum 2005: 152).

The 'illusion of intimacy' (Schickel 2000), which is a central concern of film scholars' understanding of twentieth-century stardom, then, has its earliest expression in the late eighteenth-century theatre and speaks of actresses' growing economic independence and, paradoxically, their simultaneous sexualization (Wanko 2003). Women's role in the theatre is a key arena for the first blurring of the boundary between public and private. This has twin components: female sexuality and scandal. Actresses' private lives were from the outset fodder for gossip in a way that the lives of male actors typically were not. Theatre managers understood that blurring the line between public image and intimate knowledge could heighten an actress's marketability and encouraged actresses to reveal their intimate selves; male spectators often paid a fee to visit them backstage in the hope of gaining sexual favours. It made sense for actresses to participate in this 'illusion of public intimacy' in order to increase their fame and popularity, so they deliberately tried to merge their theatrical persona with their private selves. They delivered prologues and epilogues whose secrets might entice audiences. Biographical material about these actresses also encouraged an illusion of public intimacy; when the actresses began to publish their memoirs (almost always written by men) they also blurred actress's public image and private selves. Memoirs often 'closely linked women with their stage characters, publicized personal scandals, intensified quarrels between players, and thus stimulated the patronage of the commercial theatre' (Nussbaum 2005: 151). When Peg Woffington debuted as Macheath's moll in Gay's *Beggar's Opera*, her memoirist claimed that she 'appeared to be the very Character she personated' (despite the fact that at the time of the performance she was 12 years old) (Woffington 1760: 12). Restoration theatre established a new kind of intimacy with famous performers, which was predominantly centred on female sexuality. It also established illusions of public intimacy which began with insinuations of prostitution. So while expanded social roles for women allowed for greater freedom and public prominence, these were heavily constrained within discourses of sexuality. The paradoxes that frame early female theatrical fame are part of the shape of the whole of theatrical culture and portend key issues in mass mediated celebrity culture to come. As we shall see in chapter 5, this paradox is with us today, despite the advances for women.

However, as we saw, throughout the nineteenth century the role of the theatrical star became increasingly important. When the Theatres Act of 1843 ended patent protection for legitimate theatres in Britain, respectable theatre grew. And so did the power of the theatrical star who was often both actor and theatrical manager, including female actor-managers. With their growing importance, women actor-managers attempted to control their public image and present a respectable self. Even as early as the 1830s Lucia Elizabeth Vestris, the famous contralto, managed the Olympic Theatre, where she successfully produced operatic burlesques. She also managed the Covent Garden theatre and, finally, with her husband Charles James Mathews, the Lyceum Theatre (1847–55). Madame Vestris was, however, the undisputed manager and Charles her able assistant.

A female actor-manager who directly links the theatre and the emerging cinema is Sarah Bernhardt, who is perhaps the most famous actress of the nineteenth century and the first established theatrical actress to 'star' in film. She also managed the Theatres de la Renaissance (1893–9). Bernhardt's career is a salient example of the nineteenth-century actress's oscillation between sexual scandal and respectability, which persist into the twentieth and twenty-first centuries. Her early career is marked by scandalous rumours of her sexual appetite and indiscretions. She had an affair with a Belgian nobleman; her only son was born out of wedlock. She is later rumoured to have had a passionate affair with the French Impressionist painter Louise Abbéma, who is reputed to have dedicated one of her paintings to Bernhardt, on the anniversary of their romance. Later, while married to actor Aristedes Damala, a morphine addict, Bernhardt was rumoured to have had an affair with the future King Edward VII. However, although Bernhardt maintained a flamboyant lifestyle, she worked hard later in life to move on from her courtesan past and to establish and manage a reputation as a serious and respectable actress. By the late 1870s, although the hint of scandal never entirely disappeared, her reputation was secure. Her fortunes, like other actor-managers, became tied to touring; she toured extensively and became an enormous success across the world, including the US. By the beginning of the twentieth century, with an international reputation as the Divine Sarah, she took roles in early French films, such as La Tosca (1908). Her second film in 1912, where she played Queen Elizabeth, was important in the emerging narrative film in the US, as we shall see in the following chapter in our examination of the political economy of stardom in the cinema.

We have seen that the British theatre from the end of the eighteenth century provided female actors with an opportunity to take to the public stage, but in a manner that reveals the privatization of the female figure in public through the blurring of private and public in the lives of female actors and their sexualized status. As we have seen, managers sought to profit from the illusions of intimacy between female actor and her public and this gives early shape to the public obsession with the sexualized and scandalous private sphere that marks so much of celebrity culture subsequently.

Conclusion

The structure of fame is deeply connected to the balance of class forces in different historical periods as the changes in the British and American theatre in the late eighteenth and nineteenth centuries demonstrate. In Britain, the shift from the power of the landed gentry to the power of the entrepreneurial actor-manager reflects the waning power of Court society and the rising economic and social power of the bourgeoisie, while in both the UK and the US, the separation of the production of plays from the circulation of performances speaks to the broader shifts in economic relations towards industrialization and the struggles for control over the profits therein. It is this context which saw the rise of theatrical stardom, a consequence of a variety of simultaneous phenomena, including the prestige of touring actors from the legitimate theatre undermining the stock system and making theatres more reliant on star actors, the use of star actors to market plays at a time of growing competition, the power and dominance that was then accorded to the star actor-manager, and important changes in the laws governing the theatre, which shut down the theatre of the working class in the name of free competition, and consolidated the middle-class character of the theatre. There were also important technological developments, including the growth of the railways, passenger and freight ocean liners and other forms of transportation that facilitated the touring of companies. The rise of theatrical fame was also connected to wider social and cultural trans-formations. So while different conceptions of fame from different periods overlap, the revolutionary upheaval of the late eighteenth century and the industrial revolution of the nineteenth changed the structure of society irrevocably, including the structure of public life and the shape of public renown. This period opened up the possibility of celebrity to new classes of people as social mobility and the new ideas of freedom and equality mark the transition to bourgeois modernity. We saw in the case of women in the theatre, the possibilities thrown open by these changes. But the curtailment of the democratic aims of that period also witnessed the consolidation of a new form of class power, and new forms of social hierarchy and prestige, of which stardom and celebrity were a part. And, as we saw in the case of women in the theatre, new freedoms were circumscribed in highly gendered ways. Thus celebrity parallels a key paradox of capitalist modernity – the promise of liberty, equality and fraternity which confronts the reality of domination, subordination and hierarchy. Indeed, with the rise of bourgeois culture, those who most lose out are those to whom the promises of freedom and equality were aimed, and whose tastes and predilections are said to be addressed by star and celebrity performances – the newly industrialized working class who found that much of their culture had either been shut down or co-opted into the increasingly industrialized and commercial culture.

This chapter has tried to suggest that although the development of the mass media was a central factor in the growth of celebrity, there were also other, early factors that were as important, including the broad social and economic processes to do with the transition to modernity and also the specific development of one of the main cultural forms in Europe and North America in this period of transition, the theatre. The use of an individual star performer for promotional and marketing purposes develops in the West initially in the late eighteenth- and nineteenth-century British theatre. It is significant that this was a commercial theatre from the outset, unlike some other European countries, for promotional strategies are significantly more important to an enterprise that relies on making profit rather than on patronage, and that faces market competition. The theatrical star system also provides the ground for the development of the early star system in the American cinema, as will be discussed in the next chapter.

Celebrity is consolidated in particular periods in the history of capitalism, connected to changes or developments in entertainment and media, the development of new technology, and increased competition. This chapter has argued that a key early moment in the development of modern celebrity was the rise of the star performer in the commercial British theatre and the theatre's change over the course of the nineteenth century into a commercial cultural industry. The industrialization of cultural and media businesses at the end of the nineteenth and into the twentieth century is a second key moment in the rise and spread of celebrity as the following chapter will suggest through an examination of the growth of both the mass press and the cinema in the US.

3

Celebrity and the Industrialization of Cultural Production: The Case of the Mass Press and the Cinema

Introduction

Celebrity and stardom have been consolidated in particular periods of the history of capitalism when increased commercialization, increased competition and technological change coincide to produce challenges to which celebrity seems to offer a solution. This chapter examines just such a moment at the end of the nineteenth century which saw the birth of two central media industries – the mass newspaper press and the cinema. This chapter examines how celebrity and stardom became central to these two media industries and how both, for related but distinct reasons, came to rely on the circulation of star and celebrity images. It argues that in neither instance was celebrity simply a product of audience desire to see the famous or read about them. Instead, audiences were encouraged to see stars by both industries, which, in different ways, contributed enormously to a media culture that, unlike the theatre the century before, reached millions for the first time. This chapter looks at the specific business decisions taken by the newspaper press and the cinema at a moment in which the media and entertainment businesses were becoming industrialized areas of production, and, like other industries, were prone to the twin processes of competition and the tendency towards monopoly.

The growth of star systems and the distribution of celebrity images was not the result of the practices of a single industry, as is sometimes credited to the cinema, but was the result of simultaneous developments to do with industrialization of key cultural industries alongside wider processes of industrialization, the growth and expansion of the promotional industries, such as advertising, as central sectors of the economy, and of the consolidation and maturation of capitalist relations of production. Some film critics tend to credit Hollywood with inventing stardom and celebrity, or at least perfecting it (Barbas 2001; Gabler 1994; Hampton 1970 [1931]; MacCann 1992; Schickel 1962; Walker 1970), despite the existence of the star system in the theatre throughout the nineteenth century, and the simultaneous growth of star and celebrity content with the spread of newspapers and magazines, advertising, etc. Marsha Orgeron has argued that Hollywood comes to shape definitions of success in the twentieth century by superseding all other forms of public renown. Film stardom, according to Orgeron, 'trumps' all other forms of fame, skews ideas of success in other arenas, and Hollywood dominates all other industries in the production and distribution of celebrity (Orgeron 2008: 18). Gamson also suggests that the new system of celebrity 'grew up' around the new technologies of film (1994: 23), with film manufacturers and studios quickly institutionalizing audiences' keen interests in knowledge about the stars in their promotional practices (1994: 25). However, in contrast, Ponce de Leon argues that 'it is the news media that literally create celebrities', by providing the means of distributing stories about the famous (2002: 5). This chapter suggests that both are true. It is important to attend to the interactions and interrelations between different cultural industries, particularly at a time, in the late nineteenth and early twentieth centuries, when they were rapidly expanding and first operating as mass production industries. Both the press and the cinema came to rely on stardom and celebrity as part of their business strategies, and in the process both propelled celebrity into public culture with enormous and lasting impact. Those early mass media industries established celebrity as a central component of our culture which continues today.

The Rise of the Mass Circulation Press: Standardization of the Circulation of Celebrity 1850–1900

The American mass circulation press plays an important role in the expansion of celebrity at the end of the nineteenth century. This is the period when the conventions of celebrity journalism were established. In addition, celebrity gossip contributes to the success of the nineteenth-century mass press, providing content for expanding pages and the kind of news that appeals to advertisers – the key source of revenue for newspapers then and now (Curran et al., 1980). In the rapidly expanding cities of the United States, newspaper circulation grew alongside burgeoning populations. The press in the United States became the first press to become fully industrialized (Schudson 1978) and it was out of the processes of industrialization that the conventions of celebrity journalism grew and began to become embedded in the news. Significantly there was a shift in the types of public figures whose personal lives were reported upon. Leo Lowenthal calls this a shift from the 'idols of production' of previous times, who had emanated from 'the productive life, from industry, business and the natural sciences', to 'idols of consumption' drawn from the world of leisure and consumption (Lowenthal 1961: 112),[1] although as we saw in the previous chapter, this is not only a twentieth-century phenomenon, but begins in the late eighteenth century.

New styles of reporting also developed that played a central role in the production and circulation of celebrity (Ponce de Leon 2002). Indeed, many of the techniques of reporting that have come to define celebrity journalism were pioneered in this period: the human interest story, the interview, the gossip column, sensationalist headlines and content and the focus on the private lives of public individuals (Schudson 1978: 48). These conventions continue to sustain celebrity culture today across the world, in publishing, on television and on the internet as we shall see in the following chapters.

One of the most detailed studies of the role of the press in the rise of celebrity suggests that throughout the latter half of the nineteenth century newspapers developed the genre of celebrity journalism which fully matures by the 1920s (Ponce de Leon 2002: 6). For Charles Ponce de Leon, a turning point in celebrity journalism came in the 1890s 'when journalists began crafting new techniques and rhetorical strategies for depicting celebrities' which involved focusing on representing the 'real' lives of the famous in order to portray their 'human' side (Ponce de Leon 2002: 6). The conventions of celebrity journalism overlap with those of the human interest story because of their common point of origin. However, there are important differences. Celebrity journalism relies not just on reporting the private lives of public individuals, but its structure and conventions have, from the outset, contained a duality; stories oscillate between presenting favourable reports approved by the subject of the story or her agent, and unauthorized gossip. The first kind of story is often based on a press interview and/or a review. Celebrity journalism's other set of conventions, a focus on scandal, rumour and gossip, are also established in this period, and usually do not involve authorized interviews, but rather involve door stepping, reporting gossip and speculation, reporting on already circulating quotations, often taken out of context, and reporting on stunts that the famous have staged to attract media attention. Celebrity news also emerges and contributes to the 'celebrification' of public personas from a variety of arenas, including society figures, 'it' girls, sports personalities, literary authors, some politicians, theatrical stars and later film stars.

This growing focus on the private lives of public figures develops the tendency to attempt to reveal the 'real' person behind the image or performance. As we saw in the previous chapter, these discourses of revelation actually began earlier, in the theatre, and with the memoirs of actors (Luckhurst and Moody 2005). But celebrity journalism establishes conventions about how to represent public figures for a mass audience that did not exist in the eighteenth- and early nineteenth-century theatre, and provides a model for being interested in the well-known that is readily available to be taken up in the world of film later on, including the interest in obsequious interviews with stars, a fascination with the private lives of stars and celebrities, and the revelation of their 'real' selves that continues to structure celebrity news.

The emerging discourses on celebrity and their shaping by developing journalistic conventions also occur at a time of the industrialization of the newspaper business. In the case of the newspaper industry in the US, tremendous technical innovations enabled the processes of industrialization and facilitated developments in newspaper layout (Hutt 1973: 61). It also produced standard conventions in news gathering and feature writing, such as a growing reliance on wire services and feature syndicates. This period also witnessed the emergence of newspaper chains and media empires (Baldasty 1992; Brucker 1937; Ponce de Leon 2002; Schudson 1978; Tebbel 1963).

New York became one of the first centres of a technologically advanced, industrial mass press. Prior to the 1880s, most advances in newspaper publication emanated from Europe, and Britain in particular. For instance, machine-made paper was in use in the UK by the 1820s, but was not widely available in the US until the 1840s (Hutt 1973). Newspapers in the US borrowed British techniques and bought equipment from Europe. The shift from linen-based paper to wood pulp-based paper was also significant as it enabled a cheap supply of raw material. However, by the end of the nineteenth century, the major technical advances were American (Hutt 1973; Tulloch 2000; Wiener 1996) and the newspaper business flourished, both in terms of circulation and in terms of advertising revenue (perhaps outstripping the UK performance because, unlike the UK, it was not subject to a Stamp Act). There were significant advances in the printing press in the late nineteenth century, including the development of the Hoe press. This improved the quality of print and enabled an increase in the quantity of paper that could go through the presses. This also industrialized production, including the division of labour on the shop floor necessary for large-scale industrial production. In addition, this is the time when journalism became professionalized and specialized (Schudson 1978) and was divided from other areas of professional production such as layout and design, copyediting and management.

The technological advances allowed for a substantial increase in page numbers for newspapers and contributed to improvements in layout, including multi-column headlines and line drawings. These developments contributed to the logic of celebrity news – more pages meant more pages to fill with content, and celebrity gossip proved more predictable than content based on events. In addition, the presentation of the famous was very much linked to the increased quality in the printed image. Pictures of society ladies, actors, sports stars and prominent politicians began to fill newspaper front pages. For instance, William Randolph Hearst's first newspaper, the *San Francisco Examiner*, printed 22 line drawings to illustrate its front-page story about the wedding of Miss Hattie Crocker, the daughter of banker and railroad magnate Charles Crocker on 27 April 1887 (Nasaw 2002: 75). In fact, the personal column developed in a number of papers in the US at this time, known as the 'mainly about people column' (Hutt 1973: 67).

The giants of the fin de siècle newspaper industry, particularly Joseph Pulitzer and William Randolph Hearst, advanced the conventions of a style of journalism that came to be known both as the 'new journalism' and 'yellow journalism'. New York-based proprietor, Pulitzer, more than any of his contemporaries, is said to have refined the techniques of sensational journalism pioneered by Gordon Bennett thirty to forty years earlier, but he brought them up to date to fit a modern America of cities and factories. He innovated the use of bolder and darker headlines, shorter paragraphs, cross heads, an increased use of illustrations, all aimed at drawing interest from the growing literate working classes and the newly or partially literate growing immigrant population (Seitz 1924). The intention was to make the paper easier to read, livelier and more engaging. In 1889, Pulitzer ran a two-column headline in the *World* for the first time, and by the late 1890s, in competition with Hearst, large, multi-column and screaming headlines were the norm (Schudson 1978: 96). Pulitzer was the first to regularly take scandal stories and sensational reports from wire services.[2] He also mounted stunts which gave him lively front page news: Nellie Bly racing around a globe against the fictional rival Phileas Fogg, or Henry Stanley searching for and finding a Dr Livingstone in 'darkest Africa'.

Indeed, Pulitzer developed a number of techniques, from newspaper style, to journalistic style, to story topic. Important among these innovations were those which became the key components in celebrity journalism; the human interest story, the gossip column and the interview. Adopting these conventions, according to one of Pulitzer's biographers, was part of his plans to 'publish a newspaper for the millions rather than the thousands [which] meant that it would be a sensational paper, tapping hitherto untapped audiences, and appealing to a lowest common denominator in taste and literacy' (Juergens 1966: 17). We shall see below if attempts to attract a mass audience were the only reasons that celebrity gossip became such an attractive type of journalism to newspaper owners. However, where Pulitzer went, others followed. In particular, Pulitzer's arch rival William Randolph Hearst poached Pulitzer's approach to the news. Even before he moved his operations to New York, Hearst had adopted many of Pulitzer's techniques for the *San Francisco Examiner* and turned his father's failing newspaper into a highly successful one, dramatically increasing its circulation and profits.

When Hearst moved from San Francisco to New York and bought the ailing *Morning Journal* and its German language version in 1895, he was following a path already trod by Pulitzer in 1883 when he moved from St Louis to take on the *New York World*. Hearst's move to New York saw the beginning of an intense newspaper war with Pulitzer. Hearst brought his most famous reporters from San Francisco to New York: Winifred Black, Homer Davenport the illustrator and cartoonist, and lead sports writer, Charlie Dryden. He kept the price at a penny and started a price war with Pulitzer and the *Sun*'s proprietor, Charles Dana, whose papers were sold at 2 cents. Pulitzer himself had pursued this strategy in the 1880s. On 7 November 1895 Hearst published his first issue of the *New York Journal*. Heart's biographer comments that the 'news was pedestrian, but the illustrations were spectacular' (Nasaw 2002: 100). Next day the front page carried a story of the marriage of magazine artist Charles Dana Gibson (the creator of the Gibson Girls) with high quality illustrations of Gibson and his bride.

The newly launched *Journal* was filled with spectacular illustrations and bold headlines. Crime stories and human interest stories were joined by society gossip columns. Articles began appearing about the home life and leisure activities of sportsmen like John L. Sullivan and actors like Lillie Langtry. Langtry provided the *Journal* with the scandalous speculation and gossip that was to become a hallmark of celebrity news. Langtry was an 'it' girl of the nineteenth century and, as a married woman, is rumoured to have had an affair with Prince Louis of Battenberg in 1879 and the Earl of Shrewsbury in 1880. She gave birth to a daughter in 1881, with an undeclared father, providing further fuel for gossip and speculation. Langtry took to acting in 1881, on the suggestion of her friend Oscar Wilde, and toured the US to little critical acclaim, but great public interest, and this kept her in the public eye. So too did her relationship with Frederick Gebhard between 1882 and 1891, which provided many column inches on rumours of their marriage (which never materialized) alongside comments on her theatrical performances. This kind of celebrity news – stories based on the reporting of the private lives and scandals surrounding the famous – produces a set of conventions in this period that is linked to human interest journalism but is becoming a distinct genre of news in its own right, as the press interest in figures such as Langtry demonstrates.

Michael Schudson suggests that to answer the question of why the new journalism of Pulitzer and Hearst helped boost circulation we have to remember how closely intertwined are the histories of newspapers and the history of cities (Schudson 1978: 97). The latter quarter of the nineteenth century was a time of tumultuous change; 46 per cent of the population of New York were either immigrants or their parents were. The populations of the cities grew enormously, old certainties and old communities disappeared and new ways of living developed – what Schudson calls the 'changing web of social relations' (Schudson 1978: 102). Society had become more oriented on consumption with the advent of department stores, the growth of consumer goods, and the growth of popular mass entertainment such as vaudeville, the amusement park, the matinee, and at the very end of the nineteenth century, the beginnings of film. All of this was reflected in the topics and styles of new journalism (Ponce de Leon 2002). Just as we saw in the case of the theatre in Britain (see previous chapter), the development of great cities and the process of urbanization laid the ground for an expanding culture. As large numbers of workers and migrants moved into big cities to find work, forms of leisure and communication also expanded.

This was also a period in which literacy among the population grew, providing the necessary skills for workers in developing technological employment. Hearst took advantage of the growth of literacy and the expansion of leisure pursuits to expand his media empire. Hearst told his editors that one paper could not reach the growing urban population. So, he established morning, evening and Sunday editions of his papers, and he needed gossip and scandal stories to help fill column inches. His Sunday edition of the *Journal* was 'oversized, overstocked and overwhelming' (Nasaw 2002: 108) and always carried several pages on Broadway stars, including figures such as Lillie Langtry and Sarah Bernhardt. Celebrity gossip becomes a distinct type of journalism in this period. It also becomes such a staple part of Hearst's newspaper empire that by the early twentieth century he employed Louella Parsons (1881–1972) as a full-time gossip columnist for the *Chicago Herald*. By the 1920s Parsons had become Hearst's Universal News Service syndicated Hollywood gossip columnist. As we saw in the previous chapter, celebrity sometimes provided visibility and power to women in a manner not open in other walks of life, but often in circumscribed ways. Louella Parsons is a case in point. With tens of millions of readers at her height, Parsons could make or break the career of aspiring actors. By the late 1920s studio heads were so concerned about Parsons' influence and the impact she could have on business, that they conspired to create a rival gossip columnist in the figure of Hedda Hopper, whose column was soon taken up by the *Los Angeles Times*. But the enmity between the two diminished the power of neither, and so the studio heads' plans to undermine Parsons backfired – they now faced two powerful gossip columnists.

Hearst diversified his newspaper business to establish a media empire, prefiguring media moguls such as Rupert Murdoch today. For example, Hearst developed a news wire service, International News Service. But he was also interested in film from the very early days and in an early act of media convergence, produced some of the first film newsreels, with an eye to establishing himself in the nascent film industry. He then set up the International Picture Service, a syndicate formed specifically to make newsreels and then, on the basis of this success, established the International Film Service in 1916 to make cartoon films based on the characters in his papers. He personally contacted D.W. Griffith to suggest a business partnership but Griffith declined (Nasaw 2002: 279). He later approached another mogul, Alfred Zukor (of whom we shall hear more below) to establish Cosmopolitan Productions, a New York-based film studio. Hearst's cross-media ownership provided him with a great advantage over his competitors because he owned the motion picture rights to works of some of the greatest authors of the day and many of the stories to be adapted to film had already been serialized in magazines owned by Hearst, including the studio's tie-in magazine *Cosmopolitan*. This was an important form of cross-media production in the silent era of film because audiences were already familiar with the storyline of these films.

Celebrity, the Mass Press and Popular Taste: Catering to the Public or the Advertisers?

It is a widely accepted view that the innovations in journalism were part of an effort to popularize the press, as proprietors attempted to win mass readership amongst the growing populations of American cities by providing them with crime, scandal and celebrity gossip (Ponce de Leon 2002; Schudson 1978). The rise of celebrity journalism is therefore seen as a means of catering to the tastes of the growing urban populations of workers, immigrants and the poor. However, what is omitted from this narrative on celebrity news is that the late nineteenth-century mass press became popular in large part because it contained politics – radical politics no less – not because it began to replace politics with celebrity gossip (see Williamson 2010). It is important to note that there was a vibrant working-class political culture at the time (Cantor 1979) and that these newspapers were heavily influenced both by the vibrant radical press that existed in the metropolitan centres in the US at the time (Conlin 1974; Shore 1985) and by the legacy of the Sunday papers in the UK, which became extremely popular from around the 1820s (Hollis 1970). The British Sunday papers in turn learned how to speak in the language of the working class from the radical and Chartist press of the previous three decades.[3] The US press tycoons of the 1880s and 1890s borrowed from this heritage in an attempt to build mass readerships by combining radical populism with scandal, human interest stories and gossip columns. Often, the conventions of radical populism and the human interest stories and gossip overlapped. In fact, Joseph Pulitzer took a populist, but leftwing stance on many issues of the day. His editorial style was in contrast to the standard wordy style; in a blunt and mocking tone he attacked the rich and powerful. According to John Tebbel, '[i]n New York, the war between the haves and the have-nots had already begun, and Pulitzer showed himself clearly as the friend of the have-nots' (Tebbel 1963: 97). His papers held crusades on behalf of immigrants, workers, tenement dwellers, and low-to-middle-income tax payers. He declared that the *World* was, 'dedicated to the cause of the people' (Tebbel 1963: 103). Soon after he took over the paper in 1883, he published a ten point list of '*World* doctrines':

1. Tax luxuries
2. Tax inheritances

3. Tax large incomes
4. End monopolies
5. Tax privileged corporations
6. A tariff for revenue
7. Reform the civil service
9. Punish corrupt office-holders
10. Punish employers who coerce their employees in elections.

(*World*, 17 May 1883: 4)

Expressing the politics of the poor and adopting a radical stance on key issues of the day was an absolutely essential part of catering to public taste. The sensationalist stories reported in the *World* often dug at the rich, the powerful and the corrupt. Pulitzer adopted the language of the radical press (but not necessarily the activist politics) in his exposés of corrupt politicians and business tycoons and his paper spoke directly to the political and economic concerns of the working class in their own language. Pulitzer's arch rival, William Randolph Hearst, also had to appeal to the politics of the poor to establish his New York papers and to vie with Pulitzer for readers. For instance, his paper, the *New York Journal* supported Samuel Gompers' call for the eight-hour day enthusiastically and volubly. The paper also carried articles about terrifying crimes against ordinary folk, often perpetrated at the hands of the monopolies that owned New York's municipal services. Crucially, in a burgeoning city dominated by private service monopolies, the paper called for municipal ownership of gas, electricity, transport, ice and housing (Williamson 2010). Of course, unlike Pulitzer, Hearst's populism was also often racist in its pro-labour stance (Nasaw 2002: 80).[4] Nonetheless, Hearst's success was dependent on an openly anti-trust stance and his papers' ability to reflect the anger of the growing working-class population of New York, by directing tirades against the huge corporations that were getting bigger each day.

The early conventions of celebrity journalism emerge at a time and in a press that was pro-labour and anti-trust in its outlook. At the birth of the modern daily press, the papers of Hearst and Pulitzer had to be lively, easy to read, accessible, entertaining, *and* had to cover political issues in a language and a manner that was sympathetic to the concerns of workers, immigrants and the poor, in order to attract a mass audience. To suggest that these papers attracted a mass working-class audience by removing politics and replacing it with entertainment is to wrongly counterpose the 'popular' with the 'political' and to ignore the vocal political stances central to the content of these papers. Both papers, and their competitors, carried radical populist political topics *and* entertainment topics and sometimes, as in the case of many sensational stories, they were one and the same thing (Williamson 2010).

Celebrity and the Political Economy of the Early Mass Circulation Press in the US and UK

What changed? Did readers wake up one morning and decide that they were no longer interested in how their city was governed? Did they no longer care if their services were run by exploitative municipal trusts? No. Competition and economic pressures brought about by the processes of industrialization put newspapers under enormous strains and made them more reliant on advertising, financial institutions and big business.

Advertising revenue is a crucial issue in the history of the newspaper industry and for the rise of celebrity journalism, both at the end of the nineteenth century and the first decades of the twenty-first (as we shall see in the next chapter). Newspapers could not recoup their costs, never mind make a profit, on circulation sales alone; the cost of production was higher than the revenue generated from sales of even the highest circulation newspapers and this made newspapers completely dependent on advertising revenue to stay afloat (Curran et al., 1980). This situation was exacerbated by the price wars, brought about by competition, as dailies dropped their prices in order to compete for readers. Printing technology developed rapidly in the period and buying new presses and updating technology was both expensive and imperative, in order to remain competitive. These pressures squeezed revenue and made newspapers even more reliant on advertising to produce profit. The evidence suggests that it was under these pressures in the early twentieth century that the rowdy press owners in the US dropped overt radicalism in order to please the advertisers and financial investors, upon whom they were now economically dependent (Williamson 2010). This was also a time of mergers and acquisitions when the capitalist drive to monopoly kicked in as the industry matured. Newspapers were bought up and shut down in large numbers (particularly by Hearst) and the 'chain' journalism that resulted became more dependent on banking, advertising and big business, and their editors pursued the depoliticized conventions of reporting that remained.

At the end of the nineteenth century, the American mass circulation press relied on advertising revenue and this occurred at a time when advertising itself was becoming an industry with independent mechanisms. The total revenue derived by newspaper publishers from advertising rose from 44 percent in 1879 to 49 percent in 1889 to 56 percent in 1904 to 70 per cent in 1929. More than once, Hearst saw his revenues plunge when advertisers pulled out of his paper – usually when he took stands that made the advertisers nervous, such as his German-friendly stance in the First World War (Nasaw 2002: 158). But, unlike smaller papers, Hearst had a huge fortune at his disposal and by the turn of the century had spent $8 million of his family's fortune upgrading equipment and subsidizing newspaper revenue, when sales and advertising revenue dropped. Even with this fortune at his disposal, Hearst had to borrow huge sums of money from American banks to sustain his media empire. The pressure from advertisers occurred at a time of huge competition between the dailies which resulted in increased expenditure on new technology and regular price wars, pushing down revenue further. The logic of monopoly capitalism was playing itself out in the newly industrialized newspaper industry, just as it was in the newly mushrooming entertainment industries, and it was this economic logic that resulted in 'chain journalism', devoid of political content, rather than newspapers simply serving popular taste. By the 1920s, the popular press was unrecognizable; celebrity journalism, entertainment stories and human interest stories had become a dominant feature of the daily press in the US.

In the UK, in the same period, different sections of the press catered to different publics – the Sunday papers, which had never been part of the respectable press – were joined by the arrival of the daily press in the late nineteenth century (Williams 1976). While the Sundays were radical in tone (and in order to avoid press Stamp Duty, often carried no actual news, but fictitious stories, comment and large woodcut illustrations), the daily papers on the other hand were catering to an expanding middle-class readership (Williams 1961: 190–2). After the abolition of Stamp Duty in 1855, a cheap metropolitan daily press grew, led by the *Daily Telegraph*, catering to a lower and rising middle class, with a lighter tone than the *Times*, and easier to read layout for the commuter. The cheap dailies applied their lively tone to both politics and miscellany, including stories about the rich and famous (and so scandal and human interest were not the preserve of the Sundays or of the working class). In the British case, it was the crushing of the radical opposition that led what had previously been radical Sunday papers to drop political content and focus on gossip and scandal. By the 1890s the British press underwent what has been called the 'Northcliffe Revolution', as Viscount Northcliffe (Alfred Harmsworth) imported the techniques of journalism from the US, including the innovations in reporting style and a business model based on generating revenue through advertising, investment and stunts aimed at increasing circulation in dubious ways. Northcliffe started the halfpenny *Daily Mail* in 1896 with the latest rotary print-ers. Raymond Williams argues that the Northcliffe Revolution was 'less an innovation in actual journalism than a radical change in the economic basis of newspapers, tied to a new kind of advertising' (Williams 1961: 202). Its success and expansion was based 'on a clear conception of the economic basis of a newspaper – a large volume of advertising interacting with circulation; second, it was technically in the lead, both in production and distribution methods; third, it pursued a popular political policy' (Williams 1961: 203) aimed at the lower-middle class; 'business men, clerks and artisans' (Williams 1961: 204). As in the case of the US press, newspaper ownership altered dramatically in this period. Individual proprietor-owned presses were being replaced by a speculative 'chain' ownership of whole newspaper groups, which would capitalize on one title to acquire others. It is this process of the drive towards concentration of ownership, funded through advertising, alongside mass circula-tion, that the 'real basis of the twentieth-century press was...effec-tively laid' (Williams 1961: 206). By the late 1950s, there had been a massive expansion of sales of daily and Sunday papers (doubling in the space of 20 years), but at the same time the number of papers declined by more than half, while four groups controlled 77 per cent of circulation (Williams 1961: 210). Instead of seeing a steady increase in a pluralistic press catering to all sections of the population as circulation figures increased, the biggest area of growth was in the tabloid press, building mass readerships on a 'coalition of different tastes, interests and political positions' (Tulloch 2000: 142). Williams argues that this is not the developing press of an educated democracy, but rather 'an increasingly organized market in communications, with the "masses" formula as the dominant social principle', and with the varied functions of the press increasingly limited to finding a 'selling point' (1961: 211).

We have seen that the growth of a style of journalism we now call celebrity news was born in the modern cities of America and the newspapers produced there. But unlike standard histories of the American press, this chapter has so far argued that the growth in celebrity news was as much a product of the political economy of the newspaper, its need to attract advertising in an atmosphere of intense competition and expensive technological innovation, as it was an appeal to popular tastes. The shift from popular radicalism to gossip and scandal in the early mass circulation news press occurred as part of an effort to woo advertisers rather than readers, for papers relied on advertising more than circulation sales. This new style of journalism both supported the early press and grew as a consequence. The new journalism of these newspapers and the growing number of magazines in this period were also provided with many column inches on stars and celebrities by the new cinema industry which was an enormously important industry in terms of the production, circulation and distribution of celebrity and stardom. The American film industry produced its own star system as part of an economic and marketing strategy which fused promotional and economic values to aesthetic ones, as we shall see below.

The Cinema and the Production of Stardom 1900–50

As in the case of the press, the early period in the film business was one in which production and aesthetic practices acquired a high degree of uniformity and stability (Bordwell and Staiger 1985: 96) despite the fact that cultural commodities are more unpredictable than those in other fields (Hesmondhalgh 2007) and that there are specificities around these industries such as the high cost of production and the relatively low cost of distribution (Garnham 1990). Some of the mechanisms of industrial standardization cut across various industries. For instance, we saw how important advertising practices were in shaping the mass circulation press in the nineteenth century. Advertising practices (which were well established by the end of the nineteenth century) also played a crucial role in the standardization of production practices in the film industry. Janet Staiger argues that a key instance of standardization instigated by advertising practices was an emphasis on product innovation and differentiation (that is, the discourse of the non-standard product becomes standard). This differentiation was seen to give film companies a competitive edge (1991: 99). What will be explored below is the specific historical circumstances in which the star becomes a central mechanism in the tension between standardization and differentiation which resulted.

According to Robert Allen, aesthetic and economic histories of film have erroneously treated the film industry as an 'isolated phenomenon' (1980: 1), disconnected from the surrounding entertainment industries. Similarly, accounts of the emergence of stardom and celebrity in the film industry tend to stress film's formative role in the creation of the star system. For example, P.D. Marshall observes that Alfred Zukor attempted to 'inject the aura of the theatrical star in to film by contracting the French film *Queen Elizabeth* (1912) which starred the famous theatrical actress Sarah Bernhardt'. But he argues that this was a flawed strategy because 'the most famous contract players to emerge out of Zukor's Famous Players Company were in fact known only as film stars' (1997: 81). In contrast, deCordova suggests that theatrical aura and language did help to shape the discourse of film acting (deCordova 1990) and that theatrical stars did provide allure. However, when film was in its infancy, Zukor actually relied on both strategies in an attempt to establish the most effective promotional strategies to differentiate his product from others, and crucially, he borrowed from the theatre the practice of casting a central star in the promotion of his films. Thus Hollywood created a star system, but it was one that depended, from the outset, on two other sources – the theatre and the mass circulation press. The film star system borrowed the structure and promotional purpose of the star system from the theatre – a system that had replaced repertory theatre with a system which built performances and promotional practices around stars (as we saw in chapter 2). Film stardom also relied on the already-established celebrity-oriented press and publishing industries that developed a journalism around celebrity gossip and human interest (see above) and which disseminated and circulated stories about the stars. There quickly became a symbiotic interdependence as the press and publishing industries began to depend on stories from Hollywood to boost their existing reliance on celebrity content. In June 1919 Terry Ramsaye, who was both a journalist and a film producer, wrote an article for the film magazine *Photoplay*, that identifies the growing importance of the role of the press agent in the film business (Ramsaye 1919). And according to Balio, by the 1930s, Hollywood had become the third largest news source in the US (Balio 1987: 226). Celebrity and stardom's promotional purpose grew simultaneously across a number of media, interrelating the dependence of celebrity in each industry and across industries. One of the best known examples of the mutuality between early film and the press is the case of the Florence Lawrence publicity stunt orchestrated by Carl Laemmle, head of the Independent Motion Picture Company in 1910. Laemmle pinched the 'Biograph Girl', Florence Lawrence, from Biograph and then fed the press with rumours that she had been killed in a street-car accident in New York. Laemmle later contradicted this account by taking out ads in several daily papers under the headline 'We Nail a Lie'. The ad declared that Lawrence was alive and well and promised to prove it; she would be making an appearance in St Louis in March of that year (Barbas 2001). The press and the public turned out in numbers to Lawrence's press conference, and Laemmle's studio and his leading lady received a great deal of publicity and column inches as a result.

However, the dominance of the star system in Hollywood was not inevitable. Instead, as in the case of the press and the theatre, the rise of cinematic stardom was the outcome of business decisions made in the context of the industrialization of film in the early twentieth century. We will now turn to this history.

Film Stardom and Popular Taste

This book has so far challenged the widely held view that celebrity comes to dominate the entertainment industries simply in order to cater to public tastes. We have looked at the economic demands of the British and American theatre and those of the mass circulation press in the US in the nineteenth century to examine how the business decisions taken in these contexts created a focus on celebrity. But film stardom and celebrity is similarly considered to have arisen in relation to public demand. Many scholars and commentators have argued that the star system emerged when early cinema audiences began demanding information about the anonymous screen actors and early studios eventually, reluctantly, agreed to release the names of the screen performers in response to public curiosity (Barbas 2001; Gabler 1994; Hampton 1970 [1931]; Orgeron 2008; Ramsaye 1964 [1925]; Schickel 1985; Walker 1970; Woods 1919). Frank E. Woods initiated this version of events and gave himself a starring role in this history in his October 1919 article in the magazine *Photoplay* 'Why is a Star'. Woods was an influential critic for the industry magazine the *New York Dramatic Mirror*, and he was also involved in the film business, working as D.W. Griffith's assistant and scene writer at Biograph, and later Mutual (deCordova 1990). Woods – who credits himself with providing 'the first systematic critical attention ever given to film' (1919: 117) – relates the story of a fictitious fan, Lizzie, who wanted to 'know the real honest-to-goodness names of the Bio-graph girl and the Vitagraph girl' (1919: 72). No-one was willing to give up this information to the many Lizzies who wrote to him, until Woods, 'Yours Truly' (1919: 117), came into the picture and 'answered in the columns of the paper and the lid was off' (1919: 117). Woods writes that the public began to inquire about the names of screen players, but the manufacturers refused to release names in order to avoid rising costs associated with having to pay large salaries to star players that was found in the contemporaneous theatre. But as

Bordwell and Staiger comment, this 'rising cost' argument does not hold up. Film manufacturers were competing directly with vaudeville and the theatre, both of which had star systems (1985: 101). None-theless, Woods suggests that Biograph, the last manufacturer to pub-licize films on the basis of star players, was eventually forced into line by public demand; 'So, if anybody tells you that permanent success can be gained by bucking against public demand for stars, stars, stars, you can point to the experience of the only company that ever tried it to a finish and acknowledged its own failure' (1919: 118). However, as Janet Staiger argues, 'Biograph's reluctance to promote stars could have been a poor business calculation (but it was a busi-ness calculation)' (1991: 14). Woods concludes that 'the star will continue to exist numerously and will predominate in motion pictures despite all efforts of producers and exhibitors at elimination, for the reason, as I have tried to indicate, that the public demands it' (1919: 118). In 1962, Richard Schickel repeated this account by suggesting that it was the public that first invented the stars in the early days of cinema by demanding to know about the screen players; audiences began writing to the studios for information about 'the waif' or 'the man with the sad eyes'. Schickel argues that despite the studios' efforts to keep the screen players' identities secret, 'the public had begun to find them out' (1962: 11) and Alexander Walker offers a more detailed version of this history in 1970. But this account of film history has even been partially accepted by those who acknowledge the role of advertising in product differentiation (Barbas 2001; Gamson 1994) and it is one that has contributed to the view that the emergence of stardom is automatically a democratic phenomenon – the public voting for their favourites at the box office and studios having to give in to popular demand. This is also the view promul-gated by early Independent studio heads such as Carl Laemmle, in his 'Florence Lawrence' publicity stunt discussed above. He presented himself as the 'little guy' standing against the powerful Motion Picture Patents Company (MPPC), the trust set up by Edison and Biograph to insist that film distributors and exhibitors only handled film reels and machinery licensed by Trust companies. It is true that the role of the MPPC was to provide Edison and Biograph with monopoly control over film distribution – following the monopoly logic of com-mercial capital – and that many early film producers and exhibitors operated at the edges of legality. But Laemmle insisted that his victory also belonged to the public.

However, Richard deCordova poses an apt question of this version of history: if it is the case that it was the public's desire that gave rise to the star system, 'Where did the public's desire come from?' (1990:

6). It does not, he suggests, 'arise out of thin air, unsolicited' (1990: 7). Instead, deCordova suggests that it was nurtured alongside the introduction of narrative film after 1907 which began to replace event-based photojournalism, when documenting events became too expensive and troublesome, (particularly far away wars such as the Boer War). Richard Allen makes a similar point (1980: 212) and we shall examine this view in some detail below.

By the late twentieth century, film historians had challenged the 'popular demand' account of the emergence of the star system by suggesting that rather than studios and performers being reluctant to publicize the names of performers in film, it simply did not occur to them to do so because of the particular system of production that structured the early film industry prior to 1907 (Allen 1980; Bordwell and Staiger 1985; deCordova 1990; Slide 1970). Early film was highly popular without the need for a star system because it was considered to be a form of photojournalism that was documenting events or performances. What marks this period of motion picture history is *not* the existence of an incipient star system, or the demands of fans to see stars (the first fan magazine, *Motion Picture Story Magazine*, began in late 1910) but rather, a growth in film theatres who were catering to a growing public taste for documentary. It was the resultant intense commercial competition between the manufacturers, distributors and exhibitors of the motion picture apparatus, who were each struggling to dominate the market in this new form of entertainment, that produced a shift from documentary to narrative films.

Competition and the Cinema: the Transition to Narrative Film

Between 1895 and 1896 the first viable American motion picture projector – the Vitascope – was developed. The French Lumière Cinématogrophe had already exhibited in Europe, first at the Grand Cafe in Paris on 28 December 1895 and then at the London music hall, the Empire on 9 March 1896, and the Lumières were keen to exploit the commercial potential of these machines in America. American vaudeville managers soon heard of the success of these screenings and wanted to repeat them. This instigated a moment of frantic competition to be the first to project motion pictures in American theatres. Raff and Gammon (the American duo who owned the licence to market the Vitascope) joined forces with Thomas Edison, who owned the rights to manufacture the machine,[5] to ensure that the projector debuted ahead of the European invention in an effort to dominate the market. On 23 April 1896 the Vitascope made its now renowned triumphant public debut at Koster and Bial's Music Hall in New York City, after weeks of build-up and publicity. Motion picture exhibition permanently shifted format from the peep show apparatus that Edison had used in 1894, to a projected form shown in vaudeville theatres across the US. Although the event was a great success, and demonstrated early on the significance of pre-publicity, Raff and Gammon did not succeed in closing down foreign competition, and indeed their success opened the door to new competition, because they could not meet the sharp increase in demand for projectors from vaudeville managers across the country that resulted from their success at Koster and Bial's. This left a market open for competing projectors, and new manufacturers entered the field.

Robert Allen has suggested that the reason that film took off so rapidly in the US (in comparison to Europe) is because of the extensive national network of vaudeville theatres which were available (and keen) to exhibit film; 'vast numbers of Americans were able to view this visual novelty within a very short time...providing it with an almost instant national audience' (1980: 5). In the period between 1896 and 1905, motion picture exhibition took place predominantly in vaudeville theatres, and films were exhibited alongside other 'live' acts. The films were usually short 10-minute single reel 'actuality' novelties that depicted railway journeys, yacht races, and chases, or news events and images of politicians. Biograph was the first manufacturer to cover the Spanish-American War in 1898, which was very popular with audiences. Soon after, Edison made arrangements with William Randolph Hearst to send a cameraman to Cuba on one of the yacht's rented by Hearst's *New York Journal* (Allen 1980: 138). In this early period of film production manufacturers sold films by the foot and marketed them in detachable units. Catherine Kerr describes this early mode of production as 'undifferentiated volume output' (1990: 389), which was distributed through 'newly established, often undependable, wholesale exchanges' (1990: 389).

The popularity of this novelty led to an explosion of nickelodeon theatres between 1905 and 1907. It is estimated that in 1905 there were no all-film theatres, but by 1907 this number had grown to an estimated 7–10,000 (Kerr 1990: 388).[6] Bordwell and Staiger describe these early nickelodeons as 'dank, dark, dirty, and disreputable' (1985: 128). They were small venues, seating less than 200 and were often cheaply converted storefronts situated near shopping areas or near mass transport routes (Bordwell and Staiger 1985: 128). Film historians agree that it was this period of surging demand and rapidly expanding output that heralded the shift from novelty and documentary film to narrative film. In 1902, 80 per cent of film content was made up of news, travel, documentary and sport (Allen 1980: 144). By 1908, 66 per cent of film was narrative (1980: 212). According to Robert Allen, the shift to narrative film had nothing to do with a change in public demand – there continued to be a large audience for topical films and documentaries. Instead, the growth of the nickelodeon lead to a massive increase in demand for film product from *exhibitors* who wanted to maintain a steady supply of new films, and manufacturers were finding it hard to meet that demand. Allen suggests that stories and adaptations offered a solution – narrative film could be made more cheaply and more reliably than documentary (1980: 218). For instance, the most expensive film in 1907 was about the Boxer Rebellion and cost $7000. In 1911 the most expensive film was the Edison Company's *The Prince and The Pauper*, costing less than a third at $2000. For Allen, narrative film provided manufacturers with a reliable product that did not 'depend on external events and exigencies' (1980: 218). It is in this shift to narrative film that the emergent motion picture industry began to develop star performers for promotional purposes, in order to differentiate their products and gain a competitive edge.

According to the original version of the emergence of stardom instigated by Woods, early film manufacturers refused to release the names of players until they were finally forced to by public demand. But Janet Staiger throws important historical light onto this claim. She reminds us that early in 1910 (nine years prior to Woods' article), Thomas Edison publicized his players in a full-page spread of *Nickelodean*, complete with photographs of the players and a paragraph about each. Later that year, Edison was promoting the film appearance of the famous theatrical pantomimist, Mlle Pilar Morin, in an attempt to cash in on the glamour of the theatrical star system (Staiger 1991: 10). Even prior to Carl Laemmle's stunt with Florence Lawrence, Kalem was advertising display cards of players to be put on view in the lobbies of theatres (January 1910). By 1911 manufacturers were offering slides of favourite players to exhibitors to be shown between reels in order to promote the favourite players' 'next screen appearance' (Staiger 1991: 11). Staiger suggests that the exploitation of the picture personality in film took off in 1910 because of the prevailing economic conditions – advertising and publicity were becoming important tools in marketing films to the public for exhibitors and manufacturers alike. These were hard-headed business decisions, rather than the more idealistic view of responding to irresistible public desire to know the players. So why did it make sense for the film business to promote its product in this way? Part of the answer lies, as Staiger suggests, in the film industry adapting the practices of the legitimate theatre's star system (1991). However, there was also a transformation in the manufacturers' understanding of what their product was. In the move from short single reel actuality films sold by the foot, to three- and four-reel films sold as a complete story, manufacturers (and exhibitors) began to see their product not as an undifferentiated volume output, but a highly differentiated consumer product (Bordwell and Staiger 1985: 101). A technical view of film quality, which had dominated discussions of film in early trade magazines on issues of fidelity, gave way to an aesthetic view of film (for a detailed discussion of the content of these magazines, see Allen 1980; deCordova 1990; Kerr 1990). In this context, film manufacturers adopted the techniques of brand-name competition – manufacturers began to identify their product as a unique brand.

The Star Commodity and Product Differentiation

The shift in the type of product offered by manufactures is a result of the transformation of the film business from a highly competitive field of manufacturers, each competing with the other to sell as great a volume of film as possible to exhibitors, to a vertically integrated oligopoly, which standardized schedules, distribution and output. During the years between 1912 and 1916 the film business became a corporate industry.

At the end of 1907, after a long litigation battle, the Edison Company was granted a camera patent. The following year Edison negotiated a deal with Biograph (who held another major patent), and seven of the remaining camera manufacturers to establish the Motion Picture Patents Company (MPPC). This company functioned as a cartel; it assigned production, film and camera patents. It was authorized to license each sector of the industry – manufacturing, distribution and exhibition, in exchange for the use of its patented leading-edge technology. The licence provision prohibited dealings with independent manufacturers, distributors or exhibitors (and it also gave Eastman Kodak an exclusive contract to supply film stock to the manufacturers, although it abrogated its contract in 1911 in order to put its product on the open market) (Balio 1985: 109). The MPPC established industry-wide schedules that standardized rates, release dates and prices (Kerr 1990).

The result was 'industrial peace' (Allen 1980: 251) (and MPPC's drive to monopoly control), that enabled regular distribution of film. It also provided the breathing space, according to Kerr, that facilitated the development of important innovations in narrative film which foregrounded the player. The frenetic competition that characterized the pre-MPPC trust era gave way to more stable conditions which allowed important film makers such as D.W. Griffith to experiment with film technique. Griffith was employed by Biograph, who, under the more lucrative and protected conditions of the MPPC cartel, were prepared to give Griffith the time and money to make narrative films. In this atmosphere, Griffith had the opportunity to experiment with the new medium. For example, rather than filming scenes in the standard far shot that had dominated the filming of 'actuality' films, Griffith developed scenes shot in a mixture of medium shot, two-shot and close-up. He also began parallel editing. These innovations provided Griffith's films with the ability to encourage a sympathetic audience response. His film *The Lonely Villa* (1909) uses these techniques to build suspense and elicit audience sympathy. The film tells the story of a family in danger by editing between three scenes simultaneously; robbers attacking a homestead, women inside cowering with fear, and a father racing home to save the family (Kerr 1990: 394). According to Kerr, D.W. Griffith (and others) began to 'ground commercial film in its ability to represent personalized narratives. A new business strategy accompanied their innovations as business and aesthetic structures were developed together, culminating in modern film corporations built around the star commodity' (1990: 396).

The MPPC had paved the way for competition amongst the licensees based on quality of product rather than volume. Each manufacturer attempted to differentiate their produce with brand-name styles (Bordwell and Staiger 1985: 101) This was possible because each company used the same camera operators and actors and began to adapt the styles innovated by Griffith and others. Film makers began to develop a brand style – a 'Biograph film' with the 'Biograph girl', or a 'Vitagraph film' with the 'Vitagraph girl'. Brand-name advertising became a business strategy because it was seen to provide a competitive edge. Brand advertising becomes a key mechanism for film manufacturers to differentiate their products. But film manufacturers did not invent this kind of advertising. Throughout the nineteenth century, advertising in the US had not only proliferated across different sites and technologies, it had also transformed its practices from selling generic goods, to brand name advertising. Staiger argues that early film manufacturers had this model of advertising readily available to adopt in order to promote a new 'quality product' (1991: 98). At the same time, the popular press was reporting on and encouraging a growing anti-trust sentiment as we saw in the previous section. The trusts that dominated municipal services and housing in America's rapidly growing cities were regularly lambasted in the popular press. In this anti-trust atmosphere, the MPPC was unable to prevent at least 25 per cent of exhibitors from showing unlicensed films (Kerr 1990). Indeed, independent film makers like Carl Laemmle played up their anti-trust status in their own publicity, as his stunt with Florence Lawrence demonstrates. As we saw in the case of the British theatre the century before, the size of profits was too tempting to be outweighed by the threat of prosecution.

However, it was Adolph Zukor, rather than the independents, who finally undermined the MPPC. According to deCordova, Zukor set up Famous Players in order to present 'great theatrical actors in prestigious roles' (1990: 45). These 'feature' films were three to four reels long. The MPPC was still fixing prices by the foot, a standard set in place to sell single-reel films by the volume. This priced out the new, longer, narrative films that Zukor had begun to make (1912). So in 1914 Zukor left the trust and joined forces with the Paramount Picture Corporation (over which he gained control in 1916) to be the first distributor of feature films. Despite its power, the MPPC was not an example of vertical integration. It was a classic cartel based on patents and licences, even when, in 1910, it joined forces with the General Film Company (GFC) to be its sole distributor. Within a couple of years the GFC controlled all but one distribution exchange. But, in the mode of the classic cartel, it did not determine the output of the film makers, or the programmes of the exhibitors – and it still sold film by the foot. Paramount, on the other hand, was an early example of a vertically integrated film corporation because Zukor gained large interests in first-run exhibition houses where he could guarantee prime entry for Paramount's feature films.

It was in his effort to develop a 'special features' release schedule that could charge premium prices that Zukor promoted films on the basis of star players. This promotional practice became a central plank of his distribution strategy. In 1914 Zukor promoted the film *Tess of the Storm* by publicizing Mary Pickford's central role. Indeed, the story was chosen to suit Pickford's existing fame as a picture personality. Pickford, who was already a Broadway success (deCordova 1990: 45), and had been dubbed 'Little Mary' by the movie trade press by 1910 (deCordova 1990: 70), became Zukor's biggest asset. The film was judged (and judged a success) by the movie press and by exhibitors on the basis of Pickford's appearance rather than the brand name of the company. According to Kerr, by 1916 Zukor understood his 'product' to be the star performer (1990: 387). He was the first to use the star as a link between 'film as an aesthetic form and as a product of corporate industry' (1990: 387). Zukor block-booked his first-run houses, at premium prices, with films promoted by a star. He also used this strategy to further squeeze independent film makers who could not afford to pay the kinds of salaries that stars were beginning to obtain. Zukor's main star and asset was Mary Pickford who was pulling in $1000 per week.

Pickford is an interesting example of the paradox of femininity in the system of fame. She depended on her innocent 'Little Mary' image at a time when the US was building a national culture based on the idea of wholesome American-ness, but she was also a canny business-woman behind the scenes. She renegotiated her salary from $20,000 per annum to $1000 per week as well as 50 per cent of distribution profits. She clearly understood how important she was to Para-mount's publicity machine (Kerr 1990: 406). Nevertheless, her behind-the-scenes power depended on her public conformity with a conventional view of American femininity.

Movie star products became the focal point of Zukor's business strategy. For Kerr, the star system is a product of the joint develop-ment of the aesthetics of film and its development as an industry. Manufacturers attempted to combine the new film aesthetic with a coordinated corporate structure and the star became the commodity that linked film aesthetics with corporate management (Kerr 1990: 404).

By the 1930s Zukor's Paramount corporate model was standard. The drive to monopoly (which resulted in oligopoly) and vertical integration structured the film industry. Including Zukor's Paramount Pictures, there were five major studios and three minor studios that dominated Hollywood. The five major studios were integrated con-glomerates that owned film production studios, distribution organi-zations and film theatres: Fox Film Corporation, Paramount Pictures, Warner Brothers, Loews Incorporated (the parent company to Metro-Goldwyn-Mayer)[7] and RKO Radio Pictures (the three minor studios, Universal Pictures, Columbia Pictures and United Artists were not fully integrated). Stars became the centrepiece of this mature oli-gopoly and in this period, star making was an industrial machine (Marshall 1997: 84). The powerful studios owned the stars as com-modities. Vertical integration gave the big five studios a great deal of economic power, and it also enabled a high level of control over the stars; young actors were signed to long, legally binding contracts and studios controlled the stars' images through these contracts (Gamson 1994: 25). Actors had little say in the films they appeared in, or the construction of their star image, and depended on the studio to provide them with film roles (or vehicles) to establish and maintain their careers (and their economic value). Gamson argues that many of the strategies for manufacturing stars remained intact into the 1990s and centred on the blurring of the line between screen role and off-screen personality (1994: 26). As we saw in the previous chapter, this practice has roots reaching back to the eighteenth-century theatre, and so this is not a new precedent in the promotion of entertainment figures, but Hollywood contributed a great deal the development of the machinery surrounding these processes and, of course, film arrives simultaneously with a mass press, the advertising industry, the rise of public relations and the expansion of commercial entertainment culture generally. Publicity stunts and the advertising practices engaged in by the studio built a public personality that was then linked to a star's screen roles and larger-than-life images (Gamson 1994: 26). Studio publicity departments produced publicity that would link the star's personality to the part being played. For example, Rudolph Valentino, an early sex symbol of the cinema, was promoted as such by the films he starred in for Famous Players-Lasky. But when, in a struggle between star and studio that has by now become very familiar, Valentino went on a 'one man strike' and wrote to *Photoplay* magazine to complain about his contractual lack of control, Famous Players hit back by refusing to allow him to star in Ben Hur with Metro-Goldwyn-Mayer. It is important to note that the publicity machinery that developed around the film industry was not only based in the film studios. In the face of complete studio control, stars (particularly high ranking ones) began to employ their own agents and managers in an attempt to establish independent reputations and values and to wrest control over their image from the big studios. Valentino's manager, George Ullman, appealed against the decision against Valentino and was partially successful. Although Valentino was still contractually obliged to act only with Famous Players, he was now able to work in other types of employment outside of acting. Ullman, his agent, almost immediately secured Valentino lucrative employment endorsing Mineralava Clay Beauty Company. This is an early example of how central to establishing independence from studio control the role of the agent or manager was to become.

The agent's purpose is to represent the star as an independent entity, both economically and personally (Marshall 1997: 84). Agencies representing film stars became big business in themselves and lucrative for both the actor being represented and the agency doing the representing. The business of managing stars also developed its own standards and practices as in the other businesses connected to the entertainment industry. A key practice in the business of establishing a star's independence is that of linking the star's value to audience appeal rather than to a studio. An agent's job is to 'forge an independent relationship between the star and the audience' (Marshall 1997: 85). The growth of this ancillary business sector once again demonstrates the manner in which the industrialization of cultural industries often results in the development of a set of circulating businesses upon which the original industry comes, in some ways, to rely. In addition, the business calculation upon which star management grew, was both predicated upon, and further reinforced, the discourse that it is audiences that make the stars, rather than the business practices of organizations (including star management). But as we have seen, the audiences' interest in stars was encouraged and nurtured by film manufacturers and exhibitors from the first decade of the twentieth century in order to sell their product as a differentiated consumer product, by using the branding practices of the advertising industry, to associate the quality of the film with the 'star' performer. This system has had longevity, and although the history of Hollywood is a complex one, it is a system which continues to be at the heart of the promotional strategies of the 'industry of desire'.

Conclusion

At the end of the nineteenth century and into the twentieth century, two key media industries grew up. Celebrity was a crucial part of the growth and stabilization of both the early mass circulation press and Hollywood. The press developed conventions of celebrity journalism in this period which made it an attractive prospect for advertisers upon whom it relied. In the process it plays a major role in the circulation of celebrity and star images and gossip. And just as the press came to rely on celebrity to help it secure advertising revenue, so Hollywood came to rely on the circulation of its star images through the news, thus initiating a long-standing symbiotic relationship between the two. The American film industry also promulgates stardom and celebrity by developing a system of promotion that relies on the images and personalities of its leading actors as branded commodities in the promotion and product differentiation of narrative film. The establishment of these two industries are key moments in the growth of celebrity culture and they are both essentially products of economic decisions set in the context of an expanding commercial and leisure arena, and the growth adjunct industries that also emerge with the firm establishment of consumer culture, particularly advertising.

Celebrity is now so deeply embedded in our cultural landscape that it is important to have examined its origins in commercial culture, not as an inevitable outgrowth of consumer culture, or the spontaneous desire of audiences of new media to see stars, but instead as based on business calculations and the promotional strategies they entailed at a moment in history when the cultural landscape was permanently altered as a result of the growth of the mass media. Since those early moments in media culture, celebrity has continued to expand and has continued to play an import role in the media economy. We will now turn to the modern news media and the new technology environment of the present to examine the set of circumstances in our time that once again saw a massive expansion of celebrity content in the news.

4

Celebrity and News

Introduction

In 2004, the American gossip columnist, Lloyd Grove exclaimed, 'gossip has gone mainstream' (quoted in Case 2004: 36).[1] Meanwhile, Tony Case, writing in *Presstime*, the magazine of the Newspaper Association of America, told journalists, '[g]ossip has moved off the arts and weekend sections to become a bona fide asset for newspapers...' (2004: 35). Most commentators agree that gossip, and in particular, celebrity gossip, has become increasingly embedded, not just in the popular tabloids, but also across all news media platforms, including broadsheet newspapers, television news and the internet. For Case, the mainstreaming of celebrity news is a valuable practice as a business opportunity; '[b]eefing up celebrity lures young readers and attracts the advertisers who want to reach them' (2004: 36) and some academic commentators agree that celebrity news has financial benefits for news media (Cashmore 2006; Conboy 2014). Others see democratic potential in the growth of celebrity news; it is considered to erode authority (Ponce de Leon 2002) and is seen to be boisterously democratic (Connell 1992). Celebrity news, as we saw in the previous chapter, is part of a long tradition of popular journalism that emerges with modernity and the growth of the press, and for some, rather than a blight on the landscape of public communication, is considered a sign of growing democracy (Ponce de Leon 2002). However, many journalists, editors and critics are deeply concerned about the growth of celebrity content in the news because it is said to undermine what journalism ought to do – 'to monitor, to hold to account and to facilitate and maintain deliberation' (Fenton 2010: 3). The concern is that the role of the news in a democratic society is being undermined as it shifts from providing the 'news that people need', to delivering the celebrity gossip and human interest stories that advertisers are so keen on (Goldstein 1998; Hickey 1998).

This chapter will begin by examining the debate about whether celebrity news contributes to a less well-informed citizenry or is part of a progressive erosion of authority. In doing so it will consider the extent to which the news has been 'restyled' (Corner and Pels 2003) by celebrity content and will ask why celebrity news has burgeoned in this period to the extent that some claim it has become a central structuring device of information flows today (Conboy 2014; Turner 2014). What impact does the quantity of celebrity news have on news production and the role of news in democratic societies?

Many of the claims about the democratic character of celebrity news stems from its positioning within the language of popular journalism and on the language patterns (and the experiences they reflect) of non-elite groups in society, in particular, the working class, people of colour and women. This perspective values the ability of celebrity gossip to speak to ordinary people about issues that matter to them and considers 'hard' news to belong to the world of social elites from which the mass of the population are barred. Those who critique popular journalism and human interest stories are often labelled as elitist. This chapter will offer a critical discussion of this view and will suggest that we need to focus on the specific content of human interest stories, of which celebrity contributes a significant and growing portion, and consider the values that are embedded within them (Curran and Sparks 1991). This chapter will ask if celebrity news is simply a form of journalism that speaks in the language of, and in the interests of, the masses, and if so, why has it grown so much at particular historical moments, including the present? How much can we attribute the recent explosion of celebrity journalism to audience tastes and how much to the business decisions of news organizations?

In order to answer those questions, this chapter will examine the conditions at the beginning of the twenty-first century that gave rise to the recent expansion in celebrity news, including important changes in the news industry, particularly in the US and UK. The growth of celebrity news is put into a broader context of challenges facing news organizations that have been brought about by a combined set of pressures: the introduction of new technology, shrinking advertising revenue, which continues to be an important revenue stream for the news media, increasing marketization of news, the globalization of commerce, the arrival of free newspapers, and the advent of 24-hour news. What business strategies were developed in what had been a moment of uncertainty and what role did celebrity play in helping news organizations to address those issues? Today, the future of the news looks less uncertain as operating margins are increasing, online advertising revenue is picking up and so too are audiences (Ofcom 2015). To what extent did celebrity news contribute to the stabilization of news organizations and how much has celebrity impacted on new online journalistic practices?

Celebrity gossip has long been a part of human interest journalism; the journalistic conventions of the human interest story emerged simultaneously and overlapped with the rise of celebrity journalism as we saw in chapter 3, and played a significant role in the shape of the news in the transition to an industrialized mass press. The questions for this chapter are these – why did celebrity news expand so rapidly in the contemporary news landscape, what role is it playing in the transformations in the business of news today, and what does this tell us about the long-term health of the news?

Celebrity News and the Democratization Debate

To many industry commentators and scholars, the rise of celebrity news is considered to point to a democratized public sphere. For instance, both Leo Braudy (1986) and Charles Ponce de Leon (2002) suggest that the fame produced by the mass media – the fame of celebrity, of personality and of visibility – is part of a 'sweeping democratization of fame' (2002: 13), rather than a 'degraded product of technological innovation and its mind-numbing effects on the public' (2002: 13). Ponce de Leon, in a detailed examination of the emergence of celebrity journalism in America, upbraids critics for their contempt for celebrity news and their concern about its 'pernicious influence on the news media' (2002: 3). For Ponce de Leon, the phenomenon of celebrity, and its prominence in the news media,

> is a direct outgrowth of developments that most of us regard as progressive: the spread of a market economy and the rise of democratic, individualistic values. Throughout modern history these developments have steadily eroded all sources of authority, including the aura that formerly surrounded the 'great'. The culture of celebrity is not some grotesque mutation afflicting an otherwise healthy organism, but one of its central features, a condition arising directly from the encouragement that modern societies provide for social mobility and self-invention. (2002: 4)

Yet, there is no evidence that the spread of a market economy is either progressive or a sign of growing democracy. In the case of the news, we saw in chapter 3 how the pressures of the market in the late nineteenth century led to the replacement of radical populist news with celebrity gossip. Further, accounts which make claims about the unfettered growth of democracy, social mobility and equality in liberal modernity ignore the hierarchies which structure society today, in which inequality has actually intensified and social mobility has declined (Littler 2004). The system of celebrity is part of our social hierarchy and as such it contributes to symbolic exclusion (Couldry 2000, 2014), and to a society in which the majority are structurally excluded from success. Chris Rojek terms this phenomenon 'achievement famine' and considers systems of celebrity to be central to its architecture (Rojek 2001), while Jo Littler considers celebrity to be central to supporting the myths of meritocracy (Littler 2004), including those instances when celebrity gossip seems to undermine the hierarchy of fame (Cross and Littler 2010). In addition, we shall see that the intensification of market values in the news media coincides with the growth of celebrity journalism, as the fastest growing part of a more general growth in news-as-entertainment, and the resultant decline of other types of news content, such as public affairs and foreign affairs. We will examine the relationship between the growth of celebrity news and the interests of those who provide the commercial news media with their main revenue stream – in particular advertisers.

Studies have shown that the distinction between 'hard' news and 'soft' news is becoming blurred with the substantial growth in entertainment stories and celebrity gossip in news media in the latter half of the twentieth century (Franklin 1997; Turner 2014). Today, every UK online tabloid has a section dedicated to celebrity gossip. The *Daily Mail Online*'s 'TV and Showbiz' page carries headlines such as 'No slowing down! Eight months pregnant and Kim Kardashian wears skintight dress and heels to film reality show with her sisters',[2] accompanied by a large photo. The *Mirror Online* has a dedicated 'Celebrity News' section sporting headlines such as 'Halloween Horror: Reality star Natalie Nunn poses awkwardly on red carpet and SPLITS her costume' – again accompanied by a photo.[3] The broadsheet newspapers also carry celebrity news. The 'Culture' section of the *Guardian* has interviews with the stars and articles such as 'Crush of the week: Leonardo DiCaprio'.[4] The *Telegraph* has a banner on 'Hot Topics' with hypertext links to stories on the stars of shows such as *Strictly Come Dancing*, and one simply entitled 'Spectre' whose link takes the reader to a promotional page of the film starring Daniel Craig which is not even disguised as a review.[5]

Bob Franklin (1997) warned about the dangers of rapidly spreading 'newzak' in the late 1990s, a term related to the debate on 'tabloidization', which refers to the blurring of the lines between news and entertainment, broadsheet and tabloid journalism, documentary and reality TV. Franklin argued that ' "infotainment" is rampant' (1997: 6), and he points to the dire consequences of 'market driven journalism' (1997: 7) which focuses on celebrity 'trivia' rather than information about 'significant issues and events of international consequence' (1997: 4). For Franklin, 'newzak' undermines journalism's key role in informing citizens, for without an informed citizenry, 'democracy is impoverished and at risk' (1997: 5). Some, for example Brian McNair (2003), would consider this view to be elitist, while others suggest that such an approach 'begs the question [of] what is journalism's true purpose and assumes that the coverage of celebrity does not match a higher set of ideals' (Conboy 2014: 171). For Martin Conboy, journalism 'is very often a shuttling between or a balance between' an allegiance to the democratic good and the profit motive (2014: 172).[6] Conboy suggests that there is no significant problem with the existence of celebrity news because '[j]ournalism contains information and entertainment, can divert and concentrate the mind, and is vital to democracy and to the well-oiled functioning of the rumor mill. It owes, according to many of its more principled practitioners as well as its political advocates, an allegiance to the democratic good but only persists because it can make sizable profits for global conglomerates' (2014: 172). And yet, according to Des Freedman, news has never been an 'ordinary' commodity (2010: 36); instead, a very particular set of circumstances have supported journalism's democratic role, and those circumstances were under threat at the beginning of the twenty-first century by the very market forces that Ponce de Leon and others equate with freedom. Freedman argues the public 'benefited from an arrangement whereby advertisers have been happy to pour money into bulletins and titles that provide them with desirable audiences while audiences are, in turn, provided with public affairs-oriented material that contributes to their ability to make informed choices that are the hallmark of democratic political life' (Freedman 2010: 39). However, it is not just a question of making profits – as Freedman points out '[t]his arrangement has been bolstered by the willingness both of regulators to insist on minimum levels of television news and of press proprietors to subsidize loss-making titles in pursuit of political influence (and eventual profitability)' (2010: 39). Media regulation and ownership practices both, in different ways, recognize the symbolic importance of the news and have intervened in order to support the news commodity when the market on its own could not. For instance, Rupert Murdoch's media empire supported the losses of £87.7m at the *Times* and *Sunday Times* in 2010 (Companies House records). A new set of circumstances now preside over the news business that has broken the model that 'underpinned the delivery of news for many years' (Freedman 2010).

In addition, even those areas of the news business that have traditionally made sizeable profits were under threat at the beginning of the twenty-first century because of the huge growth in competition.[7] As the then director of group finance at BSkyB explained to Freedman in an interview in 2010 '[c]ompetition...has gone exponential. It's about the rate of change. It is not that there was no competition and now there is, it's that the competition is now more numerous and the playing field changes and reinvents itself at a much faster velocity' (Andrew Griffith in Freedman 2010: 37).

The picture in the US exemplified this argument. A number of critics identified the growth of competition in the newspaper industry at the end of the twentieth century and the subsequent dominance of market values, primarily a sole orientation on short-term profit which continues to permeate the editorial room. There was a significant shift away from investigative values and objective news reporting, as newspapers were faced with ever increasing financial pressures. Hickey characterized the situation that faced the American news industry at the end of the twentieth century thus:

> A new era has dawned in American Journalism...As competition grows ever more ferocious; as the audience continues to drift away from traditional news sources, both print and television; as the public's confidence in news organizations and news people continues to decline; as mainstream print and TV news outlets purvey more 'life-style' stories, trivia, scandal, celebrity gossip, sensational crime, sex in high places, and tabloidism at the expense of serious news in a cynical effort to maximize readership and viewership; as editors collude ever more willingly with marketers, promotion 'experts', and advertisers, thus ceding a portion of their sacred editorial trust; as editors shrink from tough coverage of major advertisers lest they jeopardize ad revenue; as news holes grow smaller in column inches to cosmeticize the bottom line; as news executives cut muscle and sinew from budgets to satisfy their corporate overseers' demands for higher profit margins each year; as top managers fail to reinvest profits in staff training, investigative reports, salaries, plant and equipment – then the broadly-felt consequence of those factors and many others, collectively, is a diminished and deracinated journalism of a sort that hasn't been seen in this

country and which, if it persists, will be a fatal erosion of the bond between journalists and the public. (1998: 29)

There is evidence that these processes have been in operation in the UK news business too. So, for instance, the *Telegraph* and *Sunday Telegraph* made a profit of £55.7m in 2011 – the same year that their major competitor the *Times* and *Sunday Times* lost £45m. This profit arose from the paper putting into practice precisely those measures identified by Hickey above – it developed a new business model and engaged in substantial cost-cutting measures. The paper's staff was cut to 500 – about half the size of the staff at the *New York Times*. Sub-editing was outsourced and the editor no longer held news conferences – instead journalists sent him story ideas via iPads. The paper also cut expensive sections. For example, the features section was cut in order to save £4m per year. The *Telegraph* shifted most of its stories online – 65 per cent by 2012,[8] and included promotional links and celebrity gossip in its online click-on banner 'Hot Topics', as we saw above. As a consequence of a general shift from features to showbiz, the paper secured substantial advertising revenue and secured its financial future, but at what cost to the news?

These concerns are also shared by some scholars of celebrity culture. Recently, Graeme Turner has examined the increasing acceptance of what he terms the oxymoron of 'celebrity' 'news' – a descriptor of a genre of writing in stark contrast with values more usually associated with the news. Turner argues that celebrity news, and the journalists who deliver it, rely upon practices that are diametrically at odds with the values conventionally associated with journalism, having little interest or reliance on facts or the verifiability of a story. Instead, most celebrity news is reliant either upon gossip and speculation, or upon direct feeds from the promotional industries surrounding celebrity – and neither practice treats sources objectively. For Turner, 'celebrity news' has had a most profound impact on journalism – to the extent that we might be witnessing a 'restructuring of the industrial production of news.'

> The scale of the output, the avidity with which it is taken up, and the degree to which it has become institutionally and industrially embedded in the production practices of the news media across all platforms, entitle us to think of this as a significant restructuring of the industrial production of news journalism. (2014: 146)

Turner's disquiet today echoes that raised by media scholars in the 1990s and early 2000s who chart the growth in entertainment stories and the decline in public affairs news in the tabloids (Curran 2002;

Curran and Sparks 1991; Rooney 2000; Sparks 1988), and the broadsheets (McLachlan and Golding 2000). As we saw in chapter 3, the human interest story and celebrity news overlap but are not the same, and what Turner is pointing to is an increase in stories about celebrities, based sometimes on 'human interest' reporting on their private lives, including gossip and scandal, such as Kardashian's wardrobe during pregnancy, or the sartorial mishaps of reality TV celebrities, and sometimes reporting on their promotional or creative activities in the public domain.

Also, according to Turner, because celebrity news often depends on journalists' ability to demonstrate their closeness to their sources (and therefore their insider knowledge), selected or preferred journalists become known as expert commentators. Turner argues that celebrity journalists 'will readily foreground' their friendly and personal relations with a celebrity, which not only undermines values of independence and objectivity, but also leads to an 'interdependence' between journalist and celebrity that might be described as journalists 'being captured by their sources'.[9] Turner argues:

> Celebrity has become the home of the media event, and the journalist is invited along simply to be a witness. If the journalist turns up, if their attention is rewarded, and if they decided to record that publicly in some way, then the media event becomes news and free publicity results. The journalist, of course, is perfectly aware that they are being used as a mechanism of turning advertising into news; they cooperate, however, because they need to ensure they continue to be kept in the loop by the major promotion companies, and accorded the level of access they need to cover their beat properly. (2014: 146)

It is worth noting that the intimacy between journalist and celebrity is paralleled in other areas of the news, for example through press conferences or other protocols such as interviews, briefings and lobbying (see Ericson et al. 1989; Manning 2000). Journalists covering political news are equally reliant on a privileged relationship with, and access to, politicians – so much so, that Bob Franklin argues that '[t]he spheres of journalism and government increasing overlap as journalists and politicians have grown mutually reliant, with each pursuing goals which can only be achieved with some degree of cooperation from the other' (1997: 30). Franklin calls this a 'collusive' relationship and the strongest long-term example of this in the UK is the lobby system, which is rather like a private press conference where an exclusive coterie of journalists is briefed by Whitehall or Number 10 (see Conboy 2011). There are obvious differences in the content of a Downing Street policy briefing and a celebrity press conference, but the special access that 'expert' journalists acquire is similar.

More recently we have seen directly the cosy relationship between politicians and the press and the *hidden* entanglement of the press, politicians and celebrity culture in the *News of the World* hacking scandal that prompted the Leveson Inquiry. Illegal phone hacking became a widespread practice at the *News of the World* and was fuelled by the desire to chase audiences with salacious details of celebrities' lives. The impression we are left with is that the hacking scandal was primarily about publishing the misdeeds of celebrities, but in fact the majority of the thousands of victims of phone hacking were ordinary people, many of whom had lost family members or were victims of crimes, and whose personal trauma was splashed across the front page in an effort to sell newspapers. The conditions that gave rise to the practice of illegally invading the privacy of celebrities for 'human interest' was one in which the (also illegal) hacking, harassment and libel of ordinary people became standard practices in an effort, as Brian Cathcart puts it, 'to make a story better without the effort of reporting it properly' (2012: 26). In fact, Natalie Fenton argues that the hacking scandal must be understood in the context of the same set of economic circumstances for the news business that we have been examining in this chapter. In the drive to cut costs and return to profitability, newspapers cut staff, and did so at a time when the numbers of news outlets and platforms were increasing. This exacerbated problems of producing content, with fewer journalists having to fill more space in less time:

> If you combine the faster and shallower corporate journalism of the digital age with the need to pull readers in for commercial rather than journalistic reasons, it is not difficult to see how the values of professional journalism are quickly cast aside in order to indulge in sensationalism, trade in gratuitous spectacles, and deal in dubious emotionalism...The net result is denigration of the professional life and integrity of news journalists, leading to a detrimental impact on the quality of news journalism and a consequent damage to our democracy. (2012: 4)

In the process of its investigation, the Leveson Inquiry also revealed the close relationship between news proprietor, Rupert Murdoch and his top staff, and four British prime ministers, including Labour's Tony Blair and Conservative David Cameron. *News of the World* CEO Rebekah Brooks turned out to be good friends with both prime ministers, while ex-editor Andy Coulson had been appointed by Cameron as his director of communications soon after he was forced to resign from the paper as a result of the hacking scandal. The case of the *News of the World* hacking scandal suggests that rather than speaking to the concerns of ordinary members of the public, celebrity news grew and spread for the same economic reasons as those that led to the development of journalistic practices and styles that directly preyed on members of the public who had the misfortune to be caught in its jaw. As Fenton argues, 'Rebekah Brooks (former editor of the former tabloid newspaper *News of the World*) doesn't need to give the green light to phone hacking, it's just part of what is expected' (2012: 4). For Fenton, the phone hacking scandal is not only shocking because of the awfulness of the practice and the lack of humanity it revealed, but also because it 'exposed the heart of a system that is deeply flawed' (2012: 4). She argues that the hacking scandal revealed that 'a marketized and corporatized media cannot be relied on to deliver the conditions for a deliberative democracy to flourish. Markets do not have democratic intent at their core. When markets fail, or come under threat, or simply become too bullish, ethical journalistic practice is swept aside in pursuit of competitive and financial gain' (2012: 4). Celebrity news is burgeoning in order to give newspapers a competitive edge. In the process, are the informational and deliberative functions of the news being lost?

Celebrity News, Gossip and Scandal: the Cultural Politics of 'Tittle Tattle'

But the discussion about the 'popular' and the implicit politics and/ or democratic potential of celebrity news is often conducted on the terrain of language, in particular, the language of gossip. Once again, the longstanding debate between the 'populists' and the 'pessimists', as James Curran calls them (2002), structures the discussion. A number of media scholars have pointed to the way that popular press, both historically and today, relies on the language of the working class (Conboy 2006; Curran 2002; Curran and Sparks 1991). Martin Conboy argues that the appeal of British tabloids is located in the 'linguistic specificity' of a 'popular audience' and he points out that the link between the print media and the language of ordinary people is as old as print itself' (2006: 1). Others point to a more recent 'democratization' of the news and claim that the use of the vernacular in celebrity news has the effect of including the general population who are excluded from 'serious' news discourse and high culture (Braudy 1986; Hartley 2008; Ponce de Leon 2002).

Celebrity gossip for some is seen to be unruly and to speak in the language of the disenfranchised (Bird 1992; Van Zoonen 2003); for others celebrity news speaks to the social and economic gulf between social classes, providing a critical commentary on this reality not found elsewhere (Connell 1992), and for others it has expanded 'contemporary discourses on gender, sexual morality, politics, national identity and even mental health' (Conboy 2014: 173). But it is important to make a distinction between the language of working-class papers, that are based around working-class interests, and the populist language of the mainstream tabloid press, for they are not the same, as we saw in chapter 3 (see Williamson 2012). In addition, Marshall reminds us that there are two forms of celebrity gossip: that which is reported across the news media (and other media), which is 'structured and highly mediated', and another that is based around personal conversation and evaluation, but which 'moves the highly mediated into the interpersonal dimensions of everyday interchange' (2010: 37).

Elizabeth S. Bird conducted one of the first pieces of research with readers of popular tabloids (in this case US tabloids) to examine how the mediated gossip of the tabloids is translated into the language and lives of their readers. She suggested that the papers have huge readerships because there is an 'unusually close fit between the world view portrayed in the papers and that of their readers' (Bird, 1992: 202). Bird is writing from a perspective that was prominent in Anglo-American Cultural Studies in the 1990s which emphasized the active role of audiences in decoding the texts of popular culture. She argues that readers are 'active and playful', taking 'what they want from the papers' (1992: 203). For Bird, 'an important element in their readings is indeed a form of resistance to dominant values – an awareness, for example, that they "should" be reading about news and current affairs but find these boring and irrelevant' (1992: 204). Bird explains that part of the pleasure that readers take in reading the tabloids is 'some sense of knowing and control over things that are really out of control' (1992: 205). But while Bird acknowledges that the pleasure in *feeling* in control is not the same as *having* control, and that feeling empowered does not alter one's subordinate social position, she considers the popular engagement with tabloids to be largely positive because reading tabloids helps readers cope with their lives and feel good about themselves; it is a limited act of resistance. This is not dissimilar to Ian Connell's contemporaneous view that celebrity news brings to light and gives expression to class differences that are mostly hidden in the media (1992). This kind of coverage is seen as valuable because it offers a limited awareness of the discrepancies of wealth and belonging in Western societies. And despite the fact that these studies are now quite old, they are the precursors to a prevalent perspective in relation to the digital and online worlds as we will see in the following chapters and their premise continues to be influential.

This kind of research, which did not automatically disparage the tastes of the working class, women and other marginalized groups, and did not assume that audiences were indoctrinated by what they read or viewed, was an important challenge to the notion that the media ought to be based on the experiences and interests of the middle class and social elites, and undermined the flawed claim that audiences are merely 'dupes' of the media. However, there are a number of questions that need to be addressed – in particular the twin issues of relativism and populism. Relativism, as Curran and Sparks point out, has been 'given additional dimension by...[those] who argue that the quality of media artefacts is not intrinsic to them but is created in the process of consumption' (Curran and Sparks 1991: 218). A number of studies in the 1990s argued that the value in popular texts derived not from texts themselves, but from the meanings that were 'poached' by audiences (de Certeau 1984). The assumption of those conducting research from this perspective is that 'active' readers tend to read against the grain of the meanings embedded in a text.

Following on from this was a form of populism which designated 'active' reading as almost a priori, a form of resistance to dominant or bourgeois culture (Bacon-Smith 1999; Fiske 1987; Hobson 1982; Jenkins 1992; Radway 1984). However, there is other audience research that shows that active reading can and does coincide with preferred readings embedded in texts (Morley and Brunsdon 1999) and that, at any rate, not all counter-readings are progressive (Barker and Brooks 1998; Williamson 2005). In addition, Curran demonstrates that high circulation figures cannot be explained by pointing to a 'fit' between the views of the paper and that of the readership. For instance, despite the wholesale support for the Conservatives found in Britain's most popular daily tabloid *The Sun*, the vast majority of its readership consistently votes for the Labour Party (Curran and Seaton 2003).

Today, such approaches also tend to put celebrity culture at odds with bourgeois culture. For instance, Conboy argues that '[c]omparisons of tabloid media with idealized versions of what the news ought to be doing ignore the historical evidence that tabloid news and its various predecessors in popular print culture have always sought to contest dominant bourgeois values' (2014: 175). Counterposing popular media and bourgeois media in this manner misconstrues the media field. Both elite 'bourgeois' media and popular media are owned and controlled by economic and societal elites, are hierarchically structured and serve the interests of the controlling elite (Bourdieu 1994). The popular media, of which the tabloids and celebrity news are a part, are owned either by media barons or by huge multinational conglomerates (or a combination of both, as in the case of Rupert Murdoch) whose interests in distributing 'popular' texts is economic. As we saw in the previous chapters, the rapid spread of celebrity texts historically has tended to coincide with moments of crisis and/or increased profiteering and as we shall see below, this is also the case today. Also, it is just as possible to interpret Bird's interview material as suggesting that readers' lack of interest in public affairs is not an act of resistance to 'dominant' values, but evidence of their acquiescence to their exclusion from real participation in civic life (Bourdieu 1984).

Colin Sparks offered such an analysis, when in the late 1980s he urged scholars to take seriously the reality that most readers choose to read tabloids and therefore choose *not* to be politically informed. Sparks argues that this is explicable because 'as people have more and more experience of their place in the bourgeois democracy they display less and less interest in it' (1988: 217). For Sparks, 'political and economic power in a stable bourgeois democracy is so far removed from the real lives of the mass of the population that they have no interest, in either sense, in monitoring its disposal' (1988: 217). Sparks reasons that 'the more stable and established a bourgeois democracy is the less interest the mass of the population will have in its working and the more apolitical and "trivial" the popular press will become' (1988: 217). This is an important corrective to relativist celebrations of engagement with 'mass' popular culture as 'resistance' per se. However, there is also a sense of inevitability in Sparks' argument that is both at odds with the political content found in early mass press (see chapter 3) and with the way that capitalism, being prone to economic crisis, is also prone to instability, both economic and political. So although capitalism might have seemed stable in the era of Thatcher and Reagan, when Sparks was writing, the crash of 2008 and unsustainable levels of rising debt, as well as widespread unrest in southern Europe, parts of South America and the Arab world, make the system look far less stable today, yet celebrity news has not only remained a stable part of the news media, it has burgeoned, both online and off, while new social movements have found the means of circumventing the traditional media to spread word and develop strategies of resistance (Fenton and Barassi 2011). As we shall see below, the growth of celebrity news has less to do with what people demand of their papers and more to do with the economic structure of the news industry, the crisis that it is facing, and the business decisions and practices that have resulted.

Rather than considering readers to simply be either 'resistant' or 'acquiescent', it is important to remember that content of the press is determined by its owners, and readers have to make sense of what is in front of them in specific socio-political circumstances. In this regard, Curran and Sparks have argued that entertainment and human interest stories tend to a rather conservative world view. Events are presented either in terms of the human emotion or morality of those involved in the story, rather than a broader social explanation, or are predicated on the unpredictability of human existence, presenting a fatalistic view, which undermines the idea of human agency, rather than offering political understanding (1991: 228–9). And, significantly, through celebrity stories, consumption is presented 'as the central unifying experience common to all'; it is portrayed as a 'principal source of pleasure', 'the means by which we are able to exert control over our lives, and express ourselves creatively' (1991: 231). In this address to readers as consumers rather than citizens, celebrity news, with its focus on individuals, its 'common sense' framework of explanation and its moral rather than political solutions...provide[s] tacit support for existing power relations' (1991: 232). And even if readers entirely reject these implied values, they are still not offered political stories or news about the economy alongside these entertainment stories, and this results in 'inequalities of information provision' (1991: 228) for those who may legitimately feel themselves to be excluded from wider political culture. Curran and Sparks argue that people are denied a real choice of content because of the systematic prioritization of human interest stories (including celebrity news) over political and economic news (1991: 226).

However, the idea that celebrity gossip is generally a public good continues to inform the direction of some studies in celebrity culture. In a recent special edition of *Journalism* (2014), the editors, Dubied and Hanitzsch, espouse the perspective that celebrity news is not essentially a 'social peril' (2014: 138) and that it 'deserves its place in media content' (2014: 139). Dubied and Hanitzsch suggest that to draw an antagonistic relationship between celebrity news and other news is 'disconnected' from the realities of journalism and suffers 'from a tendency to idealizations when it comes to the social relevance of journalism' (Dubied and Hanitzsch 2014: 138). Instead, they argue that celebrity coverage brings a wide range of socially and politically relevant issues into public consciousness, and thus has the potential to widen the public sphere and to democratize access to knowledge of aspects of individuals' lives (2014: 138). Again there is something of the inevitable in their account when they suggest that the growth in celebrity news is really just journalists responding to longstanding changes in social reality.

For a start it ignores the real pressures that journalists face today, with staff and budget cuts, and multi-platform delivery systems (Phillips et al. 2010). The pressure to produce more articles in less time has led to fewer journalists gathering information outside of the newsroom and an increasing reliance on feeds from PR agencies promoting celebrity (see Fenton 2012; Rojek 2012). This had led to what Davies calls 'churnalism', by which he is referring to the 'rapid repackaging of largely unchecked second hand material', which derives either from public relations organizations or news agency sources (Davies 2008: 60). Celebrity agents and public relations organizations take advantage of the news media's need for content, and the time constraints of the newsroom, by bombarding journalists with press releases and invitations for the 'chosen few' to press conferences and other promotional devices (Rojek 2001). However, it is also the case that NGOs and other campaign organizations 'use' the celebrity voice to bring their issues to the fore in the media, which both complicates the picture that all celebrity news is straightforwardly negative, but points to the way that such organizations tend to mimic the public relations strategies of the wider promotional industries (Fenton 2010) and more generally to the pervasiveness of celebritized strategies of public engagement.

There is an important difference between analyses which accept (and apologize for) the news media as we find it, and those whose analysis of the current state of the news media leads them to call for media reform in an effort to improve its democratic potential and who are concerned with 'a time that is yet to come but is nonetheless worth aiming for' (Fenton 2010: 3). Dubied and Hanitzsch belong to the former and argue that in 'post-industrial societies' where the material resources for survival are generally secured, there has been a shift from 'survival values to self-expression values' (2014: 139). They suggest that in this new context, 'people need orientation to navigate a multi-optional space of lifestyles and to articulate their identities', and celebrity lifestyles help them to negotiate their way through this minefield of choices (2014: 139). However, there are a number of assumptions here that need to be unpicked, for the picture the authors paint of the global north as an affluent, fluid, post-industrial society (and which underpins their analysis of celebrity), is flawed.

Firstly, the claims of de-industrialization are based on hype. According to OECD (2008) data, levels of industrial production in the US, Canada and most European countries (including the UK) either remains stable or has slightly increased since the 1970s, and they cannot be considered 'post-industrial' nations, despite growth in the service sector. Secondly, at the same time, affluence has severely declined – levels of 'relative poverty' (defined as households lacking three items or activities deemed necessary for life in the UK) have risen to 23 per cent (Institute for Fiscal Studies 2012) – almost a quarter of the total population, and in 2012, 14 million people lived in 'absolute' poverty in the UK and were at risk of 'social exclusion'. In the US, according to the US Census Bureau, 16 per cent of Americans also live in 'relative poverty' (about 46 million). These statistics challenge the view that the central problems that confront people today are the 'increase in multi-optionality', and a 'need for orientation' (Dubied and Hanitzsch 2014: 140). The explanation that celebrity-oriented media offer role models, whose 'standardized lifestyles' reduce 'social complexity to a manageable array of options that are "ready to apply"' (2014: 140), is based on a picture of a well-off, de-industrialized society which does not exist, apart from, perhaps, in Switzerland or Norway.

Identifying this as the central purpose of celebrity news fits the formula against the facts. It also ignores the important role of celebrity historically in the rise of consumer capitalism and the emphasis on consumer identities rather than citizenship. And while it is true, as Marshall (2010: 36) points out, that people had to be taught to engage with consumer culture over the past 100 years (and in this respect, celebrity has been a pedagogical tool) (see chapter 6 for a discussion of this issue), it is also the case that in order to understand the huge growth of celebrity news, and its ability to take on that pedagogic role, one must look beyond the idea that celebrity news helps us navigate a cornucopia of choice for the self, or that it assists in the construction of identity (even if that may be partly true) to examine how celebrity content comes to be placed in front of us in the first place, however we then make sense of it.

'Making sense', however, is not a predetermined positive, empowering process. Indeed, Nick Couldry has argued that interest in celebrity lifestyles can be seen as a symptom of social exclusion rather than an example of role model identification. Couldry suggests that the longing for material goods, symbolized in celebrity lifestyles, by 'people who are poor or feel themselves to be poor', is an expression of a desire to be included in wider society, while recognizing that one is not (2000: 53). And 'whether you are on the outside or inside of the narratives of your culture and society' (2000: 54) is a significant dimension of inequality because it speaks to whose experiences matter and whose lives count. Couldry argues that celebrity is precisely predicated on a 'hierarchy between media and non-media people' (2002: 298); a hierarchy which serves to reinforce the lines between inclusion and exclusion, despite the addition of popular voices and ordinary language in celebrity reportage across the news media. For it isn't just the language and visibility of classed, raced or gendered groups in the media that is important – we need to analyse the content of that visibility.

It is without question the case that celebrity has an enormous socio-symbolic dimension, as has been amply demonstrated in studies of celebrity and earlier, in studies of stardom (examined in chapters 1 and 5). But, while it is important to understand the significance of celebrity for articulating and contributing to societies' central value systems, for mediating experiences of the self, and giving expression to belonging and exclusion, it is equally important to understand the material conditions of our 'expanding culture' (Williams 1961: 179) that have enabled celebrity media to thrive in order to play such an important social role. That means looking at both the broad shifts in society brought about through the transformation to capitalist modernity (see chapter 1), and the specific conditions that shaped the news media and the place of celebrity news within it.

In his discussion of the growth of the mass press, Raymond Williams warns against the acceptance of 'certain formulas' or 'assumptions' about the development of the press which have been 'fitted' to an accepted interpretation (1961: 173). One such assumption, which continues to circulate (Conboy 2011: 10), is the claim that the mass press was a product of the universal extension of literacy after the Foster Education Act was passed in 1870. This led to two further assumptions with which we are now familiar – that the result was either (a) the establishment of a democratized press, speaking to the masses in their own language, or (b) its degradation. But for Williams, the facts do not bear out the first assumption, making the latter claims superfluous, because the priorities of a commercially organized news media were flawed from the outset. He points to attempts long before 1870 to establish newspapers aimed at the non-literate working classes. One such attempt was the radical press. This was a 'press with a different social basis, among the newly organizing working class' (1961: 175) which flourished between the 1770s and the 1840s but which was crushed following the destruction of the Chartist movement. This paved the way for the subsequent development, from about the 1820s, of the Sunday paper, which was aimed at the emerging working class by mixing the politics of the radical press with stories of murders and executions and the like, whose provenance comes from ballads and chapbooks of old (see chapter 2).

In other words, explanations other than the growth of literacy must be sought to explain the growth of these papers which were collectively bought and read aloud to large numbers of the non-literate working class in coffee houses, pubs and workshops. Williams is not suggesting that the extension of literacy was completely irrelevant, but rather that it was only one factor. The accepted formula, in privileging literacy, ignores other crucial causes brought about by industrialization – such as the improvements in production and distribution through the development of technology (and not just communication technologies – the development of the railways transformed and industrialized the processes of distribution) and, in this instance, the growth of political opposition in the shape of the Chartist movement. Likewise, most accounts of celebrity focus on its symbolic importance and, while this is a significant factor, it is only *one* factor. Often overlooked in discussions about celebrity news are the economic conditions that shape the financing of newspapers without which they could not exist. In order to understand the development of celebrity news and its proliferation, we have to ask questions 'about the social organization of an industrial society, about its economic organization, and about the ways in which its services, such as newspapers, are paid for' (1961: 178). This chapter will now turn to these questions in order to examine the conditions which give rise to the rapid growth in celebrity news today.

The Political Economy of Celebrity News

As we saw earlier in this chapter, with the proliferation of online and digital news outlets, the news media in the first decade of the twenty-first century faced a crisis of competition which threatened to disrupt the traditional business models in the industry. Since the end of the twentieth century, the growth of the internet resulted in added pressure on the print press, both tabloid and broadsheet, and on commercial television news, as advertisers migrated online, leaving traditional news organizations with less advertising revenue. We saw in chapter 2, the important role that advertising has played historically in the profitability of commercial news, and today this is more significant than ever, as papers continue to be unable to make a profit on circulation figures alone (Freedman 2010).

There was a significant problem for newspapers and television news in the first decades of the twenty-first century because of the development of the internet and the migration of advertising revenue to online sources. This resulted in a decline in their share of advertising revenue, upon which newspapers and commercial television rely; instead there was a big increase in specific forms of online advertising and the news industry was unable to attract it. For instance, in the UK ad spend on the internet surpassed that of the national newspapers in 2006 (Sweeney 2008: 10). By 2014 UK digital advertising rose by 15 per cent to £7.2 billion and accounted for 39 per cent of estimated UK ad expenditure (Ofcom 2015: 16). But since 2013 there has been a year-on-year increase in ad spend on UK national newspapers, which grew across the titles by 19.5 per cent and is predicted to increase again to a further 22.8 per cent in 2015 with UK national titles expecting to attract £1.42 billion in ad spend (Advertising Association 2015). According to the Advertising Association, that increase is due to a surge in increase on digital ad spend that national newspapers now attract. Although it looks as though the crisis for news organizations is over for now, the tactics employed by newspaper groups to recover declining revenue in the years between 1990 and 2012 has had a lasting impact on the news, including an increased reliance on celebrity news, as we shall see below.

Freedman argues that the major problem facing traditional news providers was less to do with the decline in audiences and more the 'degeneration of the existing news business model that tied together news and advertising' (2010: 39). This created enormous pressure for news organizations to try to develop strategies to cope with what was a new reality of 'uncertainty and chaos' (2010: 40). One of the responses was to save money by cutting costs and increasing productivity. This is standard practice across all industry. In the news context, this meant cutting expensive staff and editorial commitments such as investigative reporting, and foreign and special correspondents (Freedman 2010: 41), and we saw above that the *Telegraph* engaged in this practice while beefing up its celebrity content. It also meant cutting staff costs such as photographers and researchers, whose skills can be replaced with outsourced providers. Again, we saw this in the case of the *Telegraph*, who outsourced sub-editing to a firm in Australia. This increases news outlets' reliance on public relations and news agencies for content, both written and photographic (Davies 2008), and makes celebrity feeds from such sources increasingly attractive, both as a cost-cutting exercise and as an attempt to reach wider audiences. In addition, online versions of newspapers began to use celebrities as 'click bait' and to insist that journalists produce celebrity 'click bait'. This has further impacted both on the quality of the news and on the conditions of service for journalists and on the kind of news they are allowed to write. For example, journalists at the Trinity Mirror group complained to the National Union of Journalists that they are being forced to write 'click bait' stories and are being set individual targets to measure their work on the 'clickability' of their online stories.[10] The pressure to write celebrity 'click bait' in this context is enormous and increases the amount of celebrity news online. One of the unintended consequences of these processes has been the growth and entrenchment of online paparazzi agencies and their influence in the online terrain (discussed further below).

Another response is to branch out from a newspaper business to a diversified group. This is a contemporary version of the drive to monopoly that we saw in chapters 2 and 3. The Daily Mail group has most fully taken this route and has spent £203 million acquiring 'high profile online recruitment, holiday, property and auto classified sites' (Freedman 2010: 42). But this creates further potential problems of 'cannibalization' – that is, 'accelerating the decline of their own print classifieds' (2010: 46). The Daily Mail group has, in turn, developed a whole new online business strategy, no longer seeing themselves as a news group, but as a wider media group, whose objective is to 'deliver the news, the information, the advertising, to their audiences in whatever form both the advertiser and the consumer want to receive it' (interview with Peter Williams of DMGT by Des Freedman 2010: 44). Des Freedman points out that the danger of this rebranding exercise is that, 'more short-sighted news organizations start to prioritize the development of their non-news services and new revenue streams at the expense of their core commitment to 'hard' news:

> [t]his is a familiar characteristic of convergence where previously distinct media forms are 'integrated' in such a way as to maximize popular appeal and audience numbers with a resulting emphasis, in the case of the news, on human interest stories, dramatic narratives, celebrity gossip and 'infotainment'. (Freedman 2010: 44)

This is precisely the route taken by the Daily Mail group in amping up its celebrity content online as we shall see below.

Another strategy has been to try to recapture readers and advertising revenue by recreating news outlets online and most news organizations now have an online presence, including celebrity and showbiz sections, which have replaced features sections and investigative journalism. The context in which newspapers and news channels have had to recreate themselves online was a challenging one. For example, news organizations were unlikely to ever be able to recreate the revenue generated from the forms of ads they previously relied on offline, because the type of advertising that dominates online advertising is quite different. The main form of online advertising is search advertising (57.6 per cent) and it is dominated by giants like Google (Freedman 2010: 45). The online operations of traditional news organizations were entering a field in which they had been cut out of almost 60 per cent of available online advertising. Although that situation has now altered, as we saw above, this produced a further strategy to increasingly rely on stories that will draw a large number of browser hits (click bait) and that would therefore attract the remaining advertisers. This created a great deal of pressure to produce celebrity news because of its popularity with most advertisers. And this is precisely what the *Daily Mail* has done with some considerable success; in particular, the *Mail Online* has drawn on reality TV as an easy pool for celebrity-based gossip. A number of critics have identified the symbiotic relationship between the tabloid press and reality TV (Conboy 2014; Turner 2010). Reality TV provides an endless stream of 'ordinary' celebrities who supply the kind of gossip, speculation and scandal that attracts advertisers (see chapter 5) and this model has been reproduced online, most profitably by the *Daily Mail*. For instance, according to *Press Gazette* figures, coverage of the UK television programme *I'm a Celebrity Get Me Out of Here* enabled the *Mail Online* to hit a new record of online traffic averaging over 12 million 'unique browsers' per day in November 2014. The site's busiest day was 20 November with 14.9 million browsers where the 'most read' stories on 19 and 20 November were covering the departure of Gemma Collins and Craig Charles from the show. In the same year, the *Daily Mail Online* reported a 49 per cent growth in digital advertising. In other words, reality TV celebrity provided the *Daily Mail* with the kind of clickable content that seemed to be able to recapture high levels of advertising.

But this kind of growth rate is not sustainable and brings its own pressures and problems. For instance, in the eleven months to the end of August 2015, the *Mail Online* saw its digital advertising revenue decline to 16 per cent at a time when overall online ad spend on UK titles was increasing. While this may still bring in a substantial amount of revenue, it will not be enough to satisfy investors who had come to expect a much higher growth rate. Indeed the analysts Exane published a note to investors warning that the *Mail Online* was likely to miss its stated revenue target of £100 million by the end of 2016.[11] The very diversification that created the conditions for the economic success of the Daily Mail group produced a new set of investor-related problems that are structural rather than cyclical, as organizations are tied to the logic of providing dividends to shareholders. The logical trajectory of this situation is to produce the kind of news that advertisers are keen on, such as celebrity news, in order to increase growth rates and keep investors happy. We seem to have moved some distance from the idea of the news as a public good.

Diversification in news organizations has created a situation in which the news industry today is obsessed with short-term profits, and the need to pay higher dividends to shareholders. As part of the process of diversification, most stock in news media is owned by big institutions such as mutual funds, retirement funds and insurance companies, who know little, and care less, about the news. The performance of these companies is graded on a weekly, monthly and quarterly basis, which puts great pressure on them to perform well – and this pressure is passed along the chain of command to the media companies who own the news and the editors who package it. Editors are now much more directly responsible for the success of the news as a business, and are offered bonuses (often larger than their annual salary) in order to persuade them to act in the interests of the shareholders rather than in the interests of news-as-a-public-good (Coyle 1998).

Meanwhile, media managers are also share owners and have a direct interest in company profit. The pressure and incentives to move away from 'hard' news and towards celebrity news are enormous and are exacerbated by the regulatory climate. For instance, in the US, by lifting ownership caps and distribution percentages, the Telecom-munications Bill (1996) led to a frenzy of acquisitions and mergers. This provided more impetus for clamping down on costs, in order to 'fatten the bottom line and make a company more attractive as a takeover target, with of course, a heavy windfall to major sharehold-ers' (Hickey 1998: 30). One of the casualties of this process was international news, because it is expensive. Hickey notes that cover-age of international events on television news in the US dropped by over 30 per cent in 30 years and he comments that 'the public are being drastically short changed in its capacity to learn about and understand what is going on in the world' (1998: 33).

Another, unintended, consequence of the staff cuts that resulted from these processes is the rise of the online paparazzi agency which has dramatically expanded the amount of images of celebrities in circulation. Kim McNamara argues that the growth in the paparazzi was a direct consequence of the decline in staff photographers (2011: 516). She also argues that whereas the paparazzi industry was once 'composed of freelance photographers, selling directly to picture editors at news and entertainment publications, the field is now dominated by multinational agencies with their own brand of mostly web-based entertainment news' (2011: 516) who cater to what is now a global market. Paparazzi agencies are a 'technology-driven industry' (2011: 517) which, according to McNamara, play *the* central role in the production and distribution of celebrity images and unbounded growth of celebrity content online. Some argue that these paparazzi agencies have played a crucial role in mainstreaming the un-posed shot of the famous (Holmes 2005; McNamara 2011; Turner 2010) and have become a new kind of news provider (McNamara 2011). The reason for the increase in importance of these agencies is that their images have played a decisive role in some of the circulation wars in the print media and their online editions, when competition and chasing advertising revenue remain salient factors in the production and circulation of news. Reporting on celebrities, celebrity TV shows and celebrity scandal have been key aspects to the medium-term success of online tabloid news. But the slowing of growth rates and the way that news providers are carved out of most online advertising streams is perhaps storing up problems for the future. It remains to be seen whether celebrity content of some form or another can solve what seem now to be structural problems for the news.

Conclusion

The growth of celebrity news in the early twenty-first century has not been inevitable, but a product of economic conditions and the business decisions made in that context. The diversified ownership and investment patterns of news organizations from the latter half of the twentieth century, encouraged by a deregulated field, resulted in a bonus culture focused on short-term profits and widespread staff cuts. This profit culture was exacerbated by coinciding with the introduction of new technology, resulting in a period of transition in the news industry as online replaced offline as the main news platform, putting pressure on the traditional advertising revenue stream for news organizations. The drive to increase advertising revenue to

satisfy investors lead news providers to increase their reliance
on celebrity news, much of which originated from the content of
television reality TV programmes. Meanwhile, the loss of experienced
journalists, specialist international affairs reporters and staff photographers as a result of staff cuts, and the pressure on journalists to
produce 'click bait' made the online news more dependent on
paparazzi agencies and packaged press releases from the entertainment industry. Thus the growth of celebrity as a news topic has less
to do with 'democratization', speaking the language of the people
or giving the punters what they want, and more to do with the patterns of ownership of the news, the economic basis of its operations
and the business practices that result. What we have witnessed at
the beginning of the twenty-first century is the deployment of celebrity gossip to ensure the financial health of the news industry, but
at the cost of news itself. This key moment in the growth of celebrity
will have lasting impacts for years to come for it has altered
the central purpose of the press to provide information in the
public interest necessary for democracy to thrive. The news media's
purpose now seems to be to fatten the bottom line for shareholders
by replacing expensive public interest journalism with lucrative celebrity news.

Celebrity can tell us a great deal about the balance of forces in
society, not only symbolic, but also economic. The rise of celebrity
news today is an indication that the profit motive in the news industry
is in the ascendant and both professional values and alternative values
are relatively weak by comparison. At the end of the twentieth
century, print news declined and online news grew at precisely the
moment when deregulation encouraged mergers, acquisitions and
consolidation – a mode of ownership that demanded that the pursuit
of short-term profiteering take precedence over traditional news practices and the values that underpinned them, leading directly to practices that have increased the volume of celebrity-based news to the
point that sheer quantity may have produced a new reality. Pushing
out international news and local news, cutting budgets for foreign
correspondents, photographers, libraries, fact checking and investigative practices occurred simultaneously with an increase in column
inches, front pages and headlines devoted to celebrity issues. The
resulting cuts in staff and other resources left online news reliant
upon the large online paparazzi agencies (themselves the direct beneficiaries of cuts of staff photographers), who grew the circulation of
celebrity images exponentially, and press agents from the wider entertainment industry. This is the context for the rise of celebrity content
in the news in the last two decades.

News organizations have most successfully made use of a free pool of celebrity gossip emanating from the kind of celebrity produced by reality TV – that is, the ephemeral here-today-gone-tomorrow celebrity that is based on the celebrification of ordinary people in the media. The following chapter will examine the rise of 'ordinary celebrity' and will examine why the television industry turned to reality TV and the celebrification of ordinary people.

5

Ordinary Celebrity

Introduction

There has been an explosion of ordinary people in the media and their subsequent 'celebrification'.[1] An endless parade of ordinary people seem to temporarily achieve celebrity status through their visibility in the media. For some, the invitation to ordinary people to participate in television shows, either as contestants or through 'the peoples' vote', is seen as a progressive form of democratic entertainment or 'democratainment', as Hartley calls it (Hartley 1999, 2008). Hartley coined this word to refer to 'the means by which popular participation in public issues is conducted in the media sphere' (1999: 209). The visibility of ordinary people, and their associated 'celebrification', is considered to be advancing the processes of democracy not only in television culture but more widely;[2] it is seen as a consumer-led form of participatory democracy as digital and online voting brings viewers into the decision-making process. This chapter will question this view by examining the economic conditions that have given rise to the 'ordinary celebrity' – and, in particular, those economic conditions in the television industry because of its central role in producing 'ordinary' celebrity. It will also question the cultural politics of the representation of ordinary people in the media and will examine the way that ordinary people are treated by those organizations who profit so well from media content based on their participation and performances. This chapter will ask if increased visibility of ordinary people in the media is a sign of democratization if, as Graeme Turner argues, there is more to democracy than the 'aggregation of preferences' (2010: 46). Has there been a slippage in the use of the idea of the democratic public sphere to discuss activity that does not directly contribute to the meaningful participation of citizens in 'decision making which involves the exercise of some form of structural power' (Turner 2010: 46)?

A number of scholars have argued that television has been particularly preoccupied with the 'ordinary' and that the rise of reality TV in the late twentieth century has played a significant role in the visibility of ordinary people in the mediated public realm (Biressi and Nunn 2005; Turner 2010). This chapter will argue that reality TV *has* been crucial to the expanded circulation of *images* of ordinary celebrity (rather than creating a significant increase in actually famous ordinary people or their democratic participation in the public sphere) and that this has occurred primarily for economic reasons. There has been much important careful scholarship that has examined the complexity of reality TV, the variety of formats found under the categorization of reality TV (Hill 2007, 2015), the differences in the types of famous personalities that are produced (see Holmes 2005; Holmes and Redmond 2006), and the complex readings and cultural politics of the versions of 'ordinary' on display (Biressi and Nunn 2005). This chapter will be drawing on the insights from that body of scholarship, but will focus primarily on the industry-specific economic conditions that gave rise to the reality formats which launched the ordinary celebrity onto the international stage in the television industry in the late twentieth and early twenty-first centuries. This context is as important as the 'appeal' of reality TV, for it speaks to the imperatives by which these types of texts became so prominent in the global television environment. As Ted Magder argues, 'Behind the creative task of bringing programs to audiences, TV is a business. That matters because the way TV conducts its business has a direct impact on the process by which programs are selected, financed, and produced' (2004: 138). In other words, we do have to attend to the conditions that bring particular types of programmes to our television screens, and these are far more complex than the notion of consumer choice found in Hartley's view of the structure of television industries. This chapter will examine why production companies and broadcasters turned to reality TV programming, why the production of ordinary celebrity became a central component of the phenomenon, and how the spread of reality formats increased the circulation of images of 'ordinary' celebrity beyond the texts of reality TV. In doing so, it argues that reality television, populated as it is by ordinary people, became a central mechanism by which the television industry addressed particular problems thrown up by changes in the television industry internationally.

Throughout this book I have argued that celebrity has expanded culturally at specific historical moments and in relation to specific (commercial) media/entertainment industries for primarily economic reasons. That is, for a variety of reasons, it made 'business sense' to develop the celebrity contribution to particular cultural and media forms. In general, celebrity has expanded in industries that have seen the combination of an increase in commercial imperatives, competition and marketing, together with the development of new technology (and not always media technology as we saw in the case of the theatre), which has either altered the prevailing conditions of production (such as in the case of the press) or seen the inauguration of new industries whose emergence coincided with the economic domination of market capitalism (such as the cinema). In the case of television, in processes parallel to those we examined in relation to the news media in the previous chapter, it was the combined pressures of the development of new technology, the resulting channel proliferation, and an intensification of commercial competition that coincided with the specific development of the reality format and facilitated its spread.

This chapter will begin with an examination of the television industry, including the political economy of television in a changing technological and socio-economic environment. It will argue that reality TV has been the driving force behind the growth in 'ordinary celebrity' and will examine the conditions in which business decisions to pursue these kinds of globally marketable formats came to the fore. In order to understand the cultural economy of ordinary celebrity, the chapter will then examine the impact that reality TV has had on the structure of the industry and on the lives of those caught up in its maws: in particular, the exploitation of ordinary people. Reality TV contributed significantly to the restructuring of the television industry, which, rather than opening up the industry democratically, has resulted in attacks on the conditions of those who work in the industry and those who try to enter the ranks of fame by this means.

While this chapter is centrally a political economy of ordinary celebrity through reality TV, it finishes with a critical examination of the politics of representation to suggest that here too, despite complexities and contradictions to be found and the diverse possibilities of audience readings, the format is not necessarily a progressive force. There is a suggestion from some academic quarters that any criticism of popular entertainment media is snobbish and patronizing (Gripsrud 1992). And it is true that many of the criticisms of reality TV and ordinary celebrity derive from elitist concerns about the 'dumbing down' of culture. Ordinary celebrities are often vilified in the press, for instance, for their lack of 'talent', education or charm – in other words for their lack of middle-class cultural capital. Such condemnation contributes to a social hierarchy that excludes non-dominant subjectivities, particularly gendered, classed and racialized subjectivities. However, this does not mean that all critiques of ordinary celebrity are elitist; one can object to the representation of ordinary people in the media on different grounds (Skeggs and Wood 2012; Williamson 2010). This chapter critiques contemporary 'ordinary celebrity' and reality TV from a different set of perspectives; firstly, by examining how the display of ordinariness is *circumscribed* in important ways; and secondly, analysing how it does not live up to its promise of opening up representation to ordinary people. Instead, it regularly denigrates working-class 'lack' for entertainment purposes, or validates non-normative identities on the basis of the neoliberal individualistic selves that are promoted in many of the programmes.

Ordinary Celebrity and the Rise of Reality TV

The growth of 'ordinary celebrity' has been driven by reality TV. Indeed, as a number of scholars have pointed out, television has, from its inception, produced a type of fame that is based on 'the personality' rather than the distant 'aura' of the film star (although that distinction is less stable today) (Bennett 2010; Langer 1981). Langer was one of the first critics to examine television's specific fame system which he identifies as a 'personality system'. For Langer, unlike other systems of fame such as that found in the classic Hollywood era, 'the personality system is not "larger than life" ' – it is 'cultivated almost exclusively as "part of life" ' (1981: 355), And while it is clear that television has also circulated stardom from different arenas (such as film, sport and music), television's specific form of fame has long been bound up with the personality – 'its ordinariness, its authenticity, its intimacy' (Bennett 2010: 2). For Langer, because television personalities play themselves, '[p]ersonalities are distinguished for their representativeness, their typicality, their "will to ordinariness", to be accepted, normalized, experienced as *familiar*' (Langer 1981: 355). Thus television has long been bound up with representations of the quotidian, and in the process seems to reduce the 'distance between itself and viewer' and to suggest 'that both television personalities and viewers exist within a common universe of experience' (Langer 1981: 363). It is perhaps for this reason that television had become the central terrain for the 'celebrification' (Driessens 2013) of ordinary people, as will be discussed below.

It has also been pointed out that television produces many types of personalities, which cannot be conflated (Bennett 2010; Bennett and Holmes 2010; Geraghty 2000). Christine Geraghty suggests that a key distinction is to be found in the personalities that populate television culture between the professionals who work in the industry (programme presenters, hosts, etc.) whose fame is based on their public persona – those who play themselves professionally and 'seamlessly' (TV chefs, celebrity gardeners, TV presenters) – and those whose fame is based on their private life and 'lifestyle', who today are called ordinary celebrities (the contestants on gamedocs, docusoaps, talent shows, etc.). This is an important distinction, for it is one exploited by the television industry across a variety of reality formats which depend upon the unpaid labour of ordinary people 'playing themselves', in contrast to often grossly overpaid professional personalities. The category of 'ordinary' celebrity is complicated by the 'will to ordinariness' that drives television, for many professional and highly paid television presenters rely on their own performance of ordinariness in their television roles. In particular, the presenters of reality TV – the genre that most regularly 'celebritifies' ordinary people – cultivate a sense of themselves as 'just like us', in an attempt to diminish the distance between themselves, the television world and the viewer. Presenters of *Big Brother* in the UK, Davina McCall and her successor Emma Willis, speak with a vernacular accent and present themselves as acting on behalf of the audience. But like other presentations of 'ordinariness', professional presenters also distinguish themselves as more than the ordinary through glamour and/or an unusually sharp wit. Those contestants from reality TV who enter the world of professional presenting, such as *Big Brother* winner and presenter Brian Dowling or *Big Brother's Bit on the Side* presenter, Rylan Clark, must navigate the line between ordinary and special even more carefully. In addition, those whose fame comes from outside of the world of television, still often become the personalities of docusoaps and also rely on the performance of their everyday life, their 'ordinariness', even while a glamorous and wealthy lifestyle is on display. Figures such as members of Kim Kardashian's family and Ozzy Osbourne's family belong to this category. Well-paid for their performances and with the opportunity to translate their 'personality' fame (in the case of Sharon Osbourne) into professional television jobs, these personalities seem to blur the distinction identified by Geraghty. However, the central component of Geraghty's distinction holds between those who are paid (often handsomely) for their professional performances, and those ordinary contestants on reality TV shows who are not, and as this chapter will demonstrate, it is an important one. This chapter is concerned mainly with the latter manifestation of television's personality system – the ordinary celebrity, a product primarily of a new generation of reality TV formats that are global, economically driven, and have altered the structure of the television industry, the news and the online environment.

Reality TV developed rapidly at the end of the twentieth century because of the way that it was able to respond to challenges and changes facing the international commercial television industry (Deery 2014; Magder 2004; Raphael 2004). Although there are national specificities to attend to in understanding this process, there are also several interlinked broad trends whose reach has been global: a policy environment which encouraged deregulation, increased competition and commercialization; the introduction of new technology and media convergence in this highly marketized moment; the resulting fragmentation of the audience; rising broadcasting costs and the simultaneous loss of revenue which led to a series of cost-cutting exercises. Colin Sparks argues that the combination of technological innovation and the ideologically driven shift in policy approaches were crucial for shaping the television industry in the 1990s. So while it is true, as Turner argues, that television companies act in their own interests, it is also the case that governments pursue ideological battles on behalf of big business which results in a favourable policy environment. The development of new technology (firstly VCR and cable, followed by satellite and digital technology) created multi-channel TV at a time when governments across the globe carried out deregulation, encouraged privatization, and favoured competition and markets. In Britain, Margaret Thatcher's Conservative government pushed through a controversial Broadcasting Act (1990) that directly encouraged market competition and allowed for mergers, abolished the existing regulator (the Independent Broadcasting Authority – IBA) and made television companies the broadcasters instead. The Act allowed for new terrestrial and satellite channels and also forced the BBC to source 25 per cent of its output from independent companies. These mergers used public money to finance the private sector and enabled the creation of large media conglomerates who dominate the field. In the US the 1996 Telecommunications Act allowed for cross-media ownership, deregulated the converging broadcasting and telecommunications markets and opened up markets to competition by removing further regulation on ownership and distribution caps. In India, which had a very small broadcasting system until the 1990s, legislation in 1991 opened up broadcasting to private and foreign companies, deregulated the market and saw an explosion of private commercial channels.

There were two interconnected consequences of the proliferation of channels, just as in the case of the news that we examined in the previous chapter; the first was the fragmentation of audiences and the second was a drop in advertising revenue. From the late 1980s, broadcasters found it increasingly difficult to win mass audiences to 'peak' or 'prime time' television programming because, as the number of channels grew, sections of the audience were tuning in to niche and specialist channels. Audiences for the large terrestrial broadcasters fell as a result. Having a smaller audience share is not intrinsically a problem if you are a public service broadcaster (although continued legitimacy of public funding may become an issue), but it is for commercial broadcasters because advertising revenue is the most common form of funding for free-to-air channels and advertisers like to reach big audiences.

Advertisers are also prepared to pay large sums to reach mass audiences and traditionally, the free-to-air channels of national broadcasting systems had oligopolistic control over advertising revenue because each system had a limited number of terrestrial channels (Sparks 2007). In combined public service/commercial systems, such as the UK, Europe and Japan, there was even less competition for advertising revenue because the 'competing' channels of public service broadcasters are publically funded. For both commercial and combined systems this environment had changed radically by the early 1990s. The result of new technology and the arrival of digital television, in a newly deregulated environment, saw the growth of the numbers of commercial channels which meant that advertising revenue was spread far more widely than before and so there was a sharp increase in competition for audiences. Broadcasters were under pressure to search for new ways of reaching both large audiences and also segments of the audience that advertisers are keen to reach, usually young adults with a disposable income. Reality TV seemed to offer a solution to the problem of falling advertising revenue by attracting large and relatively young audiences. In the US, for example, the reality TV show *Survivor* enabled CBS to compete with NBC for prime time audiences.

Thursday evening prime time is the most lucrative for networks in the US because it is the most expensive advertising slot; advertisers are willing to pay a premium to reach audiences on that evening in order to boost weekend sales. By the end of the 1990s this slot was cornered by NBC who aired *ER*, *Friends* and *Will and Grace*. A thirty-second advert during these shows cost between $465,000 and $620,000 (Madger 2004: 138). In 2001 CBS decided to air *Survivor* in direct competition with NBC at 8:00pm on a Thursday evening, a seemingly bold move because channels usually avoided direct competition with NBC and instead programmed around it. It paid off – by the end of the 2001 season of *Survivor*, CBS had doubled its Thursday evening audience from 10 to 20.5 million viewers and substantially increased its ratings among 14–49 year olds (Magder 2004: 139).

But this was not as much of a gamble as at first it might have appeared. One of the advantages of reality TV formats in the eyes of network executives is that they reduce the risk associated with new production. Broadcasters can buy in internationally traded, already successful, pre-packaged shows. Format TV, such as programmes like *Survivor*, are easily adaptable to different national cultures and television environments, cost nothing in development expenditure to broadcasters, and come with a successful track record abroad. These formats also have the ability to inexhaustibly generate new content for familiar formats (Turner 2010: 19) and this fits the needs of advertisers who want predictability for their investment. *Survivor* had already aired in Europe and had proven popular with young audiences, and this track record reduced the risk to CBS of trying out an untested programme. And CBS saved the development costs that would have had to go into original production. But more important than either of these considerations was the fact that the creator of the programme, Mark Burnett, pre-sold thirty-second advertising spots and in-show sponsorship to eight advertisers who each paid $4 million for the ad time, product placement in the show and a website link (Magder 2004: 140). It was this guarantee of advertising revenue that ensured that *Survivor* was aired on Thursday evening prime time television, and it was its status as a tried-and-tested formula that enabled Burnett to acquire advertising revenue in advance. The success of *Survivor*, then, is based on persuading advertisers to invest in the programme in advance of airing. *Survivor* is a television commodity that was successfully sold, not to audiences, but to the advertising wings of General Motors, Visa, Reebok and others. Ted Magder points out that this changed the business model for US network television. Rather than buying a license from the makers of *Survivor*, CBS shared the advertising revenue with Burnett – revenue that he generated. Magder explains 'everyone noticed, and *Survivor* became the tipping point…for the business model it offered' (2004: 141). As is the case for so many 'ordinary' people in the media, the contestants on the show became 'celebrified' (Driessens 2013: 643), in the sense that they momentarily were treated like celebrities by the media, and crucially they were both commodified and exploited, or as Richard Dyer puts it 'they are both labour and the thing that labour produces' (Dyer 2004 [1986]: 5).

A further area of pressure for broadcasters that is often overlooked is the cyclical tendency towards rising costs and soaring debts, which, as we have seen, occurs across the media and cultural industries, from theatre to film to the news media, and which are part of the economic structure of commercial television. The use of the celebrity commodity for marketing purposes is central to this rising cost structure. As Chad Raphael points out, high levels of corporate debt were incurred by the big three networks in the US after they were sold in the 1980s. This was accompanied by rising costs. For example, the cost of an hour of prime time drama climbed to over $1 million per episode by the end of the 1980s and was increasing at a rate of about 8–10 per cent per annum (Raphael 2004: 122) while the cost of the most popular shows, such as *Friends*, increased to $7.5 million for a half hour episode. This cycle of rising costs is another important aspect of the business model that structures American TV (but is also applicable to other commercial broadcasting systems). Historically, programmes were licensed by broadcasters from production studios for a set price per episode over a set number of years – usually four. If the show was a hit, the price per episode goes up on renewing the licence. This is partly because the producers can charge more for a hit, but also because 'above the line' costs for the producer tend to rise (such as direction, script writing, etc.). One of the main cost increases, however, is the 'talent' or celebrity performer. Television executives like to offset the risk associated with new programmes by marketing them on the basis of already popular celebrities, and this leads to artificial scarcity of 'talent' and inflated salaries for those performers with a track record of pulling in audiences. Take the example of *Friends* again – the six principle actors had an initial annual contract of $22,500 per episode. At the renewal of their contracts, the actors formed a group to negotiate an increase of $125,000 per episode, then $750,000 per episode, and finally $1 million per episode. This goes a long way to explaining the soaring production costs of the show. Again, the rising costs associated with star or celebrity performers is a repeat of the patterns we saw in the commercial theatre (chapter 2) and commercial film industries (chapter 3) and tells us a great deal about the illogical economic logic of commercial entertainment. The celebrity commodity, so important in terms of product differentiation and marketing, can become an exponential cost that undermines the commercial viability of the product.

As we shall see below, populating shows with unpaid 'contestants' and performers enabled producers and networks to side-step this cost. Television has utilized the unpaid or low-paid celebrity status of the contestants to provide content cheaply, to act as a celebrity commodity for marketing purposes and to generate further interest in the show via stories in the news media.

In fact, reality TV offered the television industry a way of responding to the rising costs associated with commercial television production in a variety of ways. One strategy was to commercialize programmes as fully as possible. June Deery argues that reality TV is a very 'strong example of contemporary forms of commercialization' (2014: 11). This is because of its penchant for devising new forms of advertising revenue; it experimented with old models of product placement by embedding brands into media content for a fee, whereby brands become part of the show – prizes in gamedocs, rewards in talent shows, and aids in makeovers (and as we saw above, these are pre-sold to advertisers who in effect in this way take on production costs). Another response is to embark on a series of cost-cutting exercises, and as Colin Sparks points out, one of the main ways that broadcasters sought to cut costs was by 'launching an attack on the condition of the workers who produce the programmes' (Sparks 2007: n.p.). Again, we saw such practices in the news media, with cuts in staff, increased workloads and new performance management targets based on the number of 'clicks' per online story. In the case of television, significant below-the-line staff cutbacks in broadcasting systems resulted in the US, Britain and Europe, and working conditions deteriorated significantly for those left in the industry, with short-term contracts replacing full-time jobs, lower pay and greater job insecurity.

But reality TV was attractive for another reason – it enabled producers to avoid expensive above-the-line costs such as script writing, directing and talent – none of which are necessarily central labour costs for reality TV. There is no need to pay scriptwriters, often no rights clearances for music, or rehearsals to cost, etc. These production conditions also enabled the producers of reality TV to bypass union labour and control labour unrest. According to Raphael, the 1988 writer's strike in the US 'proved crucial' to the rise of reality TV because these shows were largely unaffected by a strike which delayed the opening of the autumn season for scripted shows. The delay of the season 'gave producers and programmers the impetus to develop future shows that did not depend on writing talent' (2004: 125). Bypassing unions means lower wages for workers and worse employment contracts. In addition, to further cost cutting,

broadcasters outsourced programme production to independent production companies who, in order to cut their own costs, employed
personnel on zero-hour or part-time contracts or relied on the unpaid
labour of interns (and, of course, this outsourcing was enshrined in
law in the UK after the 1990 Broadcasting Act, as part of the attack
on public service broadcasting). These cost-cutting activities resulted
in much smaller production budgets than those needed for other types
of programming (including investigative documentaries), sometimes
over 50 per cent cheaper than the cost of drama (Raphael 2004: 127).

Unlike other industries outside of the cultural and advertising
sectors, celebrity performers constitute a significant production cost.
The artificial scarcity of talent produced by a risk-averse commercial
system leads to hugely inflated salaries for actors and other types of
celebrity performers, with a proven track record of popularity, whose
image can be used to successfully market television programmes.
Reality TV therefore does away with expensive actors altogether and
can sidestep expensive celebrity talent (at least temporarily) because
it is based on the unscripted performances of ordinary people who
are paid next to nothing, or nothing at all, for their participation. In
short, ordinary people are used by the producers and broadcasters of
reality TV as a cost-cutting solution. The celebrification of some
ordinary participants on reality TV enabled programme makers and
networks to cash in on the draw of a celebrity performer without
having the outlay of a celebrity salary. It also enabled online and print
news media to cash in on the circulation of images of ordinary celebrities as content for their publications, as we saw was the case in
chapter 4. In addition, in bypassing famous performers, programme
producers also avoided their agents, who at least in the US 'had come
to occupy the role of programme developers and packagers in the
early 1980s, and who exacted considerable fees for their services'
(Raphael 2004: 125).

Of course, the cycle of rising costs associated with commercial
television has eventually been reproduced in reality TV; born out of
the logic of competition, the genre does not escape it. The success of
reality TV, its global marketability, and its relative cheapness, has
made it highly popular with broadcasters and this has lead to a significant increase in the numbers of shows and formats available,
while the pace and scale of international distribution of reality formats
has accelerated since the 1990s (Sender 2011: 10), boosted by the
expansion of distribution networks and the consolidation of global
media companies that specialize in the development of reality TV
formats.[3]

The growth in the number of reality shows has increased competition between different shows for audiences (the most successful of which are often aired in direct competition on different channels), and broadcasters are once again forced to, or are prepared to, pay large sums of money to famous 'talent' to ensure that they continue to attract the audiences that advertisers are prepared to pay to reach.[4] But the marketability of celebrity talent that is associated with good ratings results in increased cost for talent and associated above-the-line expenditure. And so a genre that was once cheap to make, because it relied predominantly on the performances of ordinary people, is also now coming to rely once again on expensive celebrity talent whose inflated salaries push up costs. Such talent in the UK takes the shape of celebrity hosts such as the double-act Ant and Dec (Anthony McPartlin and Declan Donnelly) who have long and established careers as celebrity television presenters on reality TV shows. Ant and Dec are not 'ordinary celebrities', that is, they are not ordinary members of the public who have been celebrified by their participation on reality TV. Instead, they have television personas as 'ordinary' 'cheeky chaps' which hides the fact that they are highly paid professional presenters. Ant and Dec co-host three of ITVs most popular peak viewing shows, *Britain's Got Talent*, *I'm a Celebrity... Get Me Out of Here* and *Saturday Night Takeaway*, and were reported to have signed new contracts with ITV in 2013 of over £6 million each. This represents a 113 per cent rise in one year.[5] It seems that ordinary celebrity, which is now a major feature of our cultural landscape, did not permanently solve the problems of rising costs as was anticipated. It also seems that the inequalities of wealth that mark late neoliberal capitalism are to be found in the so-called 'democratainment' invested in reality TV, as Hartley claims. Instead, a few grossly overpaid celebrity hosts parade over the humiliation and degradation of ordinary contestants, who are hardly remunerated for their trouble, if at all, but who are lured instead by the promise of fame and escape from the grind of 'ordinary' life in neoliberal capitalism. Colin Sparks puts the appeal of celebrity status for ordinary people extremely well:

> The intense desire to be recognised, to be a celebrity, to become a *Big Brother* contestant, is not primarily about the money that comes with success, although that is surely something that is in the front of people's minds. Rather it is the desire to escape the drudgery of anonymous, alienated toil in which one counts for nothing. It is the desire to be recognised as somebody unique and distinctive by a wider circle than one's immediate family and friends. The dream of celebrity is more

than a magical escape from the constraints of relative poverty and the drudgery of routine labour. It is also, and most importantly, a magical attempt to transcend alienated labour, not by expropriating the expropriators but by evading the reality of being *only* the repository of labour power. (Sparks 2007: n.p.)

As we shall see in the following section, most ordinary contestants on reality TV do not escape the reality that they are 'only the repository of labour power'. Instead they are the unpaid or underpaid hyper-exploited ocean of unofficial workers whose performances of 'being ordinary' provides much of the programme content of these highly profitable shows. The growing visibility of ordinary people on reality TV, then, is not an altruistic move on the part of programme makers and broadcasters to open up the media to the under-represented, or to democratize 'fame'; instead, it has been a central plank in a cost-cutting strategy that included increased monetizing of the product, increased commercialization, attacks on the wages and conditions of those who worked in the industry, the temporary side-stepping of highly paid talent, and as we shall see below, the extreme exploitation of an endless sea of 'ordinary people' in search of an unrealizable dream.

The Exploitation of 'Ordinary' Celebrities

While producers make claims about the egalitarian credentials of reality TV, under the ruse that it opens up access to media and celebrity careers to those who have little other means of entry into a highly competitive field (Bazelgette 2005), and some scholars agree that this is a form of 'demonstratainment' (Hartley 1999, 2008), other critics have argued that the ordinary celebrities that emerge out of reality TV represent part of a broader shift in patterns of labour and the social relations of exploitation (Andrejevic 2003, 2011; Collins 2008; Terranova 2000). In a well-aimed challenge to media and cultural populists, Mark Andrejevic examines the issue of exploitation in some depth and argues that this shift is found in the commoditization of the processes of 'monitoring' in both reality TV and social media, or what he terms, 'the work of being watched' (2011: 18). He asks '[w]hen we are engaged in social networking on a commercial Web site such as *Facebook*, are we entertaining ourselves, socializing, or working (creating value for a third party)? The same question might be asked about reality TV cast members: are they playing, working, or socializing?' (2011: 19). Drawing on a tradition of critical thinking known as 'autonomous Marxism',[6] Andrejevic suggests that contemporary forms of exploitation have moved beyond the traditional confines of the workplace and extend out to 'the social factory' – 'the realm of leisure, domesticity, and consumption' (2011: 18). According to Andrejevic, reality TV and the online economy both rely on a form of work which can be seen to be voluntary (or 'free' as Terranova (2000) puts it – in both senses, that it is both freely chosen and unpaid). Andrejevic argues that this is a form of labour akin to the exploitation of women's domestic labour: 'the capture of value generated in non-waged forms of value-generating activity' (2011: 26). Drawing on Antonella Corsani, he argues that while domestic labour produces value based on aptitudes and services connected to affectivity and language skills, in the cases of reality TV and social media, the process of 'monitoring' transforms everyday leisure and domestic activities 'into directly profitable activities' (2011: 24). This is accomplished by means of the activity of participants who create content that makes the show or site desirable to advertisers and who also 'generate value in the form of information commodities that can be bought or sold' (2011: 24). In the case of reality TV, the camera captures the activity of ordinary people which is then sold as an entertainment commodity in which audiences are invited to monitor the behaviour on display. In the case of social media, the labour of 'building, maintaining and extending social relationships online' enables the owners of the sites to monitor and capture personal information, to be sold as data about the online activities of participants, which is the 'economic machine driving the customized targeted, and "accountable" model of interactive online advertising' (2011: 25).

Andrejevic is rightly tackling those who make claims about the ' "democratization" of access to the means of media production' (2011: 27) that is seen to reside in both reality TV and the internet and it seems unquestionably the case that both rely in some ways directly on the exploitation of unwaged or poorly paid labour, as we shall see below. However, there are a number of questions to be raised in Andrejevic's account of exploitation. Firstly, the logic of his argument rests on drawing a parallel between the activities of participants on reality TV shows and the 'consumer labour' of those using social media and in this he draws an equivalence between what are quite different practices. The unpaid labour of *Big Brother* housemates is not the same as the unpaid labour of a Facebook user who unwittingly makes available personal data for sale to third parties. They are different activities, even if both are subject to commodification. Only one can be considered exploitation of labour.

David Hesmondhalgh usefully distinguishes between the everyday sense of the term exploitation – when one group takes unfair advantage of another – and the more 'specialist technical term deriving from Marxist and socialist feminist thought' (2015: 2). In the latter case, exploitation results from lack of access to, or ownership of, the means of production combined with the appropriation of labour. The means of production are owned by one class (capitalists), while another class (the working class) is excluded from ownership and thus compelled to sell their labour power. Drawing on the work of Erik Olin Wright (1997), Hesmondhalgh suggests that within these broad social relations of production, one can distinguish between oppression (or domination) and exploitation. Oppression arises from the 'material welfare of one class [being] causally dependent on the material deprivation of another'; this is predicated on the latter's exclusion from the 'key productive resources'. Exploitation adds a further dimension to these relations of domination, and that is the appropriation of labour. It is the relations that govern this appropriation of labour that lead to exploitation.

The Marxist account of labour exploitation is based on the labour theory of value, which explains how surplus value is created and its relationship to profit. In the Marxist sense of the term 'exploitation', the unpaid/low-paid work of being watched on reality TV differs from the practice of being monitored by corporations who track and collect online (or televisual) activity to be packaged as a commodity and sold on to advertisers. Engaging in creative unpaid/low-paid labour and having one's online information mined as data are both instances of being taking advantage of certainly, but they *are* different and the value generated from the activity of each has a distinctive relationship to the production process that is not equivalent. A number of Autonomous Marxist scholars identify free labour as an homogeneous entity, a structural part of labour in late capitalism and thus collapse various free activities together. But these activities are greatly varied and we must determine whether or not they are a form of labour exploitation or some other form of economic manipulation and domination and/or one group taking unfair advantage of another, or some other practice altogether. I will argue that the participant in one activity is having her labour exploited, while the activity in the other is a form of active consumption through which companies generate revenue on the basis of exploited labour elsewhere.

Gholam Khiabany (2015) has recently pointed out that Marx draws a distinction between different forms of labour under capitalism. A key distinction is between 'productive labour' and 'unproductive labour' (Khiabany 2015: 264). For Marx, these are not moral or judgemental categories; instead they are terms used to describe the different relationship that different forms of labour have to the social relations of production and the accumulation of capital. For Marx, productive labour is 'wage-labour which, exchanged against the variable part of capital (the part of capital that is spent on wages), reproduces not only this part of the capital (or the value of its own labour-power), but in addition produces surplus-value for the capitalist' (Marx 1963: 152). Productive labour is exploited labour because it produces enough value to replenish the portion of capital spent on its wages and produces a surplus – a profit for the owner. A worker exchanges her labour for a wage from capital, but that labour produces more value than she is paid, and is hence the source of the capitalist's profit. Let's take an example from reality TV. An episode of *Britain's Got Talent* is estimated to cost £1 million to produce, including salaries to the production team and the hosts, studio and location fees, equipment, etc. But the show earns the production's two companies (Syco TV and Freemantle) and the broadcaster, ITV, an estimated £9 million per show.[7] Even if we assume that most of that £1 million goes in salaries to the production team (rather than in celebrity salaries and infrastructure and capital costs), the combined wages of the numerous producers, editors, music production personnel, vision mixers, make-up artists, post production staff, graphics and art production staff, publicists, legal affairs staff, runners, floor managers, etc., is *nine time less* than the show earns. If we split that labour into a nine-hour day (although cultural workers often work even longer hours than this), it means that each worker earns her salary (the value of her work) during the first hour at work, and for the subsequent 8 hours, her labour produces surplus value which is profit for Syco, Freemantle and ITV. This is 'productive' labour because it is exploited by capital.

In contrast to Autonomous Marxism, which considers the knowledge-based commodity to be a distinctive form that has altered the relations of exploitation, Khiabany points out that for Marx (1963: 265), the distinction is not to do with the nature of the product that is produced or even the specific features of the labour, but rather, as Marx argues, 'the social relations of production, within which the labour is realised' (Marx 1963: 157). It is not the content of a commodity that determines whether or not it is a product of exploitation (informational content or not), but the relationship of labour to capital described above. So for Marx, an actor who is in the service of a capitalist firm and who is paid less than the value she creates for her work in a film, television programme, etc., is engaged in 'productive' labour and is exploited. On the other hand, an actor who is paid to go to the house of a rich capitalist to provide the entertainment for a party is not exchanging her labour for a portion of capital and then producing surplus value above it; she is not producing profit for the capitalist; instead, she is exchanging her labour for revenue. Marx writes, 'The former's labour is exchanged with capital, the latter's with revenue. The former's labour produces a surplus-value; in the latter's, revenue is consumed' (1963: 157).

Similarly, the labour that creates online content is 'productive' labour when in the service of a capitalist, who takes away more value from that labour than is paid in wages/salary. In the early days of cyber enthusiasm, just as in the early days of contemporary forms of reality TV, this relation of exploitation was obscured by the keenness of those engaged in volunteer labour (for different reasons – in the former it was a desire to build a collective new online world, in the latter as a means of entering the media as a profession). But this enthusiasm quickly wore off; as early as 1999, 15,000 'volunteers' for AOL tried to get back-wages from the company for years of free labour (Terranova 2000: 38). Although this labour was 'free' initially, recognition of exploitation on the part of the workers quickly followed, including demands for remuneration. As David Harvey reminds us, '[c]apitalists have...acceded to various measures to reduce alienation and to emphasize incorporation' (Harvey 2006: 145), including ideology and new conceptualizations of inclusion. For Harvey, '[part] of the struggle is therefore about driving home the significance of exploitation as the proper conceptualization of how concrete labors are accomplished under capitalist social relations' (2006: 145). Therefore, this work, even if it seems on the face of it to be similar to other online activities, is, in terms of the social relations of production, different from the work of maintaining a Facebook page, Pinterest profile or Twitter feed. These 'user' activities are not 'productive' labour in the sense discussed above, in that it is not exploited for surplus value for Facebook, Pinterest or Twitter, even if their activities are part of a chain of production and distribution in which profit is extracted by exploited labour elsewhere.

So where does the profit or, rather, surplus value come from? For Andrejevic, it is generated through advertising in two ways: (1) by users creating content which makes the site attractive to advertisers, and (2) by monitoring and capturing personal data which is then packaged and sold on to advertisers. In both cases we can say that, by participating in online activity, users are unwittingly enabling the creation of value for Twitter and Facebook, in the form of advertising revenue, but their activities are not directly producing surplus value. These activities could easily take place without any advertising revenue being generated at all. Instead, profit is derived from the exploitation of another pool of labour that in various ways monitors and processes this information which is then sold. The labour of a Facebook or Pinterest user is commodified, rather than exploited labour – and this occurs in two ways. The first is that it is packaged by those who work in this industry, in order to be sold to advertisers. It is turned into a commodity by the labour of others which is then sold for profit. The second is connected to the kind of self-branded, micro-celebrity self that the software of social media encourages, and this process is the topic of the following chapter.

The real profit to be made in the arena of social media *is* in advertising, but it cannot be located in the activities of the users of social media or television – these are forms of active consumption, rather than 'productive' in the sense discussed above. Instead, in the case of the internet, it is located in the burgeoning online companies who produce the information for online advertisers, as well as the income generated from the army of workers for Facebook, Twitter and other companies whose job it is to chase advertising revenue for the company, alongside the labour of technical and other staff who maintain the site and the business. This labour is exploited because the total wages are considerably smaller than the advertising revenue generated through their labour. Of course it is the case that these sites are only able to attract advertising because of the number of users who can potentially be reached, in targeted and niche ways. All profit in any industry is ultimately realized in the act of selling (or exchange), whether it be advertising space or a fast food hamburger, but in both cases profit is generated in the act of labour rather than the act of consumption. And as Graham Murdock has argued, to see production and consumption as mutually constitutive and equivalent is to sidestep the temporal dimensions to the production process, and to ignore the inequality of influence and the role of production as a determining factor in 'exerting pressures and setting limits on interpretation and use' (2003: 16). While production and consumption are integrated, they are not identical. There are currently over 100 companies who collect data online for targeted advertising and there is substantial money to be made in this enterprise. There are standard targeting companies using real-time bidding that target ads on the basis of consumer behaviour, demographics and geography. Then there are retargeting specialists who target users who browse online, but don't necessarily buy. These companies enable advertisers to target ads at customers, even when they are on different sites, and it is estimated that 80 per cent of ads are sold and resold through third parties.[8] Finally, there are companies that track where and how ads are run to see if the advertisers got their money's worth, known as measuring conversion rates. This is a booming industry in which there is direct exploitation, not of consumers who may still be manipulated for economic gain and whose activity is commodified, but of the many different types of labour involved, whose labour is exchanged for a wage which creates a surplus for the owner: data logging and processing, technical development and maintenance, customer relations, to name a few. This labour is directly exploited (in the Marxist sense); it produces and processes user information which would not otherwise exist and which is then sold as a commodity to advertisers, who buy the right to advertise to the users of Facebook, etc. It is exploited labour because the total labour in each data collection company creates enough value to replenish the capital spent on its wages and it creates added value (surplus value) on top of this – the profit the company makes from selling that data or 'service' to advertisers. Ironically, an upcoming area of potential labour exploitation and profit is in the generation and application of 'Do Not Track Tools'. At the moment there is no way to opt out of having one's data logged, so companies are investing in capitalizing on users' increasing unease about having their activity mined in this way. Those same companies who track our activity will in the future sell us apps and other services to block that tracking activity. From the perspective of current thinking on internet exploitation, we should ask, can we consider the work of signing up to these apps a way of freeing oneself from exploitation or a form of labour exploitation? Or neither?

Another question arises about Andrejevic's equation of the practices of *audiences* watching a reality TV show and the practice of *corporate* data collection – he sees both as a form of 'monitoring'. But again, they are quite different activities with different relationships to the processes of production and, indeed, occupy different temporal moments in the production cycle. The latter, as we saw above, directly exploits the labour of the information processor in order to make profit from advertising, while the former is the customer/user to whom the commodity is sold in the form of an entertainment package (either directly through payment for satellite or broadband television packages or indirectly through advertising). Of course, the labour of the information processor depends on the availability of the raw material (which in this case is 'freely' given data by the user). So, although the Facebook user is not exploited, their data is crucial to processes by which others *are* exploited.

In addition, despite the voyeuristic potential of watching reality TV, most studies of reality TV suggest that audiences are not so much involved in activities of monitoring and surveillance as they are in judging the 'bad selves' of the contestants who lack the cultural resources to perform educated middle-class identities (Skeggs 2009; Skeggs and Wood 2012). In the process of judging the behaviour of reality TV participants, audiences are being invited to assess their own socially constituted subject positions and some can express ambivalence towards one's own perceived lack (Skeggs 2009; Stacey 1994). Indeed, according to recent research, some viewers describe feelings of shame at watching the humiliation of contestants and a feeling of complicity with a set of values that are considered unacceptable (Hill 2007). None of these viewing positions, or the emotions that can accompany them, can be likened to 'monitoring', and certainly cannot be likened to the imposed and inescapable data tracking of highly profitable companies such as Adnetik.

In fact, contestants on reality TV programmes are not so much engaged in the 'work of being watched' as they are in the work of performing 'ordinariness' – or rather, performing acceptable versions of authenticity for a viewing audience which is encouraged to judge those performances. Increasingly, particular formats within reality TV, such as the docusoap, rely on more and more overt versions of such performances. British programmes such as *The Only Way is Essex, Made in Chelsea* and *Geordie Shore* rely on a knowing performativity on the part of the participants who are judged as much on their ability to 'carry it off' as they are on the content of their behaviour. Graeme Turner argues that, '[p]erforming ordinariness has become an end in itself, and this is a rich and (or so it seems) almost inexhaustible means of generating new content for familiar formats' (2010: 19). Of course, reality TV celebrities have to perform a convincing version of ordinariness in memorable and adaptable ways. Turner argues, 'the format's apparent tolerance of a lack of exceptional talents or achievements is available as long as the person concerned can perform their ordinariness with some degree of specificity or individuality' (2010: 20).

It is clearly the case that production companies are engaged in the commercial exploitation of the 'performance of ordinariness'; this performance is *labour* carried out by individuals who create such performances. Their labour in front of the camera is as much a part of the generation of value as the technical, administrative and other creative personnel involved in the production. Furthermore, it is exploited labour in that it generates value over and above the wages paid to perform the task. Indeed, in the case of ordinary celebrity on reality TV, it is really a case of hyper-exploitation, and this has been plainly identified by the unions that protect actors and performers.

In 2011 in the UK, Equity, the trade union for professional performers and creative practitioners, produced an official *Response to the Low Pay Commission General Consultation on the National Minimum Wage*, which identified unpaid labour as a major cause for concern and identified weaknesses in the current Act which enables this form of exploitation. The report states that 'there has been an increase in the level of unpaid and low paid work being advertised in the industry under the guise of the voluntary work arrangements' (Equity 2011: 3). Equity identifies reality TV as one of the main culprits involved in this exploitation. The report states: 'Talent search programmes and reality TV formats continue to attract large audiences and are favoured by many of the large broadcasters. Contestants in programmes such as *Britain's Got Talent* are compelled to enter into restrictive contracts and because of a loophole in the National Minimum Wage Act for competitions they generally do not get paid' (2011: 3). Equity has challenged ITV for refusing to pay any of the 24 finalists of the show and objected to the fact that participants were obliged to sign contracts which required them to attend and perform each week and which 'waived away their protections under working time laws and assigned all rights in their performances to the company' (2011: 3). Equity's legal advice suggests that there is a strong case to be made that 'participants in reality TV programmes are workers and entitled to pay by production companies' (2011: 3). While the HMRC considers it unlikely that 'contestants' on reality TV can be considered workers, the BBC (which is a publicly funded, rather than commercial broadcaster) is the only broadcaster in the UK to buck the trend, and only in its own in-house talent shows such as *How Do You Solve a Problem Like Maria?*, *Any Dream Will Do* and *I'd Do Anything*, where all of the finalists were engaged on standard industry contracts, with pay rates well above the national minimum wage. Commercial production companies and broadcasters refuse to pay the participants of reality TV and often lock them into appalling contracts. In the UK the growing number of docusoaps are generating large profits for production companies, with little or no outlay in salaries for the participants. ITV2's *The Only Way is Essex* (TOWIE), one of the more popular of these shows on British television, is a case in point. During the first series of the show, which attracted audiences of 1.5 million,[9] the cast were given no remuneration at all for their performances. Unable to hold down other full-time jobs because of the time commitment necessary to appear on the show, the cast got together and threatened to quit. Unlike the cast of *Friends*, who were not so easily replaced, ITV refused to pay a salary, but compromised by offering a £50 per day appearance fee.

Split over an eight-hour period, this barely reaches the national minimum wage. In the meantime, Lime Pictures, the production company behind TOWIE, saw a pre-tax profit rise in the 2013–14 period from £10.9 million to £11.4 million. Most of this was generated in the UK and we can assume that it mostly came from TOWIE, the company's biggest success.[10]

The picture is the same in the US, where according to Sue Collins, reality TV has not only radically restructured the television business, it has undermined the unions who offer protection to workers in the field. Both the American Federation of Television and Radio Artists (AFTRA) and the Screen Actors Guild (SAG) have reported large numbers of job losses with the rise of 'unscripted' reality formats, such as the docusoap, gamedoc and talent show, over which they have no jurisdiction. This is part of the casualization of cultural work, in which 'precarity' for much of the workforce has become a central feature. These formats rely on an endless supply of ordinary contestants, all searching for fame, and because most of them are not absorbed into the system of celebrity, but instead return to obscurity, the hierarchical and stratified system of media celebrity is left intact, including the likely returns for the high levels of investment in A-list celebrities. At the same time, this endless supply of unskilled labour (ordinary celebrity) helps to spread the risk associated with all cultural products, by allowing for continual adaptation of successful formats. Collins argues that 'the field for ordinary, untalented people vying for potential fame is virtually inexhaustible, and the production of short-term, non-skilled, non-union celebrity generates novelty with minimal financial risk and greater control' (2008: 97). Collins points out that many contestants are trapped in iniquitous contracts. CBS, for instance, controls the contestants on the American version of *Survivor* by a contract which 'stipulates that contestants are subject to authorization by CBS for any media contact or appearance for three years after the show airs, including paid celebrity work not sanctioned by CBS and a 'life story rights' section that effectively binds the signatory into 'relinquishing control over his or her life story and public image' (2008: 98). In addition, a confidentiality proviso protects 'trade secrets' and any breach of this contract entitles CBS to sue the contestant for damages. As Collins points out, 'this contractual arrangement underscores the enormous differential in power relations between producer and cultural worker' (2008: 98).

Andrejevic also provides alarming examples of producer control over the life and life stories of contestants, all the more so in one of the cases that he cites which involves children. The reality show *Kid's Nation* recruited forty 8–15 year olds to inhabit a ghost town in New

Mexico as a 'social experiment' to see how they would fare. The children were taken out of school and away from their parents in exchange for $5000 and the promise of cash prizes. They were subject to contracts that stipulated they do 'whatever they were told to by the show's producers, 24 hours day, 7 days a week' and even though they were paid for their participation 'those payments or the agreement to be fully under the producer's direction did not constitute employment under the producer's interpretation and therefore was not subject to any state or federal law' (cited in Andrejevic 2011: 21). Parents and children were prohibited from discussing the experience under the threat of a $5 million fine, and a state labour inspector was turned away from the set during production. The contract, obtained by the *New York Times* stated 'CBS and the production companies, Good TV Inc. and Magic Molehill Productions, retain the rights to the children's life stores "in perpetuity and throughout the universe"' (quoted in Andrejevic 2011: 22). Furthermore, these rights included the ability to portray the children either accurately, or with fictionalization, in perpetuity. Like Collins, Andrejevic points to the huge differential in power between the media companies and the individual parents and children who were not protected by labour legislation or collective bargaining. These companies not only own the means of production, they own the very life stories of these children permanently! And according to Collins, this is a standard industry contract.

The exploitation of ordinary contestants and performers on reality TV is hidden under a blanket of unfulfilled promises and ideological constructs. Graeme Turner met several contestants of *Big Brother Australia* and New Zealand's *Popstars* while conducting research on celebrity in these countries, who explained to him that they were 'grossly misled about their career prospects before the show was produced, caricatured while the show was on air, and offered only those opportunities which would promote the franchise or the networks after the show was complete' (2010: 36). For Turner, '[t]he commodification of these contestants is relentless, even though the continuing success of the format depends on their expendability; it is important that they are easily replaced by the next series' crop of contenders' (2010: 36). The expendability of these contestants was highlighted in the 2015 UK version of *Big Brother*, where a number of contestants were evicted from the house for not providing enough 'entertainment' through their performances of the self.

Critics are right to challenge the image of empowerment conjured up by the 'democratainment' neologism (discussed above). Celebrity culture, with its new-found emphasis on ordinary people, is not becoming democratized. Instead 'ordinary celebrity' is a field consisting of exploited, poorly or unpaid individuals who are compelled to sign away their rights in a bid to 'live the dream', who lack labour law protection or that offered by collective bargaining, most of whom have little chance of having a media career and for those few who do, little control over it. Amidst much academic celebration of new media technology and television empowerment, the work of scholars such as Andrejevic, who attempt to understand the underlying relations of power, is extremely important. Andrejevic is right to point out that audiences of reality TV and users of the internet are being economically manipulated by large corporations who use their activities as a means of creating commodities for advertising revenue. However, the logical conclusion of the extension of the concept of exploitation to all activities in 'the social factory' (i.e. society as a whole) is that everything we do in society is exploited, even presumably forms of resistance. But exploitation as a concept provides an understanding not just of domination, but of the potential for resistance. Exploitation is, as has been argued in this chapter, the extraction of surplus labour and the basis of profit. But it is also a dynamic concept, for it raises the conflict at the heart of the relations of production and the means of struggling against exploitation. Capital is driven by the need to increase surplus value by cheapening the cost of labour. This is as much the case for the cultural industries as any other. As we saw in the first section of this chapter, the television industry dealt with the rising costs, which are an endemic part of the business model that structures the industry, by attacking the conditions of those who work in the industry (and in this I include unpaid or poorly paid contestants and performers). This directly clashes with workers' need to minimize the rate at which surplus is extracted from their labour (that is, the rate of their exploitation) in order to have a decent life, or at least to be able to sustain themselves. Those companies who exploit workers also directly rely on the surplus value they create, which gives the workforce in television industry and the digital economy the capacity and the potential power to resist, and in the process, potentially at least, to call for new forms of television reality, both in form and in meaning.

Raymond Williams argued that 'what is called "reality", indicating certain choices and excluding others, is in all circumstances an act of will, subject to challenge; and that the only relevant question, when such issues are at stake, is about who, in this way, set the reality up' (1989: 64). This chapter has thus far examined the 'who' of reality TV. The final section of this chapter will now turn to the 'what', that is, the meanings of ordinary celebrity that emerge from this 'reality'.

Ordinary Celebrity and Representation

We have established that 'ordinary celebrity' is a cultural form which relies on the exploitation of unpaid and poorly paid labour, the expendability of the contestants/performers, the economic manipulation of media users, the unethical and inescapable surveillance of internet users by online advertising organizations, and is premised on a huge differential in power between production companies and the ordinary people who perform on reality TV. But what of the media representation of ordinary celebrities? Has it opened up the field of representation to new social groups and classes? Does it offer an empowering vision of working-class, female and black identities that are often absent from mainstream media?

Most media discussions of ordinary celebrity either celebrate the new range of identities on display in public or vilify the individuals who have managed to carve out a place in the media, despite their perceived lack of talent or achievement. In our taste-based cultural hierarchy, reality TV is perceived as a lowly media form, and the ordinary celebrities who emerge from it are often denigrated and ridiculed for their 'lack'. The media itself has it both ways – it profits from the endless display of expendable celebrities even as it mocks them. As we saw in chapter 4, the tabloid news media depends upon celebrity content (particularly the online versions) and profits from the disparagement of ordinary celebrities. As Turner notes, the tabloid news is 'able to recount a story to its supposedly disapproving but nonetheless attentive readers in scandalous detail, while at the same time taking the moral high ground by deploring the programme involved and treating the personalities it creates with contempt' (2010: 35).

Reality television abounds with such symbolic violence. One prominent example can be found in reality makeover shows, which recruit 'spectacularly bad, excessive, out of control people' who are 'ripe for transformation' (Skeggs and Wood 2012: 216). Skeggs and Wood argue that asking participants to take part in their own humiliation in these programmes is not an act of empowerment, but of 'symbolic violence' (2012: 216). They argue that 'bourgeois standards of domesticity, femininity and individualism are offered as *the* normative standards to which the bad recruits should aspire' (2012: 218). These shows are a medium for 'making the working class perform their lack of person-value publicly' (2012: 219). For Skeggs and Wood, these shows appeal to viewers because they reiterate 'the drama of class and gender struggles over which people and standards count and matter' (2012: 218). But they also deny them, and indeed the historical and material realities of the social, through a neoliberal 'emphasis upon the individual and the naturalization of the market' (2012: 218). For Skeggs and Wood, however, this structuring conceit also contains deep contradictions. Because these formats rely on the performance of bad excessive selves and good bourgeois and/or trans-formed selves, what are generally naturalized performances of the self are turned into 'full-blown conscious performance[s]' (2012: 220) and they are therefore revealed precisely *as* performances rather than being intrinsically natural. In fact, their interviews with working-class viewers revealed outrage rather than acceptance of the advice on offer. This example points to the complex nature of meaning and interpretation, an important rejoinder to notions of media power in which domination is presented as complete. For, just as in the case of exploitation, domination contains the seeds of its opposite.

Nonetheless, even when those identities are from non-dominant backgrounds and cultures that are approved of, rather than deni-grated, it is often because the individual celebrity either displays or is constructed as possessing the values of individualism, entrepreneur-ialism and consumerism that are validated in neoliberal dominated culture. This is often the case even when the celebrity is presented as a progressive force for good. Jessalynn Marie Keller argues that Tyra Banks, a highly successful and 'visibly raced and gendered' celebrity (2014: 147), who became famous through *America's Next Top Model,* is one such celebrity. Banks has positioned herself as a positive role model for young girls by seeming to celebrate self-acceptance and through her promotion of non-normative bodies, or what she brands 'fiercely real bodies' (2014: 147). However, Banks encourages her fans to 'embrace their true selves' through consumerism, while she herself embodies the 'hegemonic hyper-femininity demanded of female celebrities' (2014: 148). After all, her brand is her body. Thus Banks '[n]avigates a subjectivity which celebrates authenticity and self acceptance, individual choice and is still acceptable to hegemonic ideals of femininity' (2014: 148).

For Keller, Banks' progressive appearance is contained within nor-mative constructions of femininity that are 'rooted in post-feminist and neo-liberal values' where consumerism is replacing feminist action. And because she is presented as having transcended the impo-sitions of gender and race, her 'brand' also relies on a post-racial identity that denies the continuation of inequalities and which 'requires profound blindness' (2014: 149) about the current realities of racism. In addition, Banks conforms to the value of entrepreneurial individualism. She is lauded for being a 'savvy' businesswoman, hardworking, ambitious and talented. Her entrepreneurial spirit shapes the context in which she promotes 'real bodies', one in which individual responsibility replaces collective responsibility, self-improvement and personal empowerment replace social welfare and one in which collective models of life are rejected in favour of individual self-discipline.

Although reality TV has undoubtedly made a version of the ordinary highly visible, including 'multiple versions of class, gender, sexuality and ethnicity' (Turner 2004: 83), it is also highly circumscribed versions of diversity, locked into normative definitions of class, gender and race, rather than 'the recognition of marginalised citizens' rights to media representation' (2004: 83). Graeme Turner has coined one of the most useful terms for thinking through the explosion of the ordinary in the media; it is what he calls 'the demotic turn'. He argues that the opening up of the media to the representation of ordinary people and/or non-dominant identities is demotic rather than democratic because there is 'no necessary connection' between the demographic changes in media representation 'and a democratic politics' (2004: 82). This is true even in relation to the celebrity system itself which remains 'an hierarchical and exclusive phenomenon, no matter how much it proliferates' (2004: 83). Contained in the idea of the demotic are the hidden limitations in celebrity culture, the disavowal of hierarchy, and the reality of exploitation, all of which are banished behind the promise of inclusivity. The demotic is driven by the profit motive in the shape of those 'large internationalised media conglomerates who, despite the demotic turn in representation and consumption, still control the symbolic economy' (2004: 84).

Conclusion

One of the central concerns of this book is to do with the role that celebrity culture plays in giving expression to the balance of forces in society, including the battle of ideas between dominant and challenging perspectives, the rise of new social groups and the decline of others. Ordinary celebrity today, even though there are various manifestations of resistance, it seems, expresses the increasing marginalization of working-class people from public culture, rather than their further integration into it, at the very moment when ordinary people are being offered the false promise of inclusion through reality TV (and the internet) precisely on the basis of being 'ordinary'. The exclusion of working-class people from participation in the creative arts, the theatre, film and television has deepened over the last thirty years, and at least in the UK is linked to a variety of both media-related issues (the prevalence of unpaid internships, the increased precariousness of work in these industries) and non-media issues (such as the abolition of university grants and the introduction of university fees, driving students away from the arts and humanities, cuts in benefits, including housing benefit, reducing actual mobility). It is also related to media representation, including the simultaneous rise of new television formats, news and internet sites that are dedicated to ridiculing the ordinary participants and teaching working-class people shame and humiliation. In fact, the marginalization of the working classes has been commented upon recently by a number of actors and artists from working-class backgrounds in the UK. In January 2014, the actors Julie Walters, David Morrissey and Stephen McGann all spoke out about lack of opportunities for aspiring working-class actors and commented that the British art, pop and acting scene is now dominated by the privately educated and privileged (*Guardian*, 26 January 2014). British artist Gary Hume commented at the same time, that whereas twenty or thirty years ago the art scene was 'full of kids from all kinds of backgrounds, mainly misfits and outsiders...art has become a respectable career path now, another professional option for the young and affluent' (*Guardian*, 26 January 2014). More recently, Salford-born Christopher Eccleston has objected to the fact that working-class actors are finding it harder than ever to make it in the industry, and he argues that British culture has become anodyne because of the dominance of those from privileged backgrounds (*Guardian*, 14 April 2015). This speaks directly against the logic of 'democratainment' – while certain types of (circumscribed) representation of ordinary people are on the increase, the actual participation of members of the working class in professional media careers is dramatically in decline. And, as Graeme Turner argues in relation to the broader political field, the activities of television audiences, users of social media or contestants on reality TV, no matter how active and participatory, 'is not the same as participating in activity which attempts to directly influence structural elements of society, whether on a national or local level' (2010: 46).

The celebrity system has long depended on the idea that an 'ordinary' person might be plucked from obscurity and thrown onto the national and international stage. For over 100 years, the idea that 'anyone can make it' has contributed to the 'myth of success' (Dyer 1979) and the idea of a meritocratic society which is said to reward 'ability' and 'talent' rather than privilege (Littler 2004). These long-established narratives of social mobility have been joined by more recent media-driven narratives of class mobility which seem to offer the trappings of fame and affluence to ordinary people without having to rely on 'talent' or the cultural capital which structures social hierarchies (and the lack of which has traditionally barred entry into public life) (Biressi and Nunn 2005: 145; Bourdieu 1993). But the idea that 'anyone can make it' *is* a myth, and one which supports inequality rather than undermining it. In fact, Jo Littler argues that meritocracy fails even on its own terms and the neoliberal dismantling of welfare systems and other 'austerity' measures have further 'exacerbated inequalities from which ' "talent" (a problematic enough concept) can be healthy enough, culturally equipped enough, or even well fed enough to "rise" through the social and cultural pool' (2004: 122). So while class identities may seem more open, 'substantial class mobility remains out of reach for the majority' (2004: 122).

In addition, ordinary celebrity does not transcend the division between the 'ordinary world' and the 'media world' but reinscribes the 'hidden injuries' of class and media power (Couldry 2000) and symbolic disempowerment found in a symbolic system which privileges mediated identities. As Nick Couldry has argued, the media symbolically categorizes people – ' "ordinary people" are not expected to be the same as "media people" ... [i]ndeed "ordinary people" are not expected to be "in" the media at all, but only to appear "on" the media in certain limited circumstances' (2007: 354). This certainly rings true of the exploitative treatment that ordinary contestants receive at the hands of television companies as we have seen.

In fact, the number of people who have taken to the public stage from ordinary or working-class backgrounds, although highly visible through an expanding media, has actually been rather limited and only a minority of the population will acquire the recognition associated with celebrity status, while the majority will suffer from 'achievement famine' and feelings of lack of recognition (Rojek 2001). Even in the current television environment, when schedules are packed with reality programmes, the number of applications for such shows vastly outnumbers the numbers of contestants chosen. *Big Brother* in the UK, for instance, has had a total of 253 contestants in its 15 years on air. In a population of 53 million adults, these numbers are miniscule. And, as a number of scholars have demonstrated, the casting of these shows is highly selective; it tends towards 'extraordinary' ordinariness (Bonner 2009; Turner 2010) and a focus on the young in order to appeal to a young demographic.

We also find that the type of self lauded in this context is one in which both the self-as-entrepreneur and the-self-as-branded commodity takes centre stage. This is a development on the television personality system identified by Langer in the early 1980s. John

Langer argues that the television personality 'overwhelmingly becomes the "central structuring category" for almost all of television's actuality and fictional forms' (1981: 363). For Langer, the effect of structuring television around personalities 'suggests that the world, first and foremost, is constructed through the actions of individuals behaving as free agents rather than by the complex relations among classes, institutions, and interest groups' (1981: 363). This process of individualization (whether expressed as individual lack or positive value) is disconnected from broader aspects of the social, and crucially, expressions of collectivity which have always been at the heart of working-class culture. What has been lost in the individualized and often competition-based versions of ordinary working-class life found in much reality TV, is the historical memory of ordinary working-class people's actual progressive impact on public life; it is worth remembering that the greatest of democratic achievements are the result of collective, usually working-class movements – universal suffrage, equal rights, equal pay, the establishment of welfare systems, etc. What is really extraordinary about working-class identity is precisely the solidarity and collectivity that is largely hidden from television representations of ordinary people, and so 'ordinary celebrity' plays an important role in banishing images of the collective in displays of pseudo-individuality.

The question of individuality is a central theme in the following chapter, which examines the relationship between the rise of social media and new celebrity culture in promoting a celebrified 'internet of me'.

6

Social Media and Celebrity: The Internet of 'Self'

Introduction

There are two influential sets of claims made in relation to social media and celebrity culture. The first is that, for a variety of reasons, social media has assisted the desire of ordinary people to become famous (Marshall 2010; Senft 2008; Turner 2014). Social media is seen to be a technology of self-presentation (Marshall 2010) and, for some, it is considered to have provided greater opportunities for the public to produce DIY celebrity or 'micro-celebrity' and to sidestep traditional gatekeepers that in the past have limited access to media (Senft 2008). Because of the accessible character of social media, and the ease with which users can produce images and text, social media is seen to significantly undermine or complicate the distinction between production and consumption as users take greater control of the process of celebrification (Marshall 2010; Senft 2008). These views are quite different from those discussed in the previous chapter, where social media use is considered to be a mode of labour which exploits users by producing data which can be captured by media organizations in various ways and turned to profit. Rather than celebrating the ability of new technologies to make us all 'prosumers', it was seen to be a mark of a new ubiquitous mode of exploitation commensurate with the prominence of media communication and digitized information in contemporary capitalism. But for many, social media (and its role in the democratization of celebrity culture) is considered to be part of a broader democratic shift brought about by the liberating potential and participatory address of new technology more generally; it is considered to undermine the power of media corporations and encourage participation (Jenkins 2008; Jenkins and Ford 2013). This chapter will pose some questions about this form of cyber-optimism by investigating the extent to which the power relations in the production of celebrity have altered as a result of social media. Claims that anyone can become a celebrity as a result of building internet fame will be challenged by examining the production of fame of the two most lauded internet celebrity sensations – Justin Bieber and Perez Hilton. This chapter will also question the broader claims about new technology as a technology of freedom (de Sola Pool 1983) that such discussions are situated within. In addition, it will ask how it is that celebrity and the processes of celebrification have come to take centre stage in some accounts of the freedom that new technology is seen to offer. How is it that online celebrity culture has, for some, taken on the appearance of the politics of democratic participation? This chapter will argue that the concept of 'participation' has been crucial in this process – 'participation' has been collapsed with practices of consumerism in a way that simply provides a new language for long discredited ideas about consumer sovereignty.

Others take a more pessimistic view of the processes of DIY celebrity. These critics argue that rather than offering new possibilities of the self, social media sites have become the home of celebrity self-promotion and the staging of the self par excellence. From this perspective, social media problematically encourages individuals to engage in forms of self-presentation that are akin to celebrity, structured by the demands of visibility and profoundly connected to consumer culture (Dean 2002; Marshall 2010; Marwick 2013; Senft 2008). Rather than democratizing online culture and the self, social media demands a self that is defined through self-promotional practices and ultimately neoliberal values. This chapter examines this tendency in social media use, particularly prevalent on Facebook and Twitter. But it will also suggest that social media is a more complicated phenomenon and that despite the promotional pull of social media platforms and the dominance of celebrity in online content, it can produce other forms of engagement. The celebrification of social media is not embedded in the technology itself but is a product of the circumstances that gave birth to social media software, a context which was structured by highly contradictory values as we shall see.

Social Media and the Production of Fame: DIY Celebrity?

Without question, the categories of celebrity have expanded in recent years. Graeme Turner points out that '[t]he opportunity of becoming a celebrity has spread beyond the various elites and entered into the expectations of the population in general' (2010: 14). It is said that the internet has seen the growth of DIY celebrity as ordinary people are said to have taken over the means of media production. But does this expansion constitute a democratization of fame, as it is sometimes claimed, where all members of the population have equal opportunity to become celebrities. How many 'ordinary' people become celebrities through the internet? What does it mean to be famous by social media and does it democratize the public realm? Or are there important differentials and hierarchies in the spread and visibility of celebrity and concomitant social values attached to the striving for celebrity that undermines rather than encourages democratic participation?

Celebrity has been central to social media almost since their inception. Twitter was launched in 2006 and even at its birth it was dominated by the West Coast celebrity-entrepreneurs of social media such as digg.com founder Kevin Rose. Today, the most popular Twitter accounts are predominantly those of pop star celebrities who come from the traditional music industry. In 2015, Katy Perry had the most Twitter followers with over 46 million, followed closely by Justin Bieber and Lady Gaga.[1] The most popular Facebook pages belong to Facebook itself, followed by Cristiano Ronaldo, Shakira, Vin Diesel, Coca Cola and Eminem, each with over 90 million fans.[2] Thus despite claims that the internet has democratized access to celebrity status, Twitter and Facebook are dominated by celebrities from the traditional (music) entertainment industries, followed by footballers, actors and corporate brands from the world of fast food; visibility in this medium is as unevenly distributed as it is in others.

So what of the potential of ordinary people to use social media as a vehicle to gain mainstream celebrity, even if it is uneven? One of the most cited examples of this form of DIY celebrity is pop star Justin Bieber. The story of Bieber's rise to fame is well known and it is mostly spin rather than substance. Bieber, it is claimed, became famous as a result of his mother posting videos on YouTube. The story told online and through Bieber's publicity machinery is that his popularity and fan base steadily grew online, and that as a result of this popularity he was finally signed by Island Records in 2008. His current Twitter popularity is attributed to his earlier DIY fame and is seen as an extension of it. We are told by Bieber's manager that on Twitter, 'the same person talking to them [his fans] before he got huge, is still talking to them now'.[3] However, Bieber's fame actually came after he was scouted and signed by marketing executive Scooter Braun, a route to musical fame that goes back to the early pop industry. The Raymond Braun Media Group relied on traditional promotional practices to bring attention to their new act, including releasing a single prior to an album release that was then vigorously promoted not only through new media outlets but through a variety of traditional outlets such as radio. In other words, Bieber is not an internet sensation, but a product of longstanding scouting and promotional practices that have formed the backbone of the music entertainment industry for many decades.

If Justin Bieber is not a DIY celebrity, there are other famous names in the media who can be seen as such. For some commentators the 'new accessibility of the means of publicity and distribution now available online does at least offer the possibility that ordinary people need no longer deal with the traditional gatekeepers to attract public attention' (Turner 2014: 150) and Perez Hilton, a savvy and sassy online blogger might be seen to be just one such case. Hilton came to fame through a notorious personal weblog, PerezHilton.com, which was a mixture of celebrity gossip and sarcastic innuendo, and within six months of its launch was named as Hollywood's most hated website.[4] This generated enormous interest in this blog as traffic to the site peaked at over 8 million in a single 24-hour period.[5] Hilton thus might be seen to represent the iconoclastic DIY celebrity the internet is credited with generating, but even if this is the case (and there are questions about this narrative), Hilton's celebrity career has taken on the contours of a normal trajectory into television light entertainment to become celebrity gossip for newspapers such as the *Daily Mail* after his appearance on *Celebrity Big Brother* UK and to profit well from his celebrity status. In fact, Turner argues that the career trajectories of figures such as Perez, 'actually end up compromising any claim one might want to make about ordinary people's capacity to generate an alternative form of celebrity through these strategies: the more their small-scale DIY presence expands, and the more followers it attracts, the more it comes to resemble those conventional forms of fame to which it may once have claimed to provide an alternative' (2014: 72). Also, Hilton already possessed the cultural capital to make the most of social media and push a blogging profile in tune with existing celebrified dominant values in the tabloids and so this might be seen as a case of amplifying certain forms of privilege (along the lines of race and class) with an iconoclastic pose.

Despite the ubiquity and dominance of 'old media' celebrity online, including news media outlets as we saw in chapter 4, discussions of digital technology continue to be accompanied by claims about its momentous potential in the service of liberation, to offer new, more equitable forms of human interaction and modes of the self. For instance, in the early years of the internet, feminists such as Donna Haraway (1985) and Sherry Turkle (1984) argued that the online world provided opportunities for new modes of the self, surmounting the impositions of gender and biology, and offering new cyborg identities (although Turkle has since readjusted her view in 2011). Another highly influential view of new media technology connects this form of media communication to ideas about its radical potential – its ability to eventually overthrow the power of big business and big government because of its empowering effects on individuals and the growth of online community (Rheingold 1993). New electronic technology promised to reinstate dialogue, to offer direct democracy, and to supersede power invested in authority (de Sola Pool 1983). The widespread impact of this view on radical politics doesn't need stating, and critical accounts have emerged to challenge the techno-enthusiasm of writers such as de Sola Pool (1983) and Castells (2010) (see Couldry 2014; Curran et al. 2016; Dean 2010). However, less remarked upon is the influence of this perspective on the claims made about the democratizing potential of the internet and celebrity culture and the yoking of consumerism more generally to a progressive politics (see Gilbert 2013). How is it that ideas and analyses that were meant to address the ability of the internet to produce a new 'horizontal' politics of networks and egalitarian modes of the self, has come to shape claims about the politics of celebrity? And conversely, how is it that online celebrity culture has, in some accounts, taken on the appearance of the politics of democratic participation? The following section will look at these questions by examining the conditions which produced the internet of 'me'. This context includes not only the broader social moment of technological development, but also the specific conditions that influenced the new wave of social media entrepreneurs and the software they developed. It will demonstrate that the highly contradictory values that circulated in this milieu and the political economy of new media have had a lasting impact on the shape of social media and its invitation to 'visibility'.

From Cyber Culture to Celebrity Culture: Fame, Popularity and the New Media Self

Social media is a contradictory phenomenon. It encourages a celebrified presentation of the self through platforms such as Facebook and Twitter, some platforms demand a marketized, entrepreneurial self, such as LinkedIn, while others encourage a hobbyist or mundane form of use, such as Pinterest. Emerging research demonstrates that many users engage predominantly in the construction of the self as a micro-celebrity (Marwick and boyd 2011; Senft 2008) and suggest that social media platforms encourage people to present themselves in a celebrified manner, locked into existing social norms around issues of gender, race and class, and also to promote a presentation of self that is in alignment with neoliberal values of the self – entrepreneurial, individualistic, competitive and incessantly visible/popular (Marwick 2013). Others point to the utilization of social media as a tool in social movements and political uprisings, with its ability to spread messages quickly and internationally, and to facilitate the cross-fertilization of oppositional politics (Juris 2005; Klotz 2004; Smith and Smythe 2004). How can we make sense of the deeply contradictory uses of, and values attached to, social media? To what extent do social networking sites encourage the presentation of the self in celebrity modes? Is celebrification implicit in the technology itself, or to do with the way that these platforms are produced?

It will be argued that the place, the time and the people that created social media was inherently contradictory and this played a role in shaping the structuring values of visibility and celebrification that are so endemic in social media sites and, at the same time, the promotion of free use and radical politics that the wider historical moment of protest tapped into and made use of. In short, social media is imbued with the dichotomous values of the Californian Ideology (Barbrook and Cameron 1996; Curran, 2016; Turner 2006).

Richard Barbrook and Andy Cameron suggest that an orthodoxy of techno-utopianism grew up around new technology because of a 'bizarre fusion of the cultural bohemianism of San Francisco with the hi-tech industries of Silicon Valley' (1996: 45). The Californian Ideology appeals, they argue, because it:

> combines the freewheeling spirit of the hippies and the entrepreneurial zeal of the yuppies. This amalgamation of opposites has been achieved through a profound faith in the emancipatory potential of new information technologies. In the digital utopia, everyone will be both hip and rich. (1996: 45)

Barbrook and Cameron point out that this optimism rests on a combination of technological determinism and a libertarian form of politics that turns a blind eye to other issues of West Coast life that used to concern the Californian counterculture – 'racism, poverty and environmental degradation' (1996: 45). The Californian Ideology, because of its hybrid origins, believes in the utopian images of both the New Left, who were opposed to convention and hierarchy, wanted fuller democracy and liberty, and the New Right, who resurrected an older form of liberalism in new clothing – economic liberalism and deregulation (1996: 50). West Coast radicals, influenced by Marshall McLuhan (2008 [1967]) and Howard Rheingold (1993), became involved in developing new technologies for an alternative press, home-brew computer clubs and video collectives. On the other hand, West Coast ideologues (particularly around the magazine *Wired*) embraced the ideology of the free market and even came to welcome the views of the extreme right wing leader of the House of Representatives, Newt Gingrich (who claimed convergence culture as an electronic marketplace), because they shared the values of enhanced 'personal' freedom, the reduction of the power of the nation state, and the idea that resourceful new media entrepreneurs were 'cool' and 'courageous' (1996: 53). In this way, the image of the rebel and that of the new tech entrepreneur were merged. According to Barbrook and Cameron '[b]y mixing New Left and New Right, the Californian Ideology provides a mystical resolution of the contradictory attitudes held by members of the "virtual class"' (1996: 56). As the rebellion of the 1960s and 1970s dissipated and/or was crushed, the 'virtual class' replaced rebellion with the acceptance that individual freedom can only be achieved within the constraints of technical progress and the working of the 'free market' (1996: 58). For Barbrook and Cameron, there was a drift to the right amongst the Californian ideologues, who shared an 'unquestioning acceptance of the liberal ideal of the self-sufficient individual' so crucial to American folklore (1996: 59).

Fred Turner agrees that techno-utopian ideology became ubiquitous by the end of the twentieth century, but instead of seeing it as an amalgamation of Silicon Valley business values and the New Left, he argues that it was made up of that section of the counterculture that broke away from the New Left, including its vision of political organization and ideas of collective struggle. Instead, techno-utopianism came out of that part of the counterculture that embraced the 'back to the land' hippie movement centred around Stewart Brand and Kevin Kelly and the *Whole Earth Catalog*, as well as the New Communalist movement of the 1970s and later *Wired* magazine. None of these movements or texts were particularly critical of 'business' and instead valued self-reliance, individualism and innovation. Fred Turner argues that Stewart Brand, Kevin Kelly and the founders of *Wired* magazine were 'network entrepreneurs' who were able to knit together formally separate intellectual and social networks that 'would include networks from the world of scientific research, hippie homesteading, ecology, mainstream consumer culture and in the 1990s would include representatives from the Defence Department, the US Congress, and global corporations such as Shell Oil, as well as the makers of all sorts of digital software and equipment' (2006: 5). For Turner this milieu 'helped to synthesize a vision of technology as a countercultural force that would shape public understandings of computers and other machines long after the social movements of the 1960s had faded from view' (2006: 6). New technology, in its market-driven architecture, came to be seen as *the* solution to the problems facing society and capitalism. In the meantime, network entrepreneurs became the highly visible micro-celebrities of the new tech scene, where promoting their vision necessarily included promoting themselves.

The language and practice of the 'network entrepreneurs' connected the idealism of the counterculture with that of big business, and in the end helped to produce and legitimate a socio-economic climate in the new communications industries that supported the goals of neoliberalism and which cut away the very community model and public accountability of businesses in this field. In fact, James Curran suggests that it was not the counterculture but the influence of a 'European welfarist tradition that had created great public health and broadcasting systems' (2016 : 40) that inspired Tim Berners-Lee to create the World Wide Web. Berners-Lee's project was publically funded by European Particle Physics Laboratory at CERN and was motivated by two key universal-access public service ideals: 'that of opening up access to a public good (the storehouse of knowledge contained in the world's computers system) and that of bringing people into communion with each other' (Curran 2016: 40). But for the West Coast scene, there was no contradiction between the culture of enterprise and public culture; a zealous belief that new technology will solve all problems, a lack of concern for proper public accountability or democratically oriented regulation, helped to shape the development and use of new technology in very particular ways. This is the ideological terrain that the creators of Web 2.0 inherited and were imbued in, one in which technologically determined idealism was wedded to notions of libertarianism, individualism and self-reliance, innovation, and entrepreneurialism *and* the value of being rich and powerful. As we shall see below, this had a profound impact on the architecture and construction of social media platforms, the political economy of these new brands, the manner in which they invite users to 'participate' online through them, and the kind of (celebritized) self that is encouraged. The new entrepreneurs of Web 2.0 come to dominate the West Coast new technology scene after the dot-com crash in 2001, reinforcing the Californian Ideology, of which they too are a product.

Social Media, the New Tech Start-up Scene and the Rise of the Celebrity Self

The social media gurus of Web 2.0 are the A-list celebrities of the tech scene. Mark Zuckerberg of Facebook, and Twitter's Evan Williams, Jack Dorsey, Noah Glass and Biz Stone are all highly visible celebrities in online and offline media and set the standards for ambitious would-be followers. As noted above, early social media entrepreneurs dominated social media platforms such as Twitter, becoming the celebrities of the new tech scene. Social media websites developed as venture capitalist-backed start-ups at the beginning of the twenty-first century in northern California, and this is no accident, not because it happened to be where the cool figures in social media 'hung out', but because the technical infrastructure and expertise that is necessary to new technology industries has been located in Silicon Valley since the 1960s. Web 2.0 reinvigorated the West Coast new technology scene with the optimism that had dissipated after the dot-com crash at the beginning of the twenty-first century, and so the Bay Area is home to the first generation of social media brands (Google, Facebook, Twitter, Instagram, Pinterest and Flickr). In keeping with their hybrid origins, there was a contradiction in the set of ideals that originally circulated around social media – it was simultaneously considered to be open, transparent and participatory as well as being seen as an opportunity to make money and get rich quick. The early ideological openness of Web 2.0 quickly gave way, however, to the more monetized version of online interaction, with the development of the Apple App store, the tightening of commercial control over data from companies such as Facebook and Twitter, and the highly commercialized environments of mobile carriers and ISPs and the increased use of advertising as the main source of revenue. But even from the outset, social media websites were designed, unlike collective endeavours such as wiki, not for social or communal use, but for individual use. At its core, social media is focused on the individual. It is the individual in social media who produces and consumes content, and she/he does so in an environment that is increasingly commercialized and marketized (Curran 2016; Lessig 1999, 2001). The individualized architecture of social media is the foundation upon which other practices of celebritized self-promotion are built and relates to a long history of liberal identification of the self with individualism (see Gilbert 2013; Inglis 2010).

P.D. Marshall points out that there is a strong link between social media and celebrity in that both are centred on the production of the self. He argues that 'self-production is the very core of celebrity activity and it now serves as a rubric and template for the organization and production of the on-line self which has become at the very least an important component of our presentation of ourselves to the world' (2010: 39). Similarly, according to Theresa M. Senft, increased access to technologies of content creation and distribution has led to the spread of 'micro-celebrities' (2008). Senft suggests that 'micro-celebrity is best understood as a new style of online performance that involves people "amping up" their popularity over the Web using technologies like video, blogs and social networking sites' (2008: 25). For Alice E. Marwick, social media tools like Twitter, Facebook and YouTube teach users the 'strategies and practices to achieve "micro-celebrity"' which combines the 'entrepreneurialism fetishized by techies and business people with marketing and advertising techniques drawn from commercials and celebrity culture' (2013: 10). The politics of Do-It-Yourself that characterized part of the early scene, has given way in the wake of social media to the politics of Do-It-About-Me, and this is due to the way that social media tools, focused on the individual, invite users to engage in a form of self-presentation that is saturated with consumerism and imbued with hierarchy amid claims of 'access for all' and horizontalism.

Social media has popularized what Marwick calls the 'attention economy' (2013: 10); it promotes attention-getting techniques such as 'self-branding' and 'lifestreaming' (2013: 10), which is why platforms like Twitter are so popular with celebrities themselves. Early adopters of Twitter include figures such as A-list celebrity Ashton Kutcher, whose acting roles include playing a geeky internet billionaire in the hit television show *Two and a Half Men*. Kutcher then used his acting fortune to become the kind start-up venture capitalist he plays in this role. Furthermore, social media can promote a celebrity-oriented neoliberal subjectivity by encouraging users to apply market principles to the self and to integrate market logic into our relationships with others. Twitter and Facebook encourage us to present ourselves in a manner to be consumed, to achieve status by gathering 'followers' and 'friends', to imagine those friends and followers as our public or fan base, and to steadily increase our visibility and popularity through ongoing image management and online activity. There are, of course, numerous important examples of social media being used in political struggles, protest movements and campaigns from Chiapas to Tunisia, from #BlackLivesMatter to #VoteJeremyCorbyn. These examples demonstrate that the use of technology is never predetermined, unchanging or predictable. Throughout the history of mass

communication technology, there has been a rich history of radicals
and rebels wielding these technologies against the grain and at odds
with social norms and conservative politics of the day (Curran 2002;
Williams 1961). These counterexamples are important when assessing
the social impact of social media.

But despite the ability and historical tendency to subvert media
usage, it is also important to note that the architecture and political
economy of digital media reinforces promotional values and, according to Murdock and Golding, has hollowed out 'the space previously
available for the reconstruction and extension of citizenship, and
refilled it with seductive promises of boundless consumption and
personal satisfaction' (2002: 126). They argue that:

> [c]orporations entering the new media marketplace work with social
> maps on which affiliations are classified by life styles and leisure inter-
> ests rather than by membership of moral communities. These market
> segments are then addressed by themed channels and internet sites.
> This produces a contradictory movement in which digital technologies
> facilitate 'the development of distinct groups organized around affinity
> and interest' while at the same time undermining the possibility of
> creating 'a public' – an active democratic encounter of citizens who
> reach across their differences to establish a common agenda of concern.
> (2002: 126)

In addition, social media tools encourage us to post 'status updates'
without any expectation of reciprocity or meaningful dialogue, and
to build an online image that appeals to others as fans rather than
encouraging collective connections (Marwick 2013). This version of
one-way communication borrows directly from celebrity culture and
the promotional practices that surround it (Rojek 2001). The reality
of the individualization of social media, and its interpellation of users
as popularity seekers, is at odds with the claims of 'dialogue' and
'participatory community' found on one side of the California
Ideology-influenced Web 2.0 coin, but is entirely in keeping with the
entrepreneurial neoliberal other side, with its emphasis on the mar-
ketizing project of the self. The enormous communicative and democratic potential of new technology and social media has been left
unrealized because of the market-driven, consumer and celebrity
saturated conditions from which Web 2.0 emerged.

Some argue that the celebrifying push of social media echoes psy-
choanalytic structures of modernity. Jodi Dean for instance, draws
on psychoanalysis to explain this online drive to celebrity. She suggests that these practices are all connected to what she terms a 'technoculture' that is premised on twin phenomena – the desire to know

and the 'drive to be known' (2002: 12). It is presumed that what matters is only what is known, and for Dean this produces an economy of subjectivity 'in which the technocultural subject is con-figured as a celebrity' (2002: 13), for the ideology of communicative capitalism rests on the subject recognizing themselves as known and positing a public that knows her/him. As Dean puts it, 'the ideology of publicity...hails subjects into being as celebrities' (2002: 122) and if one fails to recognize that call, or fails to accept the ideological construction of the self as one 'who has to present oneself as an object for everyone else', then such subjects 'don't "exist" at all' in this economy of subjectivity (2002: 125). Dean draws on Žižek's reinter-pretation of Lacanian psychoanalysis in her analysis of the 'celebrity drive' of technoculture, and while there is much insight in her notion of the technocultural celebrity self, her account seems to be missing a sense of contradiction in socio-economic systems and the self which inhabits them, and in this she seems to tie the human subject to immovable psychic structures and to deny agency, so that our very drives and desires 'bind us into the practices whereby we submit to global capital' (2002: 151). But as Murdock and Golding argue, 'the "monetizing" thrust of market-driven convergence has not gone unopposed' (2002: 127). They point to a number of struggles by those working in public cultural organizations to keep them public, publicly accountable, and free of charge. Although such struggle is fragile, it is an essential base for building a 'digital commons', one that 'mobilizes emerging communications technologies in the service of an extended and cosmopolitan ethos of citizenship rather than consumption' (2002: 127). For Murdock and Golding, finding ways to develop a vision of a digital commons and constructing an infra-structure to materially support it is 'one of the greatest challenges facing democracy over the coming decades' (2002: 127).

What we must be clear about is that a digital commons will not emerge from the commercially dominated new technology companies of northern California, nor from the milieu that surrounds it, despite its rhetoric of inclusion, participation and equality. On the contrary, Marwick's in-depth study of the West Coast new tech scene demon-strates that there is a considerable disparity between the egalitarian claims made about life in the new tech industries and the reality for those working in them. She identified a strict hierarchy in which the (young, white, male) start-up entrepreneur was mostly highly valued in the scene, and in which race and gender inequalities were rein-forced, rather than undermined. In the process of her research, she discovered that popular social software actually promoted inequality rather than countered it. She writes:

In studying this world closely, I found that, far from the revolutionary and progressive participation flaunted by entrepreneurs and pundits, social media applications encourage people to compete for social benefits by gaining visibility and attention. To boost social status, young professionals adopt self-consciously constructed personas and market themselves, like brands or celebrities, to an audience or fan base. These personas are highly edited, controlled, and monitored, conforming to commercial ideals that dictate 'safe-for-work' self-presentation. The technical mechanisms of social media reflect the values of where they were produced: a culture dominated by commercial interest. Although freewheeling creativity, rebellion, and non-hierarchical communality still exist online, they are dwarfed by social media applications that transform 'social graphs', the web of digital connections around a single user, into networks of personal brands contending for the very real benefits of high online status. These changes are deeply rooted in contemporary consumer capitalism, specifically the philosophy of deregulation and privatization known as 'neoliberalism'. (2013: 5)

Perhaps it is no surprise that the hierarchical and promotional social relations that shape consumer capitalism more generally should also shape the working environment of the new tech industries, but these relations have been obscured by their coexistence with the language of a radical project that has been the ideological terrain of Web 2.0. This is because the lofty idealism and radical rhetoric that characterized the first wave of technological utopianism also influenced the Web 2.0 second wave. But so too did free-market neoliberalism and entrepreneurialism. In fact, the term Web 2.0 was developed as a marketing ploy designed to distinguish these new companies from the old failed companies associated with the dot-com bust. Marwick's study very convincingly demonstrates that the new technology scene is built on hierarchy and status, ascribing 'high value to wealth, risk-taking, entrepreneurship, visibility, access to others, technical know-how and intelligence' (2013: 78). Marwick also shows how those working in this industry are pressurized into relentless online self-marketing through social media, where status is conferred through one's position in the business of technology, where 'having done it' is an insider's reference to starting a popular company such as Instagram and then selling it to Facebook for $1 billion, or inventing YouTube and selling it to Google for $1.65 billion. In short, the highest status one can gain is from starting a successful social media company and selling it for riches. At base, all of the ideals of entrepreneurialism in the new tech scene – know-how, risk taking, innovation – come down to the bottom line.

Another avenue to high status is through visibility and, according to Marwick, the new tech scene encourages those in the scene to engage in the practices of micro-celebrity – creating a publishable personality online, constructing a persona that will attract attention and performances of the self that will draw publicity, and putting in the hours of networking needed to maintain visibility. It is no coincidence, then, that six of the top ten Forbes Web Celebrities of 2010 were new technology gurus, Silicon Valley VIPs and social media entrepreneurs who combine high-status entrepreneurialism with a significant online presence: Michael Arrington – founder of TechCrunch and influential blogger; Pete Cashmore – founder of the website Mashable and blogger with 2 million followers; Evan Williams and Biz Stone – Twitter.com start-up entrepreneurs with 2.8 million followers; Kevin Rose – founder of Digg.com; and Guy Kawasaki – venture capitalist, entrepreneur and author who helped to launch and market the original Macintosh for Apple in 1984. The gendering of success in this industry is as visible as the famous. The only two women on the list – Heather Armstrong and Tila 'Tequila' Nguyen have both gained online celebrity, not for their business acumen or technological expertise in a male-dominated scene, but for activities traditionally designated as female – Armstrong for a blog about being fired from her job and the adventures as a 'stay-at-home mom', and Nguyen for nude modelling on MySpace and later hosting a reality TV show about dating. As in the earlier examples, these internet celebrities maintained their fame and visibility through their connection with older media forms – in the case of Armstrong, this included a publishing deal, and in the case of Nguyen, her own television show and transition to TV celebrity.

Not only are those in the tech industry expected to present a self in alignment with neoliberal values, women face an added layer of sexism, where women are defined in relation to the personal, and then are derided for it. According to Marwick, such visibility is considered 'meritless attention seeking' (2013: 139), which tries to garner fame through gossip. And as Marwick points out, while some 'micro-celebrity practitioners are able to translate their fame into a better job or a book deal, very few achieve the financial success or legitimacy given to mainstream celebrities' (2013: 142). Celebrity, like the new tech industry, is a hierarchical field, where attention seeking is encouraged and simultaneously derided, where high status is accorded to 'accomplishment', and (as in the case of ordinary celebrity in the previous chapter) those who want to be 'famous for being famous' are derided by the very system that demands such aspirations.

It is not only those in the new technology scene who are encouraged by social media to 'amp up' (Senft 2008) their popularity and behave as a micro-celebrity. The architecture of social media, as we have seen, encourages all members of the public to think of ourselves as micro-celebrities, regardless of who is paying attention, to treat one's followers as if they are fans, and to manage these online relationships in a way that will maintain and increase one's popularity. As Marwick and boyd argue, micro-celebrity involves viewing friends and family as followers and as a fan base – popularity is the goal (2011: 140). Yet still, social media pundits herald DIY celebrity as egalitarian and meritocratic – anyone can become a micro-celebrity it is said, and by-pass the need to pay agents and publicists which have traditionally acted as gatekeepers to fame. The problem with this claim, including the logic of micro-celebrity as a social aspiration, as we have seen, is that not only does a celebrified social media space re-inscribe subordination and privilege in practice (while hiding it discursively), it also normalizes the drive to celebrity as a personal and social goal, and in the process valorizes the associated values of the self as brand and the person as the site of commercially derived marketing practices. Many of the dominant discourses around social media accept celebrity as a legitimate goal rather than investigating the socio-economic conditions that have given rise to the popularity of this phenomenon. They accept the taken-for-granted assumptions that surround the pull of celebrity that obscure alternative possibilities for the self, the practices of visibility, and the shape and use of new communications technology. The following section will take a closer look at the link between celebrity and consumerism and how both come to be associated with freedom in discussions around online identity and usage. It will argue that a particular conception of the idea of 'participation' has had a significant influence on a generation of media and cultural scholars, reintroducing the 'cultural populism' (McGuigan 1992) that was so prominent in studies of popular culture in the 1990s in Britain and the US. Ideas of consumerism as participation have re-emerged in relation to the internet and have helped to shape the claims about celebrity and democratization that surround discussions of DIY and micro-celebrity.

Online Celebrity and the Politics of 'Participation'

Despite the growing critical response to cyber-utopianism, the internet is still considered by many today to provide the public with the ability to sidestep the power of big media by offering cheap tools for creating content, accessing information and taking part in the public sphere, and often this perspective is influenced by the California Ideology even today in academia. For instance, Aaron Delwiche and Jennifer Jacobs Henderson (2013) have recently suggested that

> Armed with inexpensive tools for capturing, editing, and organizing, people tap into the vast ocean of real-time data and multimedia content to promote personal and political interests. Functions once monopolized by a handful of hierarchical institutions (e.g. newspapers, television stations and universities) have been usurped by independent publishers, video-sharing sites, collaborative sustained knowledge banks, and fan-generated entertainment. (2013: 3)

For Delwiche and Jacobs Henderson 'participatory creative cultures' are 'just one aspect of a much larger cultural movement' (2013: 3) which spans activities as assorted as website reviews of books, restaurants, physicians, and college professors, to involvement in blogging or fan practices, to uploading video and other creative material, to organizing and participating in political uprisings (2013: 4). However, such an approach collapses very diverse activities into a single participatory project which is so broad as to be meaningless. Indeed, Delwiche begins his chapter by linking consumerism to the New Left. He describes a fan-based demonstration at Burbank to oppose the axing of *Star Trek* in 1968 and equates this protest with the 'earnest optimism' and 'open-mindedness' that were the 'core values of the early New Left before the movement leaders took their eyes off the prize' (2013: 10). Delwiche constructs a history of 'participatory culture' in which the consumer activism with 'Spock Ears' (2013: 10) is 'firmly situated within the cultural and political climate of the 1960s' (2013: 11) which includes demonstrations 'erupting around the globe' met by tanks in 'Paris, Warsaw, Mexico City, Tokyo and Prague' (2013: 11), the US civil rights movement and the establishment of the Students for a Democratic Society in 1962 and the Student Non-violent Coordinating Committee (2013: 12). In fact, Delwiche's history of participatory culture is deeply influenced by the California Ideology – a melding together of consumerism with the language of the counterculture and the equation of fan culture with left-wing political activism. How is it that consumerism, celebrity and fandom have become equated with the struggle for human and political rights and the struggles for freedom? I will argue that the idea of 'participation' and 'participatory culture' as conceptualized by Henry Jenkins has played a significant role in collapsing consumer activities with citizen and/or political activism. Jenkins' influence on a generation of scholars should not be underestimated.

For example, Delwiche's history of online participatory culture puts Jenkins centre stage of this 'important moment of cultural history' (2013: 10). For Delwiche, the success of the *Star Trek* demonstration at Burbank was as important because, had it failed 'Henry Jenkins (1988) might never have published...the book *Textual Poachers* (1992), sparking a wave of media fandom studies in the process' (2013: 10).

Thus, while it is the case that there are a number of ways that new technology has been conceptualized as a democratic force, the one that most concerns the question of celebrity is that which links consumerism with political participation and what are seen as the progressive processes of media convergence with commercial entertainment, and in this endeavour, Jenkins has played a significant role (Jenkins 2008; Jenkins and Ford 2013).

Convergence, according to Ithiel de Sola Pool, one of the earliest advocates of technology-as-freedom, is a technological process that refers to

> blurring the lines between media, even between point-to-point communications, such as the post, telephone and telegraph, and mass communications such as the press, radio, and television...a service that was provided in the past by any one medium – be it broadcasting, the press, or telephony – can now be provided in several different ways. So that the one-to-one relationship that used to exist between a medium and its use is eroding. (de Sola Pool 1983: 23)

The technological core of convergence is digitization which enables the transformation of different types of communication/information (print, audio, visual, data) to be reconfigured in binary code. This allows each communication/information form to be transformed into the others and to be shared, manipulated and distributed easily through merged telecommunications and computing apparatuses. According to de Sola Pool, the dispersal of the means of communication and its increased accessibility is seen to disrupt centralized control and offer freedom from vested power interests, and to promote and support concurrent values (de Sola Pool 1983: 25).

It is Henry Jenkins' intervention in discussions of new technology that links these ideas about technico-political progress to entertainment and consumerism, in his conceptualization of 'convergence culture' and 'participatory culture' as ones in which consumers are wielding new technology to remake popular culture in their own image. Jenkins makes it clear that while others may be interested in the impact of convergence culture on political culture, he is more interested 'in the impact on popular culture' (2008: 12) and in the ways that 'convergence thinking' is affecting the 'relationship between media audiences, producers, and content' (2008: 12). Nevertheless, Jenkins' rhetorical style invokes a sense of political rebellion in the activities of consumers; he declares that '[t]the promises of this new media environment raise expectations of a freer flow of ideas and content. Inspired by those ideals, consumers are fighting for the right to participate more fully in their culture' (2008: 18). Jenkins' early uncritical celebration of cyberculture has a new note of caution, as he now recognizes the power of elites to hamper the ability to 'participate' and to undermine processes of progressive change (2014: 272). He also acknowledges that convergence is a 'top-down corporate-driven process' (even while he insists that it is as much a 'bottom-up consumer-driven process') (2008: 18). However, his long-standing melding of citizen and consumer remains. The view that media fans are 'grassroots' activists, that his first book on the topic of participatory culture promulgated (*Textual Poachers*, 1992), continues to lie central to his approach to convergence culture, the major difference being that the term 'fan' has been replaced with 'consumer' (Jenkins and Ford 2013).

Jenkins views the terrain of convergence culture as one which is still in progress and where the outcomes are up for grabs, and which will ultimately be shaped by the 'struggles' of corporations and 'grassroots consumers' (sometimes in accord, sometimes in opposition, to each other) 'to redefine the face of American popular culture' (2013: 18). In a new language, Jenkins reasserts old ideas about consumer sovereignty (whereby entertainment, it is argued, is shaped by consumer preference – for 'our culture' in this formulation *is* consumer culture), but he gives them a radical gloss by attaching them to the language of democratic participation. In the process, he wrongly implies a sense of parity between corporations and consumers in these struggles and actually reinforces the conceptual division between old 'passive' consumers and new 'empowered' ones that his work claims to challenge (2013: 19).

However, it is worth pointing out that the processes of convergence are not only occurring in relation to technology, but are also taking place in other fields such as the economy, including that area of the economy related to new communications. The convergence of media and telecommunications industries through huge media mergers has concentrated media power in fewer hands over the past 20 years and provided enormous media conglomerates oligopolistic power over the communications field (Murdock and Golding 2002). In addition, there has been a convergence in the arena of regulation, such as the replacement in the UK of a number of separate regulatory bodies with the single entity Ofcom, as part of an effort by successive govern-ments to push deregulation and use policy to increase the reach of commercial media. The new converged regulatory environment has seen a decrease in powers to monitor and regulate and an increased remit to promote competition (Freedman 2008). As Murdock and Golding have argued 'digital democracy suggests a diffusion and distribution of power but, contradictorily, has exacerbated its con-centration and centralization' (2002: 125) by transferring control of the media from the state to transnational corporations, and through the development of the processes of surveillance both by the state and by corporations, as we saw in the previous chapter. As Lessig points out, the commercial technology of surveillance is now exten-sively deployed with an average of 92 per cent of commercial websites aggregating and sorting the personal data of users for economic pur-poses (1999: 1415). And Curran points to the threat posed to an open internet by the growth of legally asserted corporate intellectual property rights over software – corporate 'rights' backed up by the 1998 Digital Millennium Act (and its precursor the Copyright Act of 1976) (2016: 43). For Murdock and Golding, 'the very architecture and construction, as well as the political economy, of the new tech-nologies, are liberatory in their potential but regressive in their con-temporary reality (2002: 125).

As problematic as the equation of media conversion with partici-pation and participation with consumerism/fandom is Jenkins' amor-phous equation of the citizen subject with the consumer subject. As P.D. Marshall points out, the transformation of the individual into a consumer was, in fact, 'not the shift from production to consump-tion', or passive to active consumer, 'but a shift to a wider more pervasive *production* of the self' (2010: 36). Don Slater also reminds us that the production of the self is a central configuration of moder-nity – a shift from traditional society to one that is focused, obses-sively, on a variety of practices through which we try to produce a coherent self. For Slater, consumerism is central to the construction of the modern self because not only are we expected to choose a self, we are also expected to 'constitute ourselves as a self who chooses, a consumer' (1997: 91). Marshall is concerned with the pedagogic practices of this address to the self and he argues that with the rise of consumer capitalism, individuals not only had to be taught to consume, they also had to be taught to 'recognize the value of con-sumption for their own benefit' (2010: 36). He suggests that this is one of the social functions of celebrity throughout the twentieth century and in this way consumer culture became linked to the enter-tainment industries and to celebrity. He argues, 'the pedagogic work performed to transform a more traditional culture into a consumer culture was very much dependent upon celebrities' (2010: 36) and on their ability to embody the seeming promise of consumer culture. Celebrity culture has long been linked to advertising and other promotional industries such as public relations for precisely this reason. The flip side of 'choice' is that self is expected to take personal responsibility for all aspects of ourselves and to personalize health and well-being rather than considering them to be connected to social issues. As Slater puts it 'we could always choose to *do something* about our appearance, health, manners...everything we do has implications for the self, implications that we obsessively monitor' (1997: 91). The self is a thing one must produce and 'consumer industries stand ready with things one can buy in order to address all these technical problems in the production of the self' (1997: 91). Murdock and Golding argue that digital media further reinforce the relationship between the self and consumerism with an 'insistent promotional rhetoric that has hollowed out the space previously available for the reconstruction and extension of citizenship, and refilled it with seductive promises of boundless consumption and personal satisfaction' (2002: 126). Kim Kardashian, for example, is a prominent celebrity whose online fame knits together the promises of celebrity and consumerism, and the individualization of social issues to do with personal well-being. She exemplifies the neoliberal values attached to much contemporary celebrity today and, with over 35 million Twitter followers, is a prime example of the 'success' of market-oriented celebrification of the entire self. As a well-connected socialite, Kardashian first came to public prominence over a leaked sex tape in 2007, and the US television channel E! quickly offered her and her family a reality soap opera programme *Keeping Up with the Kardashians* (2007–). By 2010 Kim had a variety of endorsement deals for food and diet companies and had founded a clothing line with her sisters for *Bebe*. She and her sisters also wrote an autobiography *Kardashian Konfidential* (2010) which made it onto the *New York Times* best seller list later that year. Every aspect of her life, from sex, to family, to relationships, was marketed and sold. As with other internet celebrities, the Kardashians moved into the traditional arena of celebrity by transferring to television and securing a hugely promoted book deal. By 2012 the Kardashians had a range of consumer products from perfume to clothing that were also marketed on their TV fame, usually released to coincide with a highly promoted aspect of Kim's personal life (such as marriage or childbirth) and her cultivated image of glamour. Kim Kardashian's celebrity provides the template for ambitious DIY celebrities to borrow – every aspect of her life is part of her 'brand' and available as a promotional strategy, her celebrity encourages consumerism and equates the development of the self with the consumption of (highly gendered) consumer goods. It is less the case that celebrities like Kardashian borrow the social media protocol of ordinary people, as Graeme Turner has suggested (2014), and more a case that contemporary celebrity culture and social media come together to promote these practices online.

Consumer capitalism benefits enormously from individuals understanding themselves as consumers, rather than as political actors or participating citizens because consumption, no matter how boisterous or demanding, is part of the process of capital accumulation and does not challenge the logic of the commercial organization of culture, or of the commercial promotion of the self, and it supports the individualization of socio-personal issues, while active political citizenship makes economic, social and political demands outside of the logic of consumption. Indeed, as a number of critics have argued (Dean 2002; Marshall 1997; Marwick 2013; Slater 1997), consumer capitalism depends upon a self that is constructed as consumer, as well as and as much as the entrepreneurial self, and often the two are the same. As Marwick argues 'an effective neoliberal subject attends to fashions, is focused on self-improvement, and purchases goods and services to achieve "self-realization". He or she is comfortable integrating market logics into many aspects of life, including education, parenting, and relationships. In other words, the ideal neoliberal citizen is an entrepreneur' (2013: 13).

In both *Convergence Culture* (Jenkins 2008) and *Spreadable Media* (Jenkins and Ford 2013), there is a vacillation between a rhetoric of 'struggle' on the one hand, and advocating the need for academics to work within the logics of the corporate media boardroom on the other. So while Jenkins continues to assert, despite some evidence to the contrary, that we are moving towards a more 'participatory model of culture, one which sees the public not simply as consumers of preconstructed messages but as people who are shaping, sharing, reframing, and remixing media content in ways which might not have previously been imagined', he very much conceptualizes this as one of consumer choice and sovereignty – '[a]udiences are making their presence felt by actively shaping media flows, and producers, brand managers, customer service professionals, and corporate communicators are waking up to the commercial need to actively listen and respond to them' (Jenkins and Ford 2013: 2). This reiteration of the ideas of consumer power – this time called 'spreadability' – is nothing more than a reassertion of the view that commercial competition provides the public with what it 'wants' by 'listening' and 'responding' – this time aided by those very consumer-rebels who 'help to generate interest in particular brands or franchises' (2013: 7). In doing so, Jenkins and Jenkins and Ford reiterate a central corporate myth – that production (supply) and consumption (demand) are not only matched, but that production itself is driven only by demand. As we saw in previous chapters, the funding structure of much commercial media, including most social media, is based on advertising revenue. These companies are therefore driven by the need to satisfy the demands of this revenue stream (i.e. to satisfy their advertisers) rather than the public, and this in turn has led the internet giants to perfect the technical means of collection of personal data, entirely unethically (see previous chapter). In addition, any reduction of media reform to attempts to influence corporate media evacuates the possibility that the struggles over culture can be anything other than an attempt to influence the 'boardroom', or tinker with consumer culture and make tiny partial gains such as lobbying for a second season of a television programme or requesting that a character not be killed off. In justifying this turn to corporate entertainment boardrooms, Jenkins sets up a division between approaches to change that he characterizes as 'reform' (depicted as co-operative, sensible and in dialogue with industry) and 'revolution' (presented as outdated, pessimistic and out of touch with what is happening in industry) (2014). So, for instance, in response to Maxwell and Miller's (2011) critique of the myths of convergence in contrast with the realities of impending ecological destruction, driven by new modes of capital accumulation and consumption, Jenkins responds, '[s]o, is this an immutable law that negates any possibility of alternative outcomes, or are there moments of vulnerability when one system is giving into another when it makes sense to focus criticism and mobilization in hopes of impacting what happens next?' (2014: 247). A first response is that, of course, nothing is immutable; a central lesson of history is the capacity of humans to rise up and indeed there is an urgent call to do so, because ecological disaster is looking to be the increasingly likely 'outcome' of capitalism. But once again, Jenkins' rhetorical style confuses socio-economic and political systems with corporate ones. And even in relation to media systems (in which the old system – analogue, broadcast – is giving in to a new system – digital, narrowcast), Jenkins' view is one in which the commercial organization of popular culture is a given, and indeed even celebrated. Jenkins' combined celebration of new media, corporate media and technological convergence directly corresponds to the cybertarian vision of the West Coast new media gurus, including their problematic accommodation with the values of neoliberal corporate and consumer capitalism. But instead of a cyber-utopia, as Murdock and Golding argue, what we are witnessing in the new tech industries is an example of the restructuring of contemporary capitalism, and nothing more 'epochal' (2002: 112). Indeed, Murdock and Golding argue that media and communication systems have predominantly become 'enmeshed' in 'economic rather than technical' convergence which has transformed new media increasingly into the model of 'older communications forms' (2002: 112). In other words, the old media system is not giving way to a new one; the political economy and social relations that govern 'old media', now govern 'new media' (see Curran et al. 2016) and the relations of power that dominated the old media system, including the system of celebrity, are growing rather than receding. Of those who are attempting to offer a fuller critical understanding of the nature of the moment that we are living in, Jenkins writes, '[t]oo often, work in critical and cultural studies sees a narrow conception of critique as the only goal of theory-making and often seeks to protect its independence from commercial interests at the cost of making meaningful interventions in public debates' (2014: 289). However, for many progressive academics and activists, the key intervention in public debates is *precisely* to protect a variety of important sectors' *independence* from commercial interests – commercial interests that have been encroaching on all forms of public culture for the past fifty years, deregulating it, privatizing it, commodifying it, cutting it, increasing inequalities of access to it on the basis of ability to pay. This is not a 'revolution versus reform' disagreement, but rather a desperate attempt in the face of a neoliberal onslaught to fight for what public culture continues to exist (but is under constant threat), to try to regain the spaces, organizations and institutions of public culture that have already been privatized, and to equip ourselves and our students with the necessary understanding of the changes unfolding before us, not only to try to protect what we have left, but to struggle for a more inclusive future.

The crux of the matter is that 'participatory culture' should not be formulated as a catch-all concept that blurs the boardroom with the street demonstration and the political activist with the television fan. Genuine participatory culture is best served, not by fans negotiating with media conglomerates over the fate of favoured stars and celebrities, nor through the consumption of products and merchandise associated with celebrities, nor with the celebrified construction of ourselves online. Instead, participatory culture is best served though the existence of properly regulated, public organizations that are autonomous of the state, whose values are to serve the public rather than the shareholder, and whose commitment to equality is enshrined in law, in institutional policy, and in day-to-day practices. This is the key struggle for those who would like to see a culture in which all members of society can participate freely and equally. Where such institutions exist and are under attack, even in flawed form (such as the British Broadcasting Corporation), we must struggle to protect them and to increase their participatory values. Where they do not, we must struggle for reform in this direction.

A call to see political identities as parallel to consumer identities is an acceptance of a major designation of neoliberal subjectivity which hampers Jenkins' ability to see possible alternatives for cultural production. Jenkins' linking of new technology to the interwoven language of radical politics with those of consumer capitalism is part of a broader cultural configuration, to which Jenkins and those influenced by him, might be said to belong – the shift from counterculture to cyberculture (Turner 2006) and from politics to populism. And just as we saw in the previous chapter, where celebrity culture was shown to play an important role in the reconfiguration of the television industry against the interests of those who work in it, in the online world the pedagogic role of celebrity culture in the project of consumer capitalism has been revitalized by offering the public new tools to celebrify the self and new celebrities to endorse this ambition.

Conclusion

We have seen that the technology of freedom turns out to be as much the technology of self-promotion and celebrity. The practices of celebrity visibility have been part of the construction of hierarchy in an industry that proclaims its egalitarian principles and meritocratic practices. Indeed, so important has fame been to the new tech scene that it becomes welded to the architecture of Web 2.0 and an intrinsic part of its social media platforms. Behaving like celebrities themselves, social media entrepreneurs developed software in which celebrity-style visibility was embedded. But the geeks of San Francisco did not invent celebrity culture, it comes deeper from within the structure of consumer capitalism and, as in the case of other communication and entertainment industries, celebrity serves a function, this time to do with the production of status and hierarchy in an industry whose official ideology, according to Marwick (2013), is equality and inclusion. This dichotomy has also shaped the way social media invites usage, both as a technology of freedom and protest, and of the celebrification of the self. That this dichotomy constructs the famous web entrepreneur as a figure of rebellion is true, but there are others who have used the technology in the quest for radical change. The techies, however, have been joined by a chorus of other voices also proclaiming the internet a space of freedom, some of whom have compounded the ideological confusion surrounding new technology by collapsing the concept of the citizen with that of the consumer, and the practices of consumption with those of civil society. The consumerist desire differs enormously from the citizen desire; citizenship is a genuine bottom up phenomenon, the desire for the public to raise its voice and to win rights and freedoms comes from the mass of the population and not the elite. The consumerist desire is a top-down phenomenon; it must be taught and its lessons to the population endlessly renewed by those famous faces of our social hierarchy. As was argued above, celebrity culture has not only played a significant role in the development of commercial media, it has also played an important role in the pedagogy of consumption; celebrity offers a pseudo-meritocratic populist vision situated within hierarchy and an image of the pleasures of plenty in a unequal society structured in want. This chapter has argued that social media has not democratized celebrity (or vice versa), but has also suggested that perhaps this is not the right question to be asking. Instead of asking whether or not celebrity culture is more accessible today to ordinary people, perhaps we should be more concerned with how it has come to be that the whole wealth of human creativity is subordinated to the celebrity system, structured as it is in hierarchy, and turning people into promotional tools.

Conclusion

This book has argued that celebrity is a form of fame that corresponds to the growth of capitalist relations of production and their implantation onto the sphere of cultural production. However, I have also argued that the growth and spread of celebrity was not an inevitable product of our social and economic system. I have attempted to demonstrate that in the early forms of capitalist media and entertainment, celebrity and stardom were not immediately or necessarily apparent. Instead, they were developed, and public interest in celebrities was nurtured, for primarily economic reasons – namely market competition under the logic of the profit motive. Thus celebrity has become both a key promotional tool and a means of attracting advertisers in central sectors of the media.

As we saw, the first system of stardom is to be found in the commercial Georgian theatre, when, in an atmosphere of competition, traditional stock companies were undermined by provincial theatres who drew on the prestige of West End actors to promote plays to middle-class audiences. Competition to attract these audiences was partly a result of the growth in the population of Britain's burgeoning cities and partly to do with the arrival of the railways as well-to-do audiences were now able to travel to theatres for a day out for the first time. The repertory theatre that the star system eventually replaced did not depend on star actors to promote their plays, organized as they were as stable stock companies with many prominent actors and roles, rotating plays and leading parts nightly. That system was overturned by the star system over the course of several decades.

Again in the case of the early mass press at the end of the nineteenth century, we saw that the early press appealed to mass audiences with radical politics as much as human interest stories, and that
celebrity journalism comes to replace the earlier radical populism,
not as a consequence of declining readerships, but as a result of press
barons wishing to recoup declining advertising revenue from companies who increasingly aimed to advertise in commercially conducive
environments.

In the case of the cinema, we saw how the highly popular documentary film and photojournalism gave way at the beginning of the
twentieth century to fictional narrative film, once again not as a result
of declining audiences, but this time precisely the opposite. The
explosion of interest in the cinema and its new mass audience led film
makers to look for more predictable sources of film than political
events and wars, and began adapting novels and theatrical productions for film in order to produce a steady and predictable output.
We also saw that soon after, studios began to use the image of male
and female actors to differentiate their film product, and their studio,
from those of other film makers, once again in an atmosphere of
intense competition.

In each of these cases, we saw that the growth of celebrity-
dominated media and entertainment was part of the curtailment of
working-class culture and of working-class participation in the cultural arena, despite claims to the contrary. In the case of the theatre
in Britain, important changes in the laws governing the theatre in
1843 led to the closure of the theatre of the working class in the name
of free competition, as the number of legal theatres grew, but productions in non-permanent structures (which catered to the working class
and poor) became illegal. In the process, a lively and radical theatre
which drew in large working-class audiences was demolished and we
saw consolidated the middle-class character of the theatre. A similar
scenario occurred in the case of the nickelodeon film theatres in the
US over fifty years later, as the cartels and oligopolies that struggled
for control of the new burgeoning film industry developed their
dominance.

In the case of the mass press, journalism that expressed the interest
of ordinary people against big business and the growth of monopoly
trusts gave way to celebrity gossip and human interest. This is the
period in which some of the main conventions of celebrity journalism
were developed, such as the celebrity interview, the gossip column,
the celebrity human interest story and the reporting of private scandal.

In each of these cases – the theatre, the mass press and the cinema
– the growth of celebrity media and entertainment is part of the same

legal and commercial processes that also crushed working-class forms of culture and engagement, while consolidating bourgeois cultural dominance.

An historical approach to the spread of celebrity has been an important theme in this book because celebrity is now such an established aspect of contemporary culture that only an examination of its points of origin in commercial culture can throw doubt on the widely accepted claims that celebrity grew primarily as a spontaneous desire on the part of audiences of new media to see stars, or that it is simply a democratization of public culture. Instead, the rise of celebrity was based on business calculations and the promotional strategies they entailed at moments in history when the cultural landscape was permanently altered as a result of the growth of commercial culture and the rise of the mass media.

It is also important to remember that these new forms of cultural production replaced previous cultural forms that had spoken to working-class audiences in a language which belonged to them, rather than the new language of big business dressed up in the idiom of the people. And so, with the rise of bourgeois culture, those who most lost out were those to whom the promises of freedom and equality were aimed, and whose tastes and predilections were said to be addressed by star and celebrity performances – the newly industrialized working class who found that much of their culture had either been shut down or co-opted into increasingly industrialized and commercial culture.

Thus the structure of fame is deeply connected to the balance of class forces in different historical periods. Celebrity is part of a series of processes of reinforcing the commercial, economic and symbolic power of capitalist cultural production; the changes in the British and American theatre in the late eighteenth and nineteenth centuries first signal a shift from the power of the landed gentry to the power of the entrepreneurial actor-manager, as the power of the court declines in the face of a rising bourgeoisie, and later from individual entrepreneurs to investment capital and shareholders. In both the UK and the US, the separation of the production of plays from theatrical ownership and the rise of intermediaries in the shape of circuit booking agents, speaks to the broader shifts in the balance of power towards big capital and the drive to monopoly control over profits. The general patterns of that picture are seen again in the case of the mass press and the cinema; both industries saw a shift from smaller scale individual ownership patterns to the domination of these new media forms by a small handful of large, integrated corporations as the capitalist drive to monopoly came to the fore. The result in the case of the press was chain journalism and in the cinema the domination of film by five studios. And another result was the shaping of content around the profitable celebrity commodity.

This book has also suggested that celebrity has burgeoned in capitalist society when a series of conditions come together, including a general increase in commercialization, both as an organizing force in cultural and media industries and as a set of values that underpin business decisions. The conditions of celebrity growth also include the development of new technology in such a context of commercial expansion and competition. New technology under the pressures of intense competition transforms existing industries, as we saw was the case for the industrial printing press for the early mass press or digital technology in the case of the press a century later.

The context also shapes the new media industries that grew up around digital technology and the development of the internet in the second half of the twentieth century, exacerbating the pressures of competition further by increasing the numbers of media outlets competing for advertising revenue. These were circumstances of extreme uncertainty, particularly for the press and television. The press and the wider news media solved the challenges of these circumstances as they migrated online, by increasing celebrity content as 'click bait' to restore profitability by recouping lost advertising revenue, without which the commercial news cannot survive. This book has argued that in the process of restoring profitability, news media have seriously undermined the quality of journalism and have compromised their ability to provide news.

There are parallels in the case of the expansion of commercial television with the introduction of satellite, cable and digital technologies. The technological developments that restructured the television industries occurred at a time when the ideals of public service broadcasting were under attack and those advocating commercial competition as a system for television production were (and still are) in the ascendant, politically and economically. In this context, which also included high levels of competition, new business models were developed which centred on cheap but popular new reality TV formats and the 'ordinary' celebrity which they produced. Ordinary celebrity and interactive television are heralded by some as examples of 'democratainment' (Hartley 2008) and were seen to mark greater input and greater power of ordinary people in the media. But in fact, ordinary celebrity was part of a set of new operating models in television that also included a strategy of attacking the conditions of the people who work in the industry, including the ordinary people who perform on the shows.

Therefore the growth of celebrity in the early twenty-first century has not been inevitable, but instead it has been a product of economic conditions and the business decisions made in those contexts. The diversified ownership and investment patterns of media organizations from the latter half of the twentieth century were encouraged by a deregulated field, resulting in a business culture focused on short-term profits and widespread staff cuts. Celebrity has played a significant role in the fortunes of important media sectors in this environment because it has been developed as a key selling mechanism in each of these arenas. Furthermore, this has had an important impact on the forms and meanings of the products of each sector in quite distinct, but connected ways.

Although this book has focused on the economic function of celebrity in the growth of the media, it has also examined some of the contours of symbolic meaning of celebrity in these periods of transition and consolidation. Although celebrity has played a significant role in the consolidation of media capital, the symbolic meaning of celebrity can be as contradictory as the system from which it emerged. For instance, this book has argued that celebrity speaks both to the arrival of greater freedoms in the modern period, but also demonstrates the limits to those freedoms; it is a sign of the dominance of the commodity form and the idea of culture for profit, and yet is speaks to desires and cultural values outside of the logic of the economic – if it did not, it would have no economic value. Thus, this book has examined the contradictions in fame for female actors in the British theatre who simultaneously found independence and social power in the theatre, and prominence in the public domain, and yet also found themselves defined primarily by gender, sexuality and the private realm. We returned to questions of female celebrity in the case of the cinema and of ordinary celebrity because the contradiction between the arrival of greater freedom and the persistence of a lack of freedom find such strong expression in female celebrity.

Celebrity also speaks symbolically to the balance of forces in society at any given time, to the rise of some groups and social forces and the decline of others. So today, ordinary celebrity – that is, the celebrification of ordinary people in the media – seems on the surface to offer greater media visibility to a wider range of people, but actually devalues the cultural backgrounds of ordinary people (often legitimated by laughing at working-class women's 'lack' of taste or education) and this has coincided with a serious decline in the number of professionals in the media who come from working-class backgrounds. Ordinary celebrity today, even though there may be various manifestations of resistance to social norms, seems to express the increasing marginalization of working-class people from public culture, rather than their further integration into it, at the very moment when ordinary people are being offered the false promise of inclusion through reality TV (and the internet) precisely on the basis of being extraordinarily 'ordinary'. The exclusion of working-class people from participation in the creative arts, the theatre, film and television has deepened over the last thirty years, and as the economic, political and cultural force of neoliberalism rips through collective social and cultural institutions and attacks the very means by which ordinary people can flourish, celebrity culture offers up the so-called pleasures of consumerism, the lie of inclusivity, and reasserts the longstanding myth of celebrity culture – that anyone can 'make it'.

In the late twentieth century, the contemporary ubiquity of celebrity culture and a generalized increase in commercialization set the scene for the arrival of new technology that had so much promise. The internet and digital technology offered the possibility of a total transformation of media communication because it has the capacity to end the scarcity of the analogue age, to vastly expand the numbers and range of media outlets, increase access to information of all varieties and to make the means of production far more accessible to the public. But this potential was hampered by the context of its emergence – the dominance of the profit motive as the purpose for cultural production and the associated values and illogical logic of capitalist production. The basic value of cultural production is not the sharing of human creativity and cultures, the free circulation of information, or the desire to increase the levels of participation in the creation of meaning, but instead is based on 'sellability'. This is what Marxists mean when they talk of commodity fetishism – they are referring to a system of production in which relationships between human beings take on the appearance of relationships between things and in which the products of one's labour no longer belong to the producer.

We find that the type of self lauded in this new online context is one in which both the self-as-entrepreneur and the-self-as-branded commodity take centre stage. Certain social media apps such as Facebook and Twitter encourage this form of self-presentation, which potentially reduces the relationship between people to the presentation of the self in commodity form, a thing. It is this same commodity fetishism which produces systems of celebrity in other media and cultural industries, shaping and tailoring content around the celebrity commodity.

So to a large extent the technology of freedom turns out to be as much the technology of self-promotion and celebrity. The practices of celebrity visibility have been part of the construction of hierarchy in an industry that proclaims its egalitarian principles and meritocratic practices, as we saw in the previous chapter. Social media entrepreneurs, born into a world of fame-structured hierarchies, re-created it in the world of Web 2.0, putting themselves at the apex of this new arena of renown and shaping much of the architecture of social media as a commodity for the construction of the commodity self, with celebrity-style visibility an intrinsic part of some of the major social media platforms.

The rise of celebrity today is an indication that the profit motive is in the ascendant and that both autonomous and alternative cultural values are relatively weak by comparison. It does not, as some critics argue, symbolize the democratic opening up of the public sphere, nor is it a manifestation of egalitarianism. We do not live in an egalitarian society. Media organizations have produced or made use of the ephemeral here-today-gone-tomorrow celebrity as a mechanism for profit, often by ridiculing ordinary people in the media and teaching working-class people shame and humiliation.

Meanwhile, celebrity culture poses a world in which meaning and value are constructed through the actions of individuals, as Langer puts it in relation to the personality system, 'behaving as free agents rather than by the complex relations among classes, institutions, and interest groups' (1981: 363). This process of individualization, even if it is positively expressed, is disconnected from broader aspects of the social; most importantly it is detached from the expressions of collectivity and solidarity which have always been at the heart of working-class culture. What has been lost in the process of individualization that is supported by the values of celebrity culture, is the progressive impact that working-class collectivity has had on the shape of public life in the nineteenth and twentieth centuries. The most important democratic achievements have been the result of working-class struggle and collective movements – universal suffrage, equal rights, equal pay, the establishment of welfare systems, etc. What is really extraordinary about working-class identity is not the potential celebrity in each of us, but precisely the solidarity and collectivity that is largely hidden from media representations of ordinary people. I am suggesting that we ought to unlearn our desire to be (or even be 'like') celebrities and re-engage with our collective citizenship.

But there have been a chorus of voices that proclaim that the internet and new media technology have provided new spaces of citizen participation. However, as we saw in the final chapter of this book, this is based on a fundamentally flawed conflation of the concept of the citizen with that of the consumer, and the practices of consumption with those of civil society. Citizenship is fundamentally about participation in political and civic life, securing rights and freedoms, having a voice in the shape of civil society. Consumerism, on the contrary, is about defining ourselves in relation to things; things which are external to our own productive capabilities and creativity. Sliding between the two terms as if they are the same is ideological obfuscation and contributes to the continuation of domination rather than challenging it. And celebrity culture, as P.D. Marshall argues, has played an important role in the pedagogy of consumption, providing glamorous or idealized images of how to remake the self through the purchase of goods and services. Celebrity offers images of inclusion and plenty in a society shaped by exclusion and structured in want.

But, as I have argued throughout, media organizations have developed celebrity coverage and images in order to serve their own interests. The decisions in each of the industries that we have examined, to develop and spread celebrity-based content, were practical business decision made in specific sets of economic circumstances, sometimes, as in the case of the news, with dire consequences for the circulation of information to the public. So although I have suggested that celebrity has symbolic and ideological dimensions, I am not suggesting that media businesses act together to push celebrity ideology on the public; instead, they act in their own interests and usually in competition with each other. There are cumulative symbolic consequences of these decisions, including the persistence of social hierarchy which directly benefits media businesses, as we have seen throughout this book.

But it is precisely because media act in their own interests (and profit based on commercial competition is the 'interest' that they mostly share) that they are not up to the task of protecting and nurturing culture, in just the same way that the banking system is not up to the task of protecting the economy. Both share a short-term bonus culture perspective in which profits are paramount, rather than any other notion of social or economic good. In the case of the media, pursuing their economic interests has resulted in the wealth of human creativity being subordinated to the celebrity system, structured as it is in hierarchy and symbolic exclusion, and turning people, as it does, into promotional tools.

I want to end this book with one final 'but'. Thus far I have painted a bleak picture, and that is because the picture *is* bleak. But. Capitalist modernity is inherently contradictory and domination is never complete. Critics who define celebrity culture as part of a system of subjugation so total that it controls consciousness are as mistaken as those who see capitalism as a fundamentally egalitarian society and contemporary celebrity an expression of growing democracy. Instead, although capitalism is structured in dominance, including dominant ideas and practices, it is also structured by contradiction. We saw that the very relations of production are contradictory, where capital and labour have opposite interests and yet are forced together in the production process.

Contradiction also finds expression in the ideas and values of our society – including on the terrain of celebrity culture. Celebrity culture is structured by hierarchy, by who and what it excludes, but it also sometimes produces oppositional or challenging ideas and values. This can be found in the anti-austerity politics of the British comedian Russell Brand, or singer songwriter Charlotte Church, or Matt Damon's criticisms of the banking system in *Inside Job* (2010), pointing out that it was directly responsible for the 2008 financial crash, or in the anti-war politics of Susan Sarandon, the Dixie Chicks and many other celebrities. And while this may be no substitute for a collective anti-war or anti-austerity movement, it does demonstrate that celebrity is complex, and this is found not just in overt politics but also in its articulation of non-dominant ways of being human. It is complex because it is part of a system structured by contradiction. As such it holds together contradictory practices and ideas.

To see capitalist society either as fundamentally democratic or as a system of inescapable domination is to miss the central paradox of modernity – the claims of equality and freedom at the heart of a system founded on revolution contend with the persistence of inequality and the subjugation of lived experience; the disjuncture between political and economic transformation. As we saw in the first chapter, it was these social transformations that enabled the rise of new and expanded forms of public prominence from which celebrity emerged and which simultaneously established new social hierarchies. Celebrity culture is thus implicated in the contradictions of capitalist modernity and this cannot be fully symbolically or ideologically resolved; it cannot be entirely hidden or expunged from collective consciousness. So celebrity culture presents the human in commodity form, but it also consists of its opposite – the human can never be fully contained by the self-as-commodity, and the persistence of humanity is, in all circumstances, a cause for hope.

Notes

Chapter 1: What is Celebrity? The Changing Character of Fame

1 *The Tatler*, Saturday, 15 October 1709, in Donald F. Bond, ed., *The Tatler, Volume II*, Oxford: Clarendon Press, 1987. For a full discussion of this article, see Claire Brock, *The Feminization of Fame: 1750–1830*, Palgrave: Basingstoke, 2006.
2 See Braudy (1986: 381–9) for a full account of their quest for celebrity.
3 See Moody (2000) for a detailed account of Foote.
4 In 1766, he acquired a royal patent as the manager of Haymarket Theatre. But in order to perform plays of mimicry and scandal, Foote had to avoid the provisions of the Licensing Act and he did so by advertising these as instructional events for young actors rather than as theatrical performances. This surrounded Foote with an atmosphere of rebellion. (Quoted in Moody 2000: 69; her refernce is David Erskine Baker, *Biographia Dramatica; or a Companion to the Playhouse...*, 2 vols, rev. edn (London, 1782), pp. 167–8.)

Chapter 2: Celebrity and the Theatre: Modernity and Commercial Culture

1 1866 British HOC Report, p 159.
2 Including: the Brunswick Theatre (opened in 1828), The City Theatre in Cripplegate (opened in 1831), the Garrick in Leman Street (opened in 1831), the Standard in Shoreditch (opened in 1835), and the City of London in Norton Folgate (opened in 1837) (Booth 1991: 5).

3   The actor Johnston Forbes-Robertson explains his decision to go into management as late as 1895: 'several actors, younger than I, had taken up management very much earlier in their careers, and there was nothing for it but to take a theatre if I was to maintain my place' (J. Forbes-Robertson, *A Player under Three Reigns*, London 1925, 164–5, in Booth 1991: 31).

Chapter 3:   Celebrity and the Industrialization of Cultural Production: The Case of the Mass Press and the Cinema

1   Lowenthal (1961) considers this shift to be complete by the 1950s.
2   Intense competition between Pulitzer and Hearst prompted Pulitzer to try to carve Hearst out of the syndicate that controlled access to wire services; see Nasaw 2002: 110).
3   The Sunday papers retained the radical politics of the Chartist press but combined it with stories derived from older forms of popular literature; stories about murders and executions, scandal and infidelity, robberies and highwaymen (Williams 1961: 176).
4   For instance, Hearst offered to sponsor a labour train to bring white workers to replace Chinese ones. But, interestingly, no workers took it up and nothing came of it. See Nasaw (2002: 80–1) for a full account of this episode.
5   Although in name only – he had contributed nothing to the development of the Vitascope which was, in fact, invented by Thomas Armat and Francis Jenkins. Raff and Gammon simply wanted to link Edison's reputation to the machine.
6   The boom in nickelodeons was not a cultural anomaly; it was part and parcel of the expansion in popular entertainment in the US between 1905 and 1908 (Allen 1980: 202; Gamson 1994: 23).
7   Fox and Loews both started out as the owners of vaudeville theatres (Allen 1980).

Chapter 4:   Celebrity and News

1   Grove was hired by Mort Zuckerman in 2003, to join his New York *Daily News*, in an effort to challenge the popularity of the gossip column in Rupert Murdoch's *New York Post*, in a move whose rivalry is strongly reminiscent of that between the Hearst and Pulitzer presses more than a century earlier.
2   http://www.dailymail.co.uk/tvshowbiz/article-3297697/Eight-months-pregnant-Kim-Kardashian-wears-skintight-dress-heels-film-reality-sisters.html, accessed 31 March 2016.

3   http://www.mirror.co.uk/3am/celebrity-news/halloween-horror-reality-star-natalie-6739942, accessed 31 March 2016.
4   http://www.theguardian.com/lifeandstyle/2015/oct/31/leonardo-dicaprio-actor-crush-bim-adewunmi, accessed 31 March 2016.
5   http://www.telegraph.co.uk/film/james-bond-spectre/?WT.mc_id=tmgspk_nav_1122_100&utm_source=tmgspk&utm_medium=nav&utm_content=1122&utm_campaign=tm, accessed 31 October 2015.
6   On the issue of the varied functions of the media, see Sparks (1995).
7   Although this is less the case for local news where there is often only a single title or one or two regional news broadcasts. The challenge facing local news has been more to do with the decline in classified advertising (Freedman 2010).
8   http://www.theguardian.com/media/2012/apr/15/telegraph-times-profit, accessed 12 September 2015.
9   Celebrity news is not the only form of journalism that has been considered to be captured by promotional experts – see Aeron Davis' account of financial journalism being captured by financial public relations professionals in *Public Relations Democracy: Public Relations, Politics and the Mass Media in Britain* (Manchester University Press, 2004).
10 https://www.nuj.org.uk/news/votes-of-no-confidence-over-click-bait-targets/, accessed 20 October 2015.
11 http://www.theguardian.com/media/2015/sep/24/mail-online-digital-advertising-slows-down-to-16-annual-growth, accessed 8 October 2015.

Chapter 5:   Ordinary Celebrity

1   Olivier Driessens usefully distinguishes between celebrification and celebritization. Celebritization refers to a 'long term structural development' or 'meta-process' (2013: 643) which lacks a clear origin or endpoint. It is on a par with globalization, colonization or individualization. Celebrification, on the other hand, refers to the process by which ordinary people or public figures are transformed into celebrities, including their status as a commodity (2013: 643).
2   Hartley later uses the term to refer to 'plebiscitary formats' (television shows which invite audiences to vote for contestants) which he sees as a sign of democratic progress (2008). This chapter will challenge both assertions.
3   Endemol has just merged with Shine, for instance.
4   In addition, prime time drama continues to be a major source of competition as audiences continue to tune in.
5   'Ant and Dec double their earnings in one year to reach a combined income of £12 million'. *The Huffington Post*, 21 October, 2013.

Available at: http://www.huffingtonpost.co.uk/2013/10/21/ant-and-dec-earn-12-million_n_4136200.html, accessed 10 May 2015.

6   Autonomous Marxism has its origins in the Italian 'workerist' movement of the 1960s. Through various transformations it became influential through the work of post-Marxist philosophers Michael Hardt and Antonio Negri (2000, 2004). Hardt and Negri redefined the working class as moving away from the collective worker of the factory, and towards the socialized worker in the social factory. In this definition, everyone was defined as a worker, or rather the 'multitude', regardless of their position in relations of production. In my view, this work both overestimates the reach of capital and at the same time overly optimistically sees any act as an act of refusal. In the end Hardt and Negri sidestep the question of power by advocating that an alternative society already exists in the movement. The legacy of this work is considerable confusion about the question of exploitation and the relations of production in new media industries, as this chapter will demonstrate.

7   http://www.campaignlive.co.uk/news/1131211/, accessed 12 June 2015.

8   http://www.economist.com/news/special-report/21615871-everything-people-do-online-avidly-followed-advertisers-and-third-party, accessed 11 August 2015.

9   http://www.barb.co.uk/whats-new/weekly-top-30, accessed 12 June 2015.

10   http://www.insidermedia.com/insider/northwest/115688-turnover-soars-towie-producer-lime-pictures/, accessed 12 June 2015.

Chapter 6: Social Media and Celebrity: The Internet of 'Self'

1   http://friendorfollow.com/twitter/most-followers/, accessed 27 April 2016.

2   http://www.socialbakers.com/statistics/facebook/pages/total/, accessed 3 July 2015.

3   http://www.techi.com/2010/06/the-rise-of-the-bieber-how-pop-stars-become-famous-using-the-web/, accessed 3 July 2015.

4   http://www.techradar.com/news/internet/web/10-most-hated-websites-of-all-time-1083372, accessed 3 July 2015.

5   http://www.adweek.com/agencyspy/the-nielson-ratings-are-screwy-and-perez-hilton-got-14-million-views-in-one-day/3994, accessed 3 July 2015.

References

Addison, J. (1987 [1709]) *The Tatler*, Saturday, 15 October 1709. In Bond, D.F. (ed.), *The Tatler*, Volume II. Clarendon Press, Oxford.

Addison, J. (2004 [1713]) *Cato: A Tragedy, and Selected Essays* (eds. Dunn Henderson, C. and Yellin, M. E.). Liberty Fund, Indianapolis, IN.

Adorno, T.W. (1973) *Negative Dialectics* (trans. Ashton, E.B.). Routledge and Kegan Paul, London.

Adorno, T.W. (1991 [1963]) *The Culture Industries: Selected Essays on Mass Culture* (ed. Bernstein, J.M.). Routledge, London.

Adorno, T.W. (2008) *Lectures on Negative Dialectics: Fragments of a Lecture Course 1965/1966* (ed. Tiedemann, W.; trans. Livingstone, R.). Polity, Cambridge.

Adorno, T.W. and Horkheimer, M. (1973 [1944]) *The Dialectic of Enlightenment*. Routledge, London.

Advertising Association (2015) *The Advertising Association/WARC Expenditure Report*. AA/WARC, London.

Allen, R.C. (1980) *Vaudeville and Film 1895–1915*. Arno Press, New York.

Anderson, B. (2006) *Imagined Communities: Reflections on the Origin and Spread of Nationalism*. Verso, London.

Andrejevic, M. (2003) *Reality TV: The Work of Being Watched*. Rowman and Littlefield, London.

Andrejevic, M. (2011) 'Real-izing exploitation'. In Kraidy, M., Marwan, M. and Sender, K. (eds.) *The Politics of Reality Television: Global Perspectives*. Routledge, New York, pp. 18–31.

Bacon-Smith, C. (1999) *Science Fiction Culture*. University of Pennsylvania Press, Philadelphia, PA.

Baldasty, G.J. (1992) *The Commercialization of the News in the Nineteenth Century*. University of Wisconsin Press, Madison, WI.

Balio, T. (ed.) (1985) *The American Film Industry*. University of Wisconsin Press, Madison, WI.

Balio, T. (1987) *United Artists: The Company that Changed the Film Industry*. University of Wisconsin Press, Madison, WI.

Barbas, S. (2001) *Movie Crazy: Fans, Stars and the Cult of Celebrity*. Palgrave, Basingstoke.

Barbrook, R. and Cameron, A. (1996) 'The Californian ideology'. *Science as Culture*, 6(1): 44–72.

Barker, M. and Brooks, K. (1998) *Knowing Audiences: Judge Dredd – Its Friends, Fans and Foes*. University of Luton Press, Luton.

Baudrillard, J. (1983) *Simulacra and Simulations*. University of Michigan Press, Ann Arbor, MI.

Bauman, Z. (2005) *Liquid Life*. Polity, Cambridge.

Bazelgette, P. (2005) *Billion Dollar Game: How 3 Men Risked it all and Changed the Face of TV*. Little Brown, New York.

Bennett, J. (2010) *Television Personalities: Stardom and the Small Screen*. Routledge, London.

Bennett, J. and Holmes, S. (2010) 'The "place" of television in celebrity studies'. *Celebrity Studies Journal*, 1(1): 65–80.

Bernheim, A.L. (1932) *The Business of the Theatre*. Actors' Equity Association, New York.

Bingham, M. (1978) *Henry Irving: The Greatest Victorian Actor*. Stein and Day Publishers, New York.

Bird, S.E. (1992) *For Enquiring Minds: A Cultural Study of Supermarket Tabloids*. University of Tennessee Press, Knoxville, TN.

Biressi, A. and Nunn, H. (2005) *Reality TV: Realism and Revelation*. Wallflower, London.

Bonner, F. (2009) *Ordinary Television: Analyzing Popular TV*. Sage, London.

Boorstin, D.J. (1961) *The Image: A Guide to Pseudo-events in America*. Vintage, New York.

Booth, M.R. (1991) *Theatre in the Victorian Age*. Cambridge University Press, Cambridge.

Bordwell, D. and Staiger, J. (1985) *The Classical Hollywood Cinema: Film Style and Mode of Production to 1960*. Columbia University Press, New York.

Bourdieu, P. (1984) *Distinction: A Critique of the Judgement of Taste*. Routledge & Kegan Paul, London.

Bourdieu, P. (1993) *The Field of Cultural Production*. Polity, Cambridge.

Bourdieu, P. (1994) *On Television*. Polity, Cambridge.

Braudy, L. (1986) *The Frenzy of Renown: Fame and its History*. Oxford University Press, Oxford.

Brucker, H. (1937) *The Changing American Newspaper*. Columbia University Press, New York.

Calhoun, C. (2007) *Nations Matter: Culture, History and the Cosmopolitan Dream*. Routledge, London.

Cantor, M. (1979) *American Working Class Culture: Explorations in American Labor and Social History*. Greenwood Press, Westport, CT.

Case, T. (2004) 'Talking about gossip: celebrity news gets credibility on the way to page one'. *Presstime: The Magazine of the Newspaper Association of America*, May, 35–50.

Cashmore, E. (2006) *Celebrity Culture*. Routledge, London.

Castells, M. (2010) *The Rise of the Network Society*, 2nd edn. Wiley-Blackwell, Oxford.

Cathcart, B. (2012) 'Hacked off'. *Television and New Media*, 13(1): 21–6.

Collins, S. (2008) 'Making the most out of 15 minutes: Reality TV's dispensable celebrity'. *Television and New Media*, 9(2): 87–110.

Conboy, M. (2006) *Tabloid Britain: Constructing a Community through Language*. Routledge, London.

Conboy, M. (2011) *Journalism in Britain*. Sage, London.

Conboy, M. (2014) 'Celebrity journalism – an oxymoron? Forms and functions of a genre'. *Journalism: Theory, Practice and Criticism*, 15(2): 171–85.

Conlin, J.R. (ed.) (1974) *The American Radical Press 1880–1960*. Greenwood Press, Westport, CT.

Connell, I. (1992) 'Personalities in the popular media'. In Dahlgren, P. and Sparks, C. (eds.) *Journalism and Popular Culture*. Sage, London, pp. 64–84.

Corner, J. and Pels, D. (eds.) (2003) *Media and the Restyling of Politics: Consumerism, Celebrity and Cynicism*. Sage, London.

Couldry, N. (2000) *Inside Culture*. Sage, London.

Couldry, N. (2002) 'Playing for celebrity: Big Brother as ritual event'. *Television and New Media*, 3(3): 295–310.

Couldry, N. (2007) 'Media power: Some hidden dimensions'. In Redmond, S. and Holmes, S. (eds.) *Stardom and Celebrity: A Reader*. Sage, London, pp. 353–60.

Couldry, N. (2014) 'The hidden injuries of media power'. *Journal of Consumer Culture*, 1(2): 155–77.

Coyle, J.S. (1998) 'Now, the editor as marketer'. *Columbia Journalism Review*, July/Aug, 37–42.

Cross, S. and Littler, J. (2010) 'Celebrity and Schadenfreude: The cultural economy of fame in free fall'. *Cultural Studies*, 24(3): 395–417.

Curran, J. (2002) *Media Power*. Routledge, London.

Curran, J. (2016) 'Rethinking internet history'. In Curran, J., Fenton, N. and Freedman, D., *Misunderstanding the Internet*, 2nd edn. Routledge, London, pp. 34–67.

Curran, J. and Seaton, J. (2003) *Power Without Responsibility: The Press, Broadcasting and New Media in Britain*. Routledge, London.

Curran, J. and Sparks, C. (1991) 'Press and popular culture'. *Media Culture and Society*, 13(2): 215–38.

Curran, J., Douglas, A. and Whannel, G. (1980) 'The political economy of the human-interest story'. In Smith A. (ed.) *Newspapers and Democracy: International Essays on a Changing Medium*. The MIT Press, Cambridge, MA, pp. 288–348.

Curran, J., Fenton, N. and Freedman, D. (2016) *Misunderstanding the Internet*, 2nd edn. Routledge, London.

Davies, N. (2008) *Flat Earth News*. Chatto and Windus, London.

Davis, T.C. (2004) 'The show business economy, and its discontents'. In Powell, K. (ed.) *The Cambridge Companion to Victorian and Edwardian Theatre*. Cambridge University Press, Cambridge.

de Certeau, M. (1984) *The Practice of Everyday Life* (trans. S. Rendell). University of California Press, Berkeley, CA.

de Montaigne, M. (2015 [1580]) *Michel de Montaigne's Hugely Influential Essays*. British Library, London.

de Sola Pool, I. (1983) *Technologies of Freedom*. Belknap Press, Cambridge, MA.

Dean, J. (2002) *Publicity's Secret: How Technoculture Capitalises on Democracy*. Cornell University Press, Ithaca, NY.

Dean, J. (2010) *Blog Theory: Feedback and Capture in the Circuits of Drive*. Polity, Cambridge.

Debord, G. (1984 [1967]) *The Society of the Spectacle*. Black and Red Press, Detroit, MI.

deCordova, R. (1990) *Picture Personalities: The Emergence of the Star System in America*. University of Illinois Press, Urbana, IL.

Deery, J. (2014) 'Mapping commercialization in reality television'. In Ouellette, L. (ed.) *A Companion to Reality Television*. Wiley Blackwell, Chichester.

Delwiche, A. (2013) 'The New Left and the computer underground: recovering political antecedents of participatory culture'. In Delwiche, A. and Jacobs Henderson, J. (eds.) *The Participatory Cultures Handbook*. Routledge, New York, pp. 10–21.

Delwiche, A. and Jacobs Henderson, J. (eds.) (2013) *The Participatory Cultures Handbook*. Routledge, New York.

Driessens, O. (2013) 'The celebritization of society and culture: Understanding the structural dynamics of celebrity culture'. *International Journal of Cultural Studies*, 16(6): 641–57.

Dubied, A. and Hanitzsch, T. (2014) 'Studying celebrity news'. *Journalism: Theory, Practice and Criticism*, 15(2): 137–43.

During, S. (2007) *The Cultural Studies Reader*, 3rd edn. Routledge, London.

Dyer, R. (1979) *Stars*. BFI, London.

Dyer, R. (2004 [1986]) *Heavenly Bodies*. BFI Macmillan, London.

Eagleton, T. (2004) *After Theory*. Penguin, London.

Equity (2011) *Response to the Low Pay Commission General Consultation on the National Minimum Wage*. Equity, London.

Ericson, R.V., Baranek, P.M. and Chan, J.B.L. (1989) *Negotiating Control: A Study of News Sources*. Open University Press, Milton Keynes.

Evans, J. and Hesmondhalgh, D. (2005) *Understanding Media: Inside Celebrity*. Open University Press, Milton Keynes.

Fenton, N. (ed.) (2010) *New Media Old News*. Sage, London.

Fenton, N. (2012) 'Telling tales: Press, politics, power and the public interest'. *Television and New Media*, 13(1): 3–6.

Fenton, N. and Barassi, V. (2011) 'Alternative media and social networking sites: The politics of individual and political participation'. *The Communication Review*, 14(3): 179–96.

Fiske, J. (1987) *Television Culture*. Methuen, London.

Franklin, B. (1997) *Newszak and News Media*. Arnold, London.

Freedman, D. (2008) *The Politics of Media Policy*. Polity, Cambridge.

Freedman, D. (2010) 'The political economy of the "new" news environment'. In Fenton, N. (ed.) *New Media Old News*. Sage, London, pp. 35–51.

Gabler, N. (1994) *Winchell: Gossip, Power and the Culture of Celebrity*. Knopf, New York

Gamson, J. (1994) *Claims to Fame: Celebrity in Contemporary America*. University of California Press, Berkeley, CA.

Garnham, N. (1990) *Capitalism and Communication*. Sage, London.

Geraghty, C. (2000) 'Re-examining stardom: Questions of texts, bodies and performance'. In Gledhill, C. and Williams, L. (eds.) *Reinventing Film Studies*. Arnold, London.

Gilbert, J. (2013) *Neoliberal Culture*. Lawrence and Wishart, London.

Gitlin, T. (2002) *Media Unlimited: How the Torrent of Images and Sounds Overwhelms Our Lives*. Picador, London.

Goldstein, T. (1998) 'Does big mean bad? As the century winds down, media power continues to concentrate. Here are some tools for thinking about that'. *Columbia Journalism Review*, Sept–Oct, 52–4.

Gripsrud, J. (1992) 'The aesthetics and politics of melodrama'. In Dahlgren, P. and Sparks, C. (eds.) *Journalism and Popular Culture*. Sage, London.

Hampton, B. (1970 [1931]) *History of the American Film Industry* [originally *A History of the Movies*, Covici-Friede, New York, 1931]. Dover Books, New York.

Haraway, D. (1985) 'A cyborg manifesto: Science, technology and socialist-feminism in the late twentieth century'. *Socialist Review*, 80, 65–108.

Hardt, M. and Negri, A. (2000) *Empire*. Harvard University Press, Cambridge, MA.

Hardt, M. and Negri, A. (2004) *Multitude: War and Democracy in the Age of Empire*. Penguin, New York.

Hartley, J. (1999) *Uses of Television*. Routledge, London.

Hartley, J. (2008) *Television Truths*. Blackwell, Oxford.

Harvey, D. (2006) *Spaces of Global Capitalism: Towards a Theory of Uneven Geographical Development*. Verso, London.

Hesmondhalgh, D. (2007) *The Cultural Industries*. Sage, London.

Hesmondhalgh, D. (2015) 'Exploitation and media labor'. In Maxwell, R. (ed.) *The Routledge Companion to Labor and Media*. Routledge, London.

Hickey, N. (1998) 'Money lust: How pressure for profit is perverting journalism'. *Columbia Journalism Review*, July/August, 28–36.

Hill, A. (2007) *Restyling Factual TV: Audiences and News, Documentary and Reality TV*. Routledge, London.

Hill, A. (2015) *Reality TV*. Routledge, London.

Hobsbawm, E. (2003 [1969]) *Bandits*. Abacus, St. Ives.

Hobson, D. (1982) *'Crossroads': Drama of a Soap Opera*. Methuen, London.

Hollis, P. (1970) *The Pauper Press: A Study in Working-Class Radicalism of the 1830s*. Oxford University Press, Oxford.

Holmes, S. (2005) 'Off-guard, unkempt, unready? Deconstructing contemporary celebrity in Heat magazine'. *Continuum: Journal of Media and Cultural Studies*, 19(1): 21–38.

Holmes, S. and Redmond, S. (2006) *Framing Celebrity: New Directions in Celebrity Culture*. Routledge, Abingdon.

Howe, E. (1992) *The First English Actresses: Women and Drama 1660–1700*. Cambridge University Press, Cambridge.

Hutt, A. (1973) *The Changing Newspaper: Typographic Trends in Britain and America 1622–1972*. Gordon Fraser, London.

Inglis, F. (2010) *A Short History of Celebrity*. Princeton University Press, Princeton, NJ.

Institute for Fiscal Studies (2012) *Living Standards, Poverty and Inequality in the UK: 2012*. Available at: http://www.ifs.org.uk/publications/6196.

James, C.L.R. (2001 [1938]) *The Black Jacobins: Toussaint L'Ouverture and the San Dominican Revolution*. Penguin, London.

Jameson, F. (1991) *Postmodernism: or, the Cultural Logic of Late Capitalism*. Verso, London.

Jenkins, H. (1992) *Textual Poachers: Television and Participatory Culture*. Routledge, London.

Jenkins, H. (2008) *Convergence Culture: Where Old and New Media Collide*. New York University Press, New York.

Jenkins, H. (2014) 'Rethinking "Rethinking convergence/culture"'. *Cultural Studies*, 28(2): 267–97.

Jenkins, H. and Ford, S. (2013) *Spreadable Media*. New York University Press, New York.

Juergens, G. (1966) *Joseph Pulitzer and the New York World*. Princeton University Press, Princeton, NJ.

Juris, J. (2005) 'The new digital media and activist networking within anti-corporate globalization movements'. *The Annals of the American Academy*, 597: 189–208.

Kaplan, R.L. (2012) 'Between mass society and revolutionary praxis: The contradictions of Guy Debord's *Society of the Spectacle*'. *European Journal of Cultural Studies*, 15(4): 457–78.

Keller, J.M. (2014) Fiercely real? Tyra Banks and the making of new media celebrity'. *Feminist Media Studies*, 14(1): 147–64.

Kerr, C.E. (1990) 'Incorporating the star: The intersection of business and aesthetic strategies in early American film'. *Business History Review*, 64(3): 381–408.

Khiabany, G. (2015) 'Uneven and combined independence of social media in the Middle East: Technology, symbolic production and unproductive labor'. In Bennett, J. and Strange, N. (eds.) *Media Independence: Working with Freedom or Working For Free*. Routledge, New York.

Kinservik, M.J. (2007) *Sex, Scandal, and Celebrity in Late Eighteenth-Century England*. Palgrave Macmillan, Basingstoke.

Klotz, R. (2004) *The Politics of Internet Communication*. Rowman and Littlefield, Lanham, MD.

Langer, J. (1981) 'Television's "personality system"'. *Media, Culture and Society*, 3(4): 351–65.

Lessig, L. (1999) 'Open codes and open societies: Values of internet governance'. *Chicago-Kent Law Review*, 74(3): 1405–20.

Lessig, L. (2001) 'The internet under siege'. *Foreign Policy*, 27: 56–65.

Littler, J. (2004) 'Celebrity and "meritocracy"'. *Soundings: A Journal of Politics and Culture*, 26: 118–30.

Lowenthal, L. (1961) *Literature, Popular Culture, and Society*. Prentice-Hall, Englewood Cliffs, NJ.

Luckhurst, M. and Moody, J. (2005) *Theatre and Celebrity in Britain, 1660–2000*. Palgrave Macmillan, Basingstoke.

MacCann, R.D. (ed.) (1992) *The Stars Appear*. The Scarecrow Press, Metuchen, NJ.

McDayter, G. (2009) *Byromania and the Birth of Celebrity Culture*. SUNY Press, Albany, NY.

McGuigan, J. (1992) *Cultural Populism*. Routledge, London.

McLachlan, S. and Golding, P. (2000) 'Tabloidization in the British press: A quantitative investigation into the changes in British newspapers, 1953–1997'. In Sparks, C. and Tullochs, J. (eds.) *Tabloid Tales: Global Debates over Media Standards*, Rowman & Littlefield, Lanham, MD, pp. 75–90.

McLuhan, M. (2008 [1967]) *The Medium is the Massage*, 9th edn. Ginko Press, Berkeley, CA.

McNair, B. (2003) *News and Journalism in the UK*. Routledge, London.

McNamara, K. (2011) 'The paparazzi industry and new media: The evolving production and consumption of celebrity news and gossip websites'. *International Journal of Cultural Studies*, 4(5): 515–30.

Magder, T. (2004) 'The end of TV101: Reality programs, formats, and the new business of television'. In Murray, S. and Oullette, L. (eds.) *Reality TV: Remaking Television Culture*. New York University Press, New York, pp. 137–56.

Manning, P. (2000) *News and News Sources: A Critical Introduction*. Sage, London.

Marshall, P.D. (1997) *Celebrity and Power: Fame and Contemporary Culture*. University of Minnesota Press, Minneapolis, MN.

Marshall, P.D. (2010) 'The promotion and presentation of the self: Celebrity as a marker of presentational media'. *Celebrity Studies*, 1(1): 35–48.

Marwick, A. (2013) *Status Update: Celebrity, Publicity and Branding in the Social Media Age*. Yale University Press, New Haven, CT.

Marwick, A. and boyd, d. (2011) 'To see and be seen: Celebrity practice on Twitter'. *Convergence*, 17(2): 139–58.

Marx, K. (1963) *Theories of Surplus Value: Part I*. Lawrence and Wishart, London.

Marx, K. (1993 [1858]) *Grundrisse* (trans. Nicolous, M.). Penguin Classics, London.

Marx, K. (2008 [1852]) *The Eighteenth Brumaire of Louis Bonapart.* Cosimo Classics, New York.

Marx, K. (2014 [1859]) *A Contribution to the Critique of Political Economy* (trans. Stone, N.I.). Echo Library, Fairford.

Marx, K. and Engels, F. (1970 [1848]) *Manifesto of the Communist Party in Selected Works.* Lawrence and Wishart, London.

Maxwell, R. and Miller, T. (2011) 'Old, new and middle-aged media convergence'. *Cultural Studies*, 25(4/5): 585–603.

Miège, B. (1989) *The Capitalization of Cultural Production.* International General, Amsterdam.

Mole, T. (2009) *Romanticism and Celebrity Culture, 1750–1850.* Cambridge University Press, Cambridge.

Moody, J. (2000) *Illegitimate Theatre in London, 1770–1840.* Cambridge University Press, Cambridge.

Morin, E. (1960) *The Stars: An Account of the Star-System in Motion Pictures* (trans. Howard, R.). Grove Press, New York.

Morley, D. and Brunsdon, C. (1999) *The Nationwide Television Studies.* Routledge, London.

Murdock, G. (2003) ' "Back to work": Cultural labor in altered times'. In Beck, A. (ed.) *Understanding the Cultural Industries.* Routledge, New York.

Murdock, G. and Golding, P. (1977) 'Capitalism, communication and class relations'. In Curran, J., Gurevitch, M. and Woollacott, J. (eds.) *Mass Communication and Society.* Arnold, London, pp. 12–43.

Murdock, G. and Golding, P. (2002) 'Digital possibilities, market realities: The contradictions of communications convergence'. *Socialist Register*, 38: 111–28.

Nasaw, D. (2002) *The Chief: The Life of William Randolph Hearst.* Gibson Square Books, London.

Nussbaum, F. (2005) 'Actresses and the economics of celebrity 1700–1800'. In Luckhurst, M. and Moody, J. (eds.) *Theatre and Celebrity in Britain, 1660–2000.* Palgrave Macmillan, Basingstoke, pp. 148–68.

OECD (2008) *Annual Report 2008.* Available at: https://www.oecd.org/newsroom/40556222.pdf.

Ofcom (2015) *The Communications Market Report.* Available at: http://stakeholders.ofcom.org.uk/binaries/research/cmr/cmr15/CMR_UK_2015.pdf.

Orgeron, M. (2008) *Hollywood Ambitions: Celebrity in the Movie Age.* Wesleyan, Middletown, CT.

Pascal, B. (1983 [1670]) *Pensées* (trans. Cruickshank, J.). Grant & Cutler, London.

Ponce de Leon, C.L. (2002) *Self Exposure: Human Interest Journalism and the Emergence of Celebrity in America, 1890–1940.* University of North Carolina Press, Chapel Hill, NC.

Phillips, A., Couldry, N. and Freedman, D. (2010) 'An ethical deficit? Accountability, norms and the material conditions of contemporary journalism'. In Fenton, N. (ed.) *New Media, Old News*. Sage, London, pp. 51–68.

Powell, K. (1997) *Women and Victorian Theatre*. Cambridge University Press, Cambridge.

Radway, J.A. (1984) *Reading the Romance: Women, Patriarchy, and Popular Literature*. University of North Carolina Press, Chapel Hill, NC.

Ramsaye, T. (1919) 'How do they get that way? Revelations of a press-agent'. *Photoplay*, June, 68–71 and 123.

Ramsaye, T. (1964 [1925]) *A Million and One Nights: A History of the Motion Picture Industry*. Simon and Schuster, New York.

Raphael, C. (2004) 'The political economic origins of Reali-TV'. In Murray, S. and Oullette, L. (eds.) *Reality TV: Remaking Television Culture*. New York University Press, New York, pp. 119–34.

Redmond, S. (2013) *Celebrity and the Media*. Palgrave Macmillan, London.

Rheingold, H. (1993) *The Virtual Community: Homesteading and the Electronic Frontier*. MIT Press, Cambridge, MA.

Ritzer, G. (2007) *McDonaldization of Society*, 5th edn. Sage, London.

Rogers, N. (1998) *Crowds, Culture, and Politics in Georgian Britain*. Clarendon Press, Oxford.

Rojek, C. (2001) *Celebrity*. Reaktion, London.

Rojek, C. (2012) *Fame Attack: The Inflation of Celebrity and its Consequences*. Bloomsbury Academic, London.

Rooney, D. (2000) 'Thirty years of competition in the British tabloid press: The Mirror and the Sun 1968–1998'. In Sparks, C. and Tullochs, J. (eds.) *Tabloid Tales: Global Debates over Media Standards*. Rowman and Littlefield, Lanham, MD, pp. 91–110.

Rowell, G. (1978) *The Victorian Theatre 1792–1914: A Survey*. Cambridge University Press, Cambridge.

Schickel, R. (1962) *The Stars*. The Dial Press, London.

Schickel, R. (1985) *Common Fame: The Culture of Celebrity*. Pavilion/ Michael Joseph, London.

Schickel, R. (2000) *Intimate Strangers: The Cult of Celebrity in America*. Ivan R. Dee, Chicago, IL.

Schudson, M. (1978) *Discovering the News: A Social History of the American Newspapers*. Basic Books, New York.

Seitz, D.C. (1924) *Joseph Pulitzer: His Life and Letters*. Simon and Schuster, New York.

Sender, K. (2011) 'Real worlds: Migrating genes, travelling participants, shifting theories'. In Kraidy, M.M. and Sender, K. (eds.) *The Politics of Reality TV: Global Perspectives*. Routledge, London, pp. 1–11.

Senft, T. (2008) *Camgirls: Celebrity and Community in the Age of Social Networks*. Peter Lang, Oxford.

Shore, E. (1985) 'Selling socialism: The *Appeal to Reason* and the radical press in turn-of-the-century America'. *Media Culture and Society*, 7(2): 147–68.

Sichel, E. (1911) *Michel de Montaigne*. Constable, London.

Skeggs, B. (2009) 'Haunted by the spectre of judgement: Respectability, value and affect in class relations'. In Sveinsson, K.P. (ed.) *Who Cares About the White Working Class*. Runnymede, London, pp. 36–45.

Skeggs, B. and Wood, H. (2012) *Reacting to Reality Television: Performance, Audience and Value*. Routledge, London.

Slater, D. (1997) *Consumer Culture and Modernity*. Polity, Cambridge.

Slide, A. (1970) *Aspects of American Film History Prior to 1920*. Scarecrow Press, Metuchen, NJ.

Smith, P. and Smythe, E. (2004) 'Globalization, citizenship and new information technologies: From MAI to Seattle'. In Malkia, M., Anttiroiko, M. and Salovainen, R. (eds.) *eTransformation in Governance*. IGI Publishers, Hershey, PA, pp. 289–317.

Sparks, C. (1988) 'The popular press and political democracy'. *Media, Culture and Society*, 10(2): 209–24.

Sparks, C. (1995) 'The media as a power for democracy'. *Javnost – The Public*, 2(1): 45–61.

Sparks, C. (2007) 'Reality TV: The Big Brother phenomenon'. *International Socialism Journal*, 114. Available at: http://isj.org.uk/reality-tv-the-big-brother-phenomenon/.

Stacey, J. (1994) *Star Gazing: Hollywood Cinema and Female Spectatorship*. Routledge, London.

Staiger, J. (1991) 'Seeing stars'. In Gledhill, C. (ed.) *Stardom: Industry of Desire*. Routledge, London, pp. 3–17.

Sweeney, M. (2008) 'Internet ad spending will overtake television in 2009'. *Guardian*, 19 May.

Taylor, G. (1989) *Players and Performers in the Victorian Theatre*. Manchester University Press, Manchester.

Tebbel, J. (1963) *A Compact History of the American Newspaper*. Hawthorn Books, New York.

Terranova, T. (2000) 'Free labor: Producing culture for the digital economy'. *Social Text*, 18(2): 35–58.

Thomas, J. (1984) *The Art of the Actor-Manager*. Bowker Publishing, Epping.

Tulloch, J. (2000) 'The eternal recurrence of new journalism'. In Sparks, C. and Tullochs, J. (eds.) *Tabloid Tales: Global Debates over Media Standards*, Rowman and Littlefield, Lanham, MD, pp. 131–46.

Turkle, S. (1984) *The Second Self: Computers and the Human Spirit*. Granada, London.

Turkle, S. (2011) *Alone Together: Why We Expect More from Technology and Less from Each Other*. Basic Books, New York.

Turner, F. (2006) *From Counter Culture to Cyber Culture: Stewart Brand, the Whole Earth Network, and the Rise of Digital Utopianism*. University of Chicago Press, Chicago, IL.

Turner, G. (2004) *Understanding Celebrity*. Sage, London.

Turner, G. (2010) *Ordinary People and the Media*. Sage, London.

Turner, G. (2014) 'Is celebrity news, news?' *Journalism: Theory Practice and Criticism*, 15(2): 144–52.

Van Zoonen, L.(2003) ' "After Dallas and Dynasty we have … Democracy": Articulating soap, politics and gender'. In Corner, J. and Pels, D. (eds.) *Media and the Restyling of Politics: Consumerism, Celebrity and Cynicism*. Sage, London, pp. 99–117.

Walker, A. (1970) *Stardom: The Hollywood Phenomenon*. Stein and Day, New York.

Wanko, C. (2003) *Roles of Authority: Thespian Biography and Celebrity in Eighteenth-Century Britain*. Texas Tech University Press, Lubbock, TX.

Wiener, J.H. (1996) 'The Americanization of the British press, 1830–1914'. In Harris, M. and O'Malley, T. (eds.) *Studies in Newspaper and Periodical History Annual*. Greenwood Press, Westport, CT, pp. 238–51.

Williams, R. (1961) *The Long Revolution*. Chatto and Windus, London.

Williams, R. (1976) *Communications*, 3rd edn. Penguin, Harmondsworth.

Williams, R. (1989) *On Television: Selected Writings* (trans. and ed. O'Connor, A.). Routledge, London.

Williamson, M. (2005) *The Lure of the Vampire: Gender, Fiction and Fandom from Bram Stoker to Buffy*. Wallflower Press, London.

Williamson, M. (2010) 'Female celebrities and the media: The gendered denigration of the "ordinary celebrity" ', *Celebrity Studies*, 1(1): 118–21.

Williamson, M. (2012) 'When "popular" was "radical": The mass circulation US press in the 1890s, emerging celebrity journalism and popular taste', *Media History*, 18(2): 115–27.

Williamson, M. (2014) 'Celebrity, gossip, privacy and scandal'. In Carter, C., Steiner, L. and McLaughlin, L. (eds.) *The Routledge Companion to Media and Gender*. Routledge, London, pp. 311–21.

Wilson, E. (2004) *Bohemians: The Glamorous Outcasts*. Rutgers University Press, New York.

Woffington, M. (1760) Memoirs of the celebrated Mrs Woffington, interspersed with several theatrical anecdotes; the amours of many persons of the first rank; and some interesting characters drawn from real life. No publisher name, British Library Holdings, London.

Woods, F.E. (1919) 'Why is a star'. *Photoplay*, October, 70–2 and 117–18.

Wright, E.O. (1997) *Class Counts: Comparable Studies in Class Analysis*. Press Syndicate of the University of Cambridge, Cambridge.

Index